RENEWALS 458-4574
DATE DUE

WITHDRAWN
UTSA LIBRARIES

Managing Buyer–Supplier Relations

This highly practical book gives vivid insight into the real-world challenges facing industrial companies. It is useful for both purchasing professionals and all senior executives involved in the product creation process.

Antony M. Sheriff, Executive Director, Product Development, Fiat Auto S.p.A.

If I were to recommend a single book for Procurement Management it would be this.

Jean Michel Paulange, Snr. Vice President, Electrolux AB (Purchasing)

Reading this book has inspired me to look at Product Development in a different light altogether.

Kjell Ake Eriksson, Vehicle Line Executive, Saab Automobiles AB

Managing suppliers is a complex process that is often underestimated. This book presents research carried out by a practising manager in the automotive industry, coupled with five hundred interviews in the automotive, aircraft and white goods industries, in order to describe the tools and techniques needed to manage suppliers better.

The book offers a specification perspective, and includes analysis of models of outsourcing, visions for suppliers for capability building, the meaning of specifications, models of specification flow and the future of managing suppliers, including systems supply and digital procurement.

Students, academics and practitioners in the field of buyer–supplier relations, or involved in examining the impact of outsourced design or team-based design processes, will find this an invaluable work.

Rajesh Nellore received his degree in Electronics Engineering from BMS College of Engineering in India. He then obtained a postgraduate Diploma in International Business from the University of Birmingham and an MBA from the University of Wales in Cardiff. He recently obtained his Doctorate of Business Administration from the University of Newcastle. He has published extensively in different journals and serves as a reviewer for many journals. He has global operational experience with Saab Automobiles, Scania, General Motors and Electrolux and serves as a consultant for many large corporations. He is currently the director responsible for global telematics at Fiat Auto S.p.A. and can be e-mailed at Nellorerajesh@hotmail.com.

Routledge Studies in Business Organizations and Networks

1 **Democracy and Efficiency in the Economic Enterprise**
 Edited by Ugo Pagano and Robert Rowthorn

2 **Towards a Competence Theory of the Firm**
 Edited by Nicolai J. Foss and Christian Knudsen

3 **Uncertainty and Economic Evolution**
 Essays in honour of Armen A. Alchian
 Edited by John R. Lott Jr

4 **The End of the Professions?**
 The restructuring of professional work
 Edited by Jane Broadbent, Michael Dietrich and Jennifer Roberts

5 **Shopfloor Matters**
 Labor-management relations in twentieth-century American manufacturing
 David Fairris

6 **The Organisation of the Firm**
 International business perspectives
 Edited by Ram Mudambi and Martin Ricketts

7 **Organizing Industrial Activities Across Firm Boundaries**
 Anna Dubois

8 **Economic Organisation, Capabilities and Coordination**
 Edited by Nicolai Foss and Brian J. Loasby

9 **The Changing Boundaries of the Firm**
 Explaining evolving inter-firm relations
 Edited by Massimo G. Colombo

10 **Authority and Control in Modern Industry**
 Theoretical and empirical perspectives
 Edited by Paul L. Robertson

11 **Interfirm Networks**
 Organization and industrial competitiveness
 Edited by Anna Grandori

12 **Privatization and Supply Chain Management**
 Andrew Cox, Lisa Harris and David Parker

13 **The Governance of Large Technical Systems**
 Edited by Olivier Coutard

14 **Stability and Change in High-Tech Enterprises**
 Organisational practices and routines
 Neil Costello

15 **The New Mutualism in Public Policy**
 Johnston Birchall

16 **An Econometric Analysis of the Real Estate Market and Investment**
 Peijie Wang

17 **Managing Buyer–Supplier Relations**
 The winning edge through specification management
 Rajesh Nellore

Managing Buyer–Supplier Relations

The winning edge through specification management

Rajesh Nellore

London and New York

First published 2001
by Routledge
11 New Fetter Lane, London EC4P 4EE

Simultaneously published in the USA and Canada
by Routledge
29 West 35th Street, New York, NY 10001

Routledge is an imprint of the Taylor & Francis Group

© 2001 Rajesh Nellore

Typeset in Baskerville by Keystroke, Jacaranda Lodge, Wolverhampton
Printed and bound in Great Britain by MPG Books Ltd, Bodmin

All rights reserved. No part of this book may be reprinted or reproduced or utilised in any form or by any electronic, mechanical, or other means, now known or hereafter invented, including photocopying and recording, or in any information storage or retrieval system, without permission in writing from the publishers.

British Library Cataloguing in Publication Data
A catalogue record for this book is available from the British Library

Library of Congress Cataloging in Publication Data
Nellore, Rajesh
    Managing buyer–supplier relations : the winning edge through
    specification management/Rajesh Nellore.
        p. cm.
    Includes bibliographical references and index.
    1. Industrial procurement. 2. Relationship marketing. I. Title.
    HD39.5 .N45 2001
    658.8′12–dc21   2001016597

ISBN 0–415–25303–9

This book is dedicated to my grandparents Bhuma and T.V. Srinivasan, my mother Revathi Vasan, my sister Anandi Nellore and my father N.S. Vasan who was tragically killed in the Kenya Airways plane crash on the 31st of January 2000 in Abidjan.

Contents

List of figures ix
List of tables xi
Foreword xiii
Acknowledgements xv
List of abbreviations xix

Introduction 1

1 A theoretical perspective on specifications 6

2 Specifications: do we really understand them? 41

3 Visionary-driven outsourced development 51

4 Redefining the role of product specifications 64

5 Mapping the flow of specifications 81

6 Applications of specifications in outsourcing: building on Quinn and Hilmer 98

7 Applications of specifications in outsourcing: portfolio approaches 115

8 Contracts to help validate specifications 133

9 Managing systems suppliers: an uphill task 157

10 Digital procurement 168

Bibliography 186
Index 193

Figures

1.1	The view of specifications	10
1.2	Content variables	13
2.1	The continuum from narrative to quantitative specifications	46
2.2	Contents of a specification	48
2.3	Supplier network depicting the development and manufacture of an armrest	49
3.1	Solution options to fix alternator noise in the car	55
3.2	The matching process	56
3.3	Creation of visions for suppliers	57
3.4	The vision for suppliers	58
3.5	Integrated means of guidance-related capability and generation model	62
4.1	Specification–supplier framework	72
4.2	Triangulation	73
4.3	Comfort curve in an automobile	77
5.1	The specification process at an auto OEM	82
5.2	Breakdown of specifications	83
5.3	Risk analysis	89
5.4	Bottleneck analysis	90
5.5	Material groups in the aircraft OEM	91
5.6	A process model for specifications in the aircraft OEM	91
5.7	Elaboration of the MSS	93
5.8	Generation of specifications	94
5.9	Validations, problem analysis and feedback	95
5.10	Proposed specification model	96
6.1	Strategic sourcing	102
7.1	The Olsen and Ellram portfolio model	118
7.2	The specification generators	122
7.3	Analysis of supplier relationships	129
9.1	The systems supplier framework	163
9.2	The mega-systems approach	165
9.3	The supplier–knowledge importance link	167
10.1	A summary of procurement	184

Tables

1.1	List of authors and content variables	14
2.1	Meaning of a specification	42
2.2	Categorisation of definition areas	43
2.3	Supplier–communication mode interface	44
3.1	Employee-defined visions	53
3.2	Current state of capabilities	59
3.3	Future state of capabilities if negative trend continues	60
4.1	Problem areas identified through the survey	65
4.2	Categorisation of problem areas	65
5.1	After-sales requirements on specifications	85
6.1	A comparison of the different outsourcing models	103
6.2	Activities in the auto OEM classified according to competitive advantage	104
6.3	Activities in the auto OEM classified according to strategic vulnerability	105
6.4	Activities in the truck OEM classified according to strategic vulnerability	106
6.5	Comparison of essentially qualitative specifications	108
6.6	Comparison of the mixed specifications	109
6.7	Comparison of essentially quantitative specifications	110
6.8	The procurement matrix	111
6.9	The procurement matrix complemented by contract relationships	113
7.1	Portfolio approaches in purchasing	117
7.2	The specification–portfolio link	125
8.1	The contract data	140
8.2	Contract parameters, sequenced	142
8.3	Regrouping contract parameters	143
8.4	Different contractual possibilities	145
8.5	Validation criteria for entry and remaining in the business	154
9.1	Why are you a systems supplier?	159
9.2	Categorisation of reasons	159
9.3	Life span of items in the car	161

9.4	Different types of supplier	164
10.1	Websites for information on digital trade	170
10.2	Existing e-B2B organisations	175
10.3	Risks and benefits of e-B2B	176
10.4	Released savings thanks to e-business	177
10.5	Distribution of paper	182
10.6	Net savings	183

Foreword

The act and art of purchasing are subjects nearly every adult has first-hand experience of and therefore, need no introduction to engage in a discussion regarding the subject. It is one of the facts of modern life that society requires commerce to deal with its daily purchases from a very small scale to a very large one. Despite the need for this skill, the professional act of purchasing is hardly ever taught or studied in schools until the advanced college levels for a very focused career in purchasing. It is assumed that buying is easily learned in life's normal course of events.

However, in modern business, where millions of dollars and the future market success of a company's product are at stake, professional purchasing is extremely critical. Identification of the right suppliers, at the right time, based on mutually agreed expectations is not as easy as one might think, due to the complexities of the marketplace and the fact that much of the process relies on human execution.

One of the most important elements of a successful commercial arrangement is clarity of expectations and specifications accompanying the contract. Many a failure in execution can be traced back to unclear specification. Thus the study of the role specifications play in successful purchasing, as discussed in this book, will be an invaluable tool for all levels of your organisation from the buyer to the Chief Executive Officer. Purchasing is a complex, team sport cutting across all functions in an organisation and needs to be treated very seriously if your company is to be successful.

I have personally learned a lot from this book. There are many lessons for us as a company, which we have been challenging and implementing. The lessons described in this book are not limited to one country but apply across the United States and Europe, and are strategic in nature. I would strongly recommend this book for companies who wish to engage in the management of change and increasing profitability for all levels of management.

James E. Taylor
Vehicle Line Executive
General Motors Corporation
Detroit, USA

Acknowledgements

This book is the result of four years of full-time research carried out in many different companies commencing in late 1996. It has been my aim to provide both researchers and practitioners in the field of outsourced product development with tools and techniques to help improve productivity by exploring fields that previously have been little investigated. The chapters give a global perspective on better managing buyer–supplier relationships for the different layers of personnel within a corporation; from top management to the front line engineer who deals with the suppliers directly. I gained a better appreciation of the problems facing corporations in outsourced product development and have learnt to appreciate them better during the course of this journey.

My initial interest in the field of buyer supplier relations was sparked off during my MBA studies (1994–95) at the University of Wales, College of Cardiff under the expert tutelage of Professors Dan Jones, Peter Hines and Owen Jones. This led me to explore the possibility of doing research work in the automotive industry. Saab Automobiles in Sweden agreed to my request and funded me. The funds were approved by the Chief Engineer at that time, Kjell Ake Eriksson who currently leads a Vehicle Line Team in the United States for Saab Automobiles. Without his help, support, encouragement and the countless hours spent explaining to me the problems and challenges facing the automotive industry, this research would never have been possible. He is a close friend and my grateful thanks to him and his wife for their support. Nutek – a Swedish government body provided limited funding which is also acknowledged. A few Swedish colleagues; Jan Eklof and Christer Norr deserve a special mention for their help.

Along with my research work at Saab Automobiles I was also employed as a full-time Assistant Project Leader for the key project (1997–98) in the Electronics department. A special thanks to all my friends and colleagues who helped me at Saab Automobiles. I can only just name a few of them due to space restrictions. They are Johan Rosendahl, Lief Ivarsson, Christer Hyleen, Jimmy Ordberg, Urban Johansson, Kerstin Johansson, Gary Siddall, Peter Moller, John Arle, Stig Nodin and Hakan Karlsson. Limited research work was also carried out at Saab Aircrafts, Sweden; UTI, Sweden; Lear Corporation, Sweden; Nissan Motor Manufacturing, United Kingdom; Rolls Royce, United Kingdom; BMW, Germany; Electrolux, Sweden; Volvo Aero Corporation, Sweden; Volvo Car xvi *Acknowledgements*

Corporation, Sweden; Toyota Motor Corporation, Japan; and six supplier companies who prefer to remain incognito. The co-operation of these firms is gratefully acknowledged. Special thanks to Ken Foxley of Nissan, Bengt Olof Elfstrom of Volvo Aero Corporation, Paul Bertrand and Jean Michel Paulange of Electrolux, Steven Newton and Graham Lewis of Rolls Royce, Michel Erussard of Renault, Antony Sheriff of Fiat Auto, Stafan Quensal of Atlas Copco, and Wilhelm Becker of BMW. I would particularly like to thank Jean Michel Paulange for his special contribution as both my former boss and current close friend.

I was then offered the opportunity to start an Advanced Procurement Planning group at Scania in Sweden, (1998–99). Hakan Samuelsson, the former Executive Vice President and current CEO of Mann trucks in Germany, offered me a position. I learnt a lot from the Scania experience, which is a modular company. Special thanks to my friends and colleagues; Peter Carlsson, Sven Berg, Ingmar Stoor, Rolf Thomer, Bertil Rengfelt, Magnus Boman, and many others.

Bob Hendry, the former President of Saab Automobiles and current Chairman of Adam Opel AG in Germany, encouraged me to speak to General Motors Corporation (GM) in the United States. I was offered a position by Harold Kutner, the Group Vice President of Purchasing, to work with issues related to Advance Purchasing. Jim Taylor, the Vehicle Line Executive of the prestige car line and my mentor, encouraged me to broaden my experience by working on issues related to his car line. At the same time I was involved with issues related to technology management under the guidance of Dr Larry Burns – Vice President in charge of Research and Development and Planning. These operational experiences have helped me to broaden my scope and make the research work more accessible. Special thanks to my friends and colleagues at General Motors with whom I have spent countless hours discussing my research and, in particular, Bo Andersson – Executive in charge of GM Purchasing and David Coon – Asia Pacific Liaison Manager.

Jim Taylor made arrangements for me to complete part of my studies at the University of Newcastle, for which I shall remain ever grateful. This also allowed me the opportunity to spend six months in France on an overseas assignment for General Motors during 2000. Special thanks to my professors and friends: Jean Jacques Chanaron, Ian McLoughlin, Klas Söderquist and Roger Vaughan for helping me to complete this.

This research has benefited greatly from reviewer suggestions which have helped improve it and bring a broader perspective from the eyes of a practitioner cum researcher. Being presented with the Academy of Management award for the best student paper in 1999 was a great boost to my contributions being acknowledged along with rest of the publications in peer-reviewed journals. This has been a difficult path and many long hours have been spent on this research.

Finally, I would like to thank my parents, Revathi Vasan and Nellore Srinivasan, my grandparents, Bhuma and T.V. Srinivasan, and my sister, Anandi Nellore, for their help and support in making this a success.

Last but not least, I would like to thank the editorial team at Routledge who have gone beyond the call of duty to help me complete the book. Michelle

Gallagher, Annabel Watson and James Whiting deserve special mention for their help and support for my writings.

Despite all the input from practising managers, questionnaire surveys and university colleagues, the insights posed, errors and omissions in this book are my sole responsibility. My research on this exciting topic continues and this book is a partial display of my research to date.

The author and publishers would like to thank the copyright holders for permission to use the following material:

Chapter 2 is a revised version of 'Specifications: do we really understand what they mean?', *Business Horizons* (1999), vol. 42, no. 6, pp. 63–69 by R. Nellore, K. Söderquist, G. Siddall and J. Motwani. Copyright *Business Horizons*, with permission from *Business Horizon*.

Chapter 3 is a revised version of 'Visionary-driven outsourced product development', *Journal of Supply Chain Management* (2001), vol. 37, no. 1, by R. Nellore. Copyright NAPM, with permission from NAPM.

Chapter 4 is a revised version of 'Black box engineering: the role of product specifications', *Journal of Product Innovation Management* (1998), vol. 15, no. 6, pp. 534–549, by C. Karlsson, R. Nellore and K. Söderquist. Copyright Elsevier Science, with permission from Elsevier Science.

Chapter 5 is a revised version of 'A specification model for product development', *European Management Journal* (1999), vol. 21, no. 1, pp. 50–63, by R. Nellore, K. Söderquist and K.A. Eriksson. Copyright Elsevier Science, with permission from Elsevier Science.

Chapter 6 is a revised version of 'Strategic outsourcing through specifications', *Omega* (2000), vol. 28, no. 5, pp. 525–540, by R. Nellore and K. Söderquist. Copyright Elsevier Science, with permission from Elsevier Science.

Chapter 7 is a revised version of 'Portfolio approaches – the missing link to specifications', *Long Range Planning* (2000), vol. 33, no. 2, pp. 245–268, by R. Nellore and K. Söderquist. Copyright Elsevier Science, with permission from Elsevier Science.

Chapter 8 is a revised version of 'Validating specifications – a contract-based response', *IEEE Transactions in Engineering Management* (2001), by R. Nellore. Copyright IEEE, with permission from IEEE.

Chapter 9 is a revised version of 'Managing systems suppliers – an uphill task', *Purchasing Today* (2001), vol. 12, no. 1, pp. 14–16, by R. Nellore. Copyright NAPM, with permission from NAPM.

Chapter 10 is a revised version of 'Digital procurement – a stand alone practice? An example of sourcing paper', PRACTIX-CAPS RESEARCH (2001), by R. Nellore. Copyright CAPS, with permission from CAPS. Additional data provided by Jean Jacques Chanaron of ESC-Grenoble.

Abbreviations

B2B	business to business
B2C	business to customers
CAD	computer-assisted design
CD	compact disk
CTS	component technical specification
CVP	component validation plan
DINKS	double income, no kids
EDI	electronic data interchange
GM	General Motors
HVAC	heating ventilation and air conditioning system
IVTS	initial vehicle technical specification
MRP	materials requirement planning
MSS	market segment specification
OEM	original equipment manufacturer
PCA	potential competitive advantage
PDS	product design specification
PDT	product development team leader
ppi	paper price index
R&D	research and development
RDS	radio data system
SSTS	sub-system technical specification
SSVP	sub-system validation plan
SV	strategic vulnerability
Sys	systems supplier
VTS	vehicle technical specification
VVP	vehicle validation plan

Introduction

Purchasing is a fascinating subject. It has emerged from a role of little or no importance to an increasingly strategic role contributing to company success. In fact, it has achieved such importance that companies often order their purchasing organisations to make price savings of x per cent every year in order to reach the promised financial goals for the company shareholders. Purchasing managers in almost every industry wait for these telephone calls from management informing them of the projected savings requirement. This sets off a chain of events whereby the purchasing managers force the required numbers on their suppliers, which may or may not be within the capability of the suppliers. This, however, is not a concern of the purchasing managers. The suppliers are thereby pushed to their limits and have little or no manoeuvrability. Let us illustrate this situation with an example. The white goods industry purchases a large quantity of flat steel every year from major steel manufacturers, more than a million tones per year. The steel industry is capital-intensive and requires to be run at full capacity though demand can be full of peaks and troughs. When squeezed by the purchasing managers of the white goods manufacturer for price reductions during a period of price troughs, the steel mills have little or no option but to accept these price reduction demands. This squeezing of suppliers is not limited to those from the purchasing department but all departments involved in buying direct (components, systems) and indirect (stationery, computers, advertising) goods from suppliers try it. This new role of 'supplier squeezing' has often been termed the domain of the 'procurement function' instead of the purchasing function as it is a focused and tactical activity.

Is 'supplier squeezing' a necessary evil? Practitioners and academics would offer opposite views. My research supports the proposition that 'supplier squeezing' is a necessary evil and that 'Original Equipment Manufacturer (OEM) internal squeezing' is necessary in order to achieve the same targets harmoniously together with the suppliers. My research prefers internal control methods within an OEM rather than external unilateral supplier squeezing to achieve value added. Even if the OEM unilaterally generates the cost savings from the suppliers as projected by management, the suppliers almost always tend to cover their losses by asking OEMs to pay for every single change made in the original requirements which were the basis of the relationship. This supports the proposition that internal reforms become more important than external supplier squeezing as the projected cost savings are rarely achieved on a company-wide basis, though they may be visible on the purchasing budget. Research has proved that supplier involvement is beneficial to companies though the focus has always been on squeezing suppliers rather than the adjustments that need to be made internally within an OEM to achieve cost savings. I would like to approach the complex subject of supplier involvement in product development from this angle. The benefits of supplier involvement are many, such as reduction of lead times, continuous innovation, ability to focus on core capabilities, etc. However, 'how to involve suppliers' to achieve sustained profitability has been little investigated. Looking at internal reform this book will attempt to contribute to the understanding of 'how to involve suppliers' through specification management for sustained profitability.

This book is based on interviews with over 500 managers in one automotive OEM, one aircraft OEM, one truck manufacturer and six first tier suppliers of auto OEMs, all based in Europe. The auto OEM is the main case study for this research and 450 questionnaires, with qualitative questions, sent to global automotive suppliers were also used for supplementary data collection along with interviews at the 'world-class' Toyota Motor Corporation. Issues that cut across the organisation regarding internal reforms were investigated, revealing the voice of the development people to be deterministic of the outcome. A specification is not only the written description of goods and services but also the written communication of development personnel, including the communication from suppliers. Unfortunately, the term specification conjures up memories of engineering work and few are inclined to dwell on it. However, since it involves all levels and all departments within a firm it is important for organisations to understand the importance of specifications. This book is anchored in the specification basis and elaborates on this as a means for increased profitability.

Specifications are a difficult issue to understand. Sometimes, they represent totally different concepts internally within a company and between buyers and suppliers. We will concentrate on the latter as the focus of the book. First, I will introduce the term specifications and demonstrate its characteristics. This presents a practitioner's overview of the spectrum of requirements that a complete vendor-supplied product should meet. The discussion is timely and reflects current thought about vendor relations within the concept of an extended supply chain. The content fits well within the triple definition of quality based on quality of design, quality of conformance and quality of performance. The underlying emphasis is on the prevention of quality problems in the supply chain through careful communication of product requirements. Following this, I will give an example of how visions for suppliers based on the specifications can be used as a powerful governance mode in companies, thereby affecting the core capabilities within an organisation. This is necessary, as even if the specifications are separated for the different types of suppliers, attempts must still be made to understand the fact that different types of suppliers exist. This is a very difficult task as it involves changing the mindset of the people within an organisation. In order to manage the specifications to achieve sustained profitability, companies need to manage and build their competence. I will describe the competence building scenario with many examples from the automotive industry.

Then the flow of specifications is mapped out so that corporations can understand the areas which need to be emphasised. The flow of specifications represents an excellent integration of methodologies. What it offers is the development and thought process involved in this integration and that is the primary contribution of this book. Integration is a valuable lesson in efficiency and synergy. This is followed by a discussion of the role of specifications in decisions on outsourcing.

There are two approaches to understanding this issue that are discussed. The first approach is based on an extension of Quinn and Hilmer's model of decision-making in outsourcing published in *Sloan Management Review* in 1994. Quinn and Hilmer's model was selected, as it is the only model that covers the entire spectrum of make/buy decisions. The second is the use of the portfolio approach to make decisions on outsourcing. This suggests a means to better manage and control the purchasing process. It adds more depth to the notion of 'portfolio management' in the area of managing supplier relationships. Firms that look at purchasing with the broad view described in this chapter should be able to manage the supplier relationships better and hence, the quality of the incoming materials, and delivery, speed and other supplier quality dimensions. Portfolio models have been used in a limited way in supplier selection research and there is a dearth of literature in this area. This is followed by a thorough analysis of how contracts can help validate the specifications.

Finally, two futuristic concepts are introduced, namely, systems suppliers and digital procurement. Both of these have ramifications for the management of specifications as they change the nature of the game within the industry. Global conclusions and overall managerial implications for the corporate manager are presented towards the end of every chapter.

Overview of the book

The organisation of the book is as follows. Chapter 1 presents a theoretical framework and lays the ground for the research conducted and results presented in this book. It discusses existing research in the area of specifications and explores its limitations. The theoretical framework builds on research conducted by both academics and practitioners.

Chapter 2 explains the various elements that make up the specification. This will help both the buyer and the supplier to understand the set requirements in same manner, thereby leading to planned products.

Chapter 3 describes how visions can affect specification management especially in outsourced product development. Through in-depth case studies this chapter explains how visions affect specification management and, thus, outsourced development. If visions are used as a strategic tool in outsourcing, then they can be used to drive the core capabilities and thus achieve planned products.

Specifications are central to product development and have to be managed such that the buyer–supplier interactions are as unproblematic as possible. In order to aid the interaction process Chapter 4 proposes a specification supplier framework to improve and sustain specification management. This framework is built on the context and causal conditions of existing problems faced in the automotive industry.

Chapter 5 explores the specification processes in the automotive and the aircraft industries and recommends a specification flow process to make integrated products. This process could help OEMs to develop high quality, low cost and well-interfaced products.

Chapter 6 researches existing models in outsourcing and then explores their advantages and disadvantages. Only one model, namely, the Quinn and Hilmer model of outsourcing, was found to be applicable to the entire spectrum of make/buy decisions. This chapter expands on their model, connecting it to specifications and applying it to real-life situations.

Chapter 7 expands on the application of portfolio models in purchasing. Research has been carried out on the limited applications of portfolio models in purchasing and found them to be lacking in dimensions such as that of specifications. It elaborates on the outsourcing process at the world-class Toyota Motor Corporation and links these specifications within the help of portfolio models.

Specifications need to be validated, i.e., checked for conformance to the plans. Often suppliers do not deliver to the specifications and then the contracts are used to legally oblige them to pay for non-conformance. Chapter 8 explains that contracts are not only a legal document but can be used as a commercial document with explicit parameters to ensure that the suppliers deliver to the specifications. This type of validating contract is explored in this chapter.

With specifications becoming increasingly complex and organisations increasingly outsourcing, there is a need to develop supply structures that can help in this transition. In other words, there is a need for organisations to be surrounded by suppliers that can understand high level specifications. The automotive industry in particular has been promulgating the concept of 'systems suppliers' to deal with high level specifications. Chapter 9 sets out to explain the characteristics of such a supplier and the associated supply network.

Chapter 10 explores the dynamics of digital procurement. Sourcing that was previously done by face-to-face contact and paperwork is becoming digital. This chapter explores digitalisation and concludes with some of the challenges for specification management. Digital or not, the challenge of specification management still exists.

Methodology

Throughout the research interviews were used as the primary data collection mode. The extensive data collected from interviews were analysed using the open coding technique (Strauss and Corbin, 1990). In this technique, data are first broken down by separating an observation, a sentence, or a paragraph and giving a name to each separate idea or event. Data are then grouped in categories that pull together groups of ideas and events. These become sub-categories. The next step in the method – axial coding – regroups and links the categories to each other in a logical manner. The objective of axial coding is to identify main categories (phenomena) and make connections between them and their sub-categories, leading to the development of a series of propositions clarifying context and causal conditions to phenomena.

In order to improve reliability and repeatability of the data collection procedures, data from interviews, open discussions and observations are collected and maintained in three forms:

- directly taken field notes from interviews and observations;
- expanded typed notes made as soon as possible after the field work (this includes comments on problems and ideas that arise during each stage of the fieldwork and that will guide further research);
- a running record of analysis and interpretation (open coding and axial coding).

Accuracy of the data and intermediate findings was improved through the use of multiple sources of evidence, the establishment of a chain of evidence, and letting key informants review draft result reports. Documents, semi-structured interviews and observations provided multiple data sources of the same phenomenon. Establishing a chain of evidence is ensured by the existence of documents such as the interview notes, transcriptions, and notes made immediately after the fieldwork. Finally, interview reports and the up-to-date analyses were sent to key people for validation and comments. Our analysis confirmed the existence of the four key areas identified by the task force. The questionnaires that were used to gather the opinions of the suppliers were analysed with the help of the open coding technique.

Aims of the book

I hope that this book will be a useful guide for top managers in pursuit of ever improving their organisations. Partial results have been published in different journals and permission from them is gratefully acknowledged. It would be a pleasure to get feedback from readers and comments and suggestions for improvement are always welcome. My journey into this fascinating world of specification management continues and will be shared through subsequent publications.

1 A theoretical perspective on specifications

Today firms are more actively involving suppliers in their integrated development processes and have identified suppliers as a source of competitive advantage (Cusumano and Takeishi, 1991; Nishiguchi and Beaudet, 1998; Quinn and Hilmer, 1994; Richardson, 1993). That means that there is room for development and identification of factors that could help sustain or improve the relationship between the buyer and the supplier in outsourced product development. There are various factors that one could look into when trying to improve or sustain the buyer–supplier relation such as Just In Time, location of suppliers, trust, specialised investments, specifications and contracts (Cusumano and Takeishi, 1991; Harris *et al.*, 1998; Lamming, 1993; Sako, 1992). With the exception of specifications, the literature dealing with buyer–supplier relationships is very rich. Supported by few existing references (Smith and Reinartsen, 1991; Kaulio, 1996; Harris *et al.*, 1998), this book sets out to explore the role of specifications in product development.

Setting the scene

In order to grasp the essence of specifications, one must go back in time to the era of craftsmanship and observe the changing role of specifications in the automotive industry, as it was the first to be hit by the 'Japanisation' of industries. We will first discuss the evolution of work practices from craftsmanship to lean production, then study the varying demands on the services of the suppliers in the work practices discussed above, and finally analyse the changing role of specifications in these eras.

Evolution of the automotive industry and the changing role of suppliers

In the era of craftsmanship there was a direct link between the customer and the shop floor personnel. A classic example of an automotive firm from the craftsmanship era is P&L – Panhard & Levassor (Womack *et al.*, 1990) which was the leading automotive company in 1894. There were no car dealers and no standards in the late 1800s. Each car was tailored to individual customers. Since there was no standardisation, there was a need for rework such as filing and shaping parts so as to make them fit. There were a number of individual sub-contractors working directly in the P&L plant (ibid.). There were obvious problems with the craftsmanship style due to the following reasons:

- high production costs;
- reliability problems as no two cars were alike;
- inability on the part of the independent sub-contractors to innovate.

The problems inherent to the craftsmanship era (in automobiles) gave rise to mass production. In the beginning of mass production 'Fordism' was developed by Henry Ford (manufacturer of the Model T car). Ford started by using standard gauges, and thus standardising the work procedures so that the components could be interchangeable (Womack *et al.*, 1990). Ford also pulled everything in-house, manufacturing everything that was required to make an automobile under one roof. The parts were standard and, thus, did not require skilled personnel, unlike during the craftsmanship era. During the 1950s, Ford outsourced components that were previously made in-house. The outsourcing was price-based and the supplier with the lowest quote got the orders. Low profit margins meant that the suppliers could not invest in research and development and thus innovate for the customer. The pioneer continuous flow system developed by Ford – steel and rubber came into the factory and ready-to-drive cars came out (Krafcik, 1988) – had to be complemented by a number of managerial principles before it was possible to set up a traditional model of mass production. Though Ford was successful, he did not provide the customers with variety. However, Alfred P. Sloan of General Motors did.

Womack *et al.* (1990) and Berggren (1992) emphasise the importance of the development at General Motors during the 1920s under Alfred Sloan. Sloan provided variety to the customer and also created independent profit centres within the General Motors group to make components. Sloan developed stable sources for outside funding, created new professions within marketing and finance to complement the engineering professions, etc. In the 1980s, General Motors tried to outsource many components that were made by the in-house profit centres, but since this was met with internal resistance, the outsourcing percentage remained quite small and was still price-based. Sloan's ideas combined with Ford's manufacturing system (technology) and Taylor's scientific management (organisation) were instrumental in developing the traditional mass production system (Berggren, 1992).

Over time, each firm goes through significant changes in its strategy, experiences deep crises and/or strong growth, and changes in its geographical penetration (market and manufacturing investments in new regions, or withdrawals) (Boyer and Freyssenet, 1995). The specific trajectory of Japanese manufacturing and, in particular, Toyota, gave rise to the lean production system. Krafcik (1988) was the first to coin the name 'lean production'. In the lean production paradigm, independent suppliers are involved to a large extent and the OEM is restricted to vital systems or the whole product, in this case, the car

(Lamming, 1993). Large numbers of components and systems may be outsourced according to the lean production paradigm. Womack and Jones summarise the main elements of the lean enterprise as follows:

- focusing on a limited number of activities within each firm;
- strong collaborative ties with clear agreements on target costing;
- joint definition on levels of process performance;
- joint definition on rate of continuous improvement and cost reduction;
- consistent accounting systems;
- a well-defined formula for splitting the losses and gains. In the lean enterprise, each participant adds value to the production chain;
- reduction of waste that gives the potential for significant performance improvement;
- rotation of middle and senior managers between company operations; suppliers and foreign operations are the central elements of this new industrial structure.

(Womack and Jones, 1994)

It will be observed from the above that the role of the supplier has changed. In the craftsmanship era, the role of the supplier was to take charge of making parts and components that were fitted together by the main assembler. Sloan provided variety for the customer in the mass production era and set up independent profit centres within the General Motors group, though once again there was limited outsourcing that was price-based. In the era of lean production, the supplier involvement shot up from no or little involvement to increased involvement and responsibility.[1] Suppliers are now responsible for entire systems and subsystems. In the current era of lean production, supplier management is considered to be very important and many manufacturers are concentrating on their core competencies, leaving the rest to the suppliers (Leenders *et al.*, 1994).

Evolution of the role of specifications

We saw that the role of the supplier has changed from the craftsmanship era to the lean production era. The changing roles of suppliers have obvious implications for the specifications because the more involved the suppliers are, in terms of time and complexity of the systems, the more they will presumably be involved in the specifications.

The specifications in the case of craftsmanship were very loose as the goods arriving at P&L were described as having 'approximate specifications'[2] (Womack *et al.*, 1990). General Motors had well-defined specifications,[3] as otherwise it would have been hard to estimate the lowest cost during the bidding process for the part in question. In cases where the specifications were not well defined, General Motors suffered losses[4] as the suppliers could exploit them, i.e., by charging money for changes in specifications. In lean production, since supplier involvement is probably the highest as compared to all the other eras, the specifications would require joint involvement. Hence, the role of specifications has been changing from a loose specification in the craftsmanship era, to a tight specification, and finally to a joint specification (where both the OEM and the suppliers collaborate in the writing of the specification). There can be problems with each and this was quite evident considering the losses in the craftsmanship era and the mass production era (ibid.).

Understanding specifications

In the product development process there are various activities that take place between the buyer and supplier, for example, joint testing, computer-assisted design (CAD) data exchange, joint operational design, etc. Specifications are also exchanged between the buyer and the supplier. Specifications have been defined in a number of different ways. In order to understand the actual term specifications, the term design needs to be explained. Vincenti (1990) describes the term design[5] and takes it to mean two things, namely, the contents of a set of plans and the process by which these plans are produced. A set of plans for the product is equivalent to the written description of products (Smith and Reinartsen, 1991) and may be seen as a narrow definition of specification. Specification could also correspond to the process of producing the plans (Kaulio, 1996). This may be seen as a broad definition of specification. In other words, the broad definition of specifications not only includes the process of arriving at the specification, but also encompasses the document called the specification (ibid.).

Specifications could also be seen as representing two different perspectives, namely the commissioning perspective and the mediating perspective (Kaulio, 1996).[6] In the commissioning perspective, there is one-way communication and the contents of the specifications are essentially ready and simply have to be worked on. In the mediating perspective, the specification is a forum for dialogue and, thus, the specification is created by the joint effort of the different actors in the development process. Kaulio further comments that the commissioning perspective corresponds to the narrow definition of specifications, while the mediating perspective corresponds to the broad definition of specifications.

It is difficult to comment on which is superior: the narrow definition or the broad definition. Even in the narrow definition, the process is present because without the process there will be no specification. Essentially this discussion indicates that there are two processes involved. The first is the process of getting to a final specification document, and the next is to execute the contents of the specification document and to realise the product. For the purposes of this book the following definitions of specification (Figure 1.1) will be used. The specifying process is defined as the process involved in getting to the final written document. This is done by creating and repeating a number of draft documents (through sub-processes).

The specifications are a means of conducting dialogue in the development process between both internal and external actors. They assist in the co-ordination and integration of the design activities (Kaulio, 1996). The creation

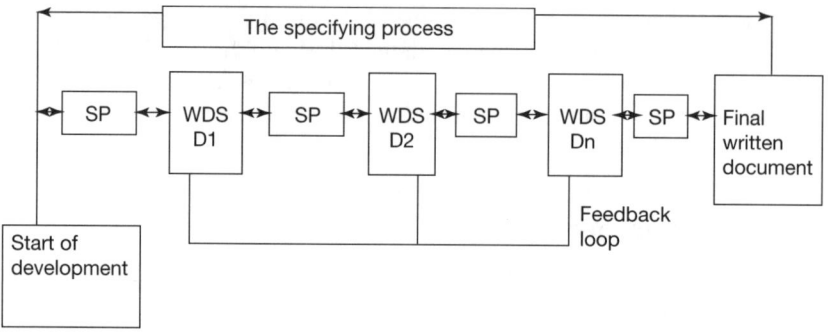

Figure 1.1 The view of specifications

Notes: SP = Specification Sub-Process (continuous development of the specification documents)
WDS = Written document called the specification
D1 = Draft 1, D2 = Draft 2, Dn = nth draft of the specification document

of interdependent tasks linked to each other and performed by specialised participants brings a need for co-ordination (Karlson, 1994). If the specifications were falsely interpreted by the supplier or the buyer due to a faulty process, the output would be chaotic. This means that the specifications may have to consider both the internal process of the supplier/buyer as well as the external process (the patterns of specification interaction between the buyer and the supplier). Imai *et al.* (1985) comment that information is a key resource and is of utmost importance in the new product development process. In outsourced product development, the buyer and the supplier each deal with a separate part of the environment and these tasks need to be linked to each other (Lawrence and Lorsch, 1967), thereby necessitating a high degree of co-ordination between the buyer and the supplier and thus in the information flow. This means that the flow of information between and within processes is very crucial for the success of the product development process and is a vital component for the survival of the product development process as a whole. In other words, no information flow would mean no co-ordination and thus the new product development process would be affected.

This move towards increased supplier involvement requires both internal and external co-ordination between and within the OEM and supplier firms. This is because organisations, due to external contingencies, become segmented into units, each of which is given a special task of dealing with a specific part (ibid.). This means that the buyer and suppliers engage in specialised tasks and these have somehow to be linked together. These tasks are interrelated and interdependent and cannot be performed in isolation. This division of labour and the interdependence between the tasks that are carried out by the OEM firm and the suppliers make the need for co-ordination all the more important (Karlson, 1994).

Many analysts fail to recognise the importance of co-ordination which results in problems when making the product (Karlson, 1994). Simon (1976) sees organisations as 'decision making and information processing systems', which, according to Karlson (1994), moves the focus from how people are grouped to the decision process itself. Galbraith (1973) subscribes to the idea of co-ordination being a decision process.[7] The greater the uncertainty,[8] the more information that will need to be processed (ibid.). Simon[9] (1976) argues that co-ordination is a process consisting of three steps, namely, the development of a plan of behaviour for the members of the group, the communication of that plan to the members, and finally, the acceptance of the plan by all the members. This indicates that the co-ordination of the specific activities and competencies (suppliers focus on parts/ components while the OEM focuses on the overall architecture) is essentially a decision process in which transformation of communication and information is important. This focus on communication by both Galbraith (1973), and Simon (1976) could mean that if more emphasis is put on communications (quality, amount, time, etc.), co-ordination would be more positive.

Solutions to the problems of communication include putting specialist groups together in the same location, providing them with tools to communicate, etc. (Karlson, 1994). Karlson suggests that the interdependency between the tasks requires co-ordination to be performed on an ongoing basis. Co-ordination could be facilitated by procedures, plans, standardised product structures, the organisational members themselves, etc. According to Galbraith (1973), the organisation can handle task uncertainty in two major ways, namely, by reducing the need for information processing (creation of slack resources and self-contained tasks) and, second, increasing the capacity to process information (investment in vertical information systems and creation of lateral relations). These elements are as follows:

- Slack resources – Uncertainty is reduced by increasing the amount of slack, for example, having tolerances, increasing the lead time to delivery, etc., though this will be at a cost to the customer. The specifications[10] allow the creation of slack as the development personnel could make the different trade-offs with respect to the whole product, described by the specification.
- Self-contained tasks – Having a number of skills pooled together in a group reduces uncertainty. This reduces the diversity faced by the group and facilitates the collection of all the resources required to solve a problem. The specifications may be worked on by the different groups in charge of the different areas of the final product. The specifications thus facilitate the creation of self-contained tasks.
- Vertical information systems – The changes in the specifications or targets are used to create a new plan instead of updating the old plan. The frequency of updates would depend on the amount of uncertainty faced. The more frequent the updates, the fewer the number of exceptions referred upwards. The specifications, if updated very frequently, could help the developers make their decisions on the latest information rather than relying on outdated information.
- Creation of lateral relations – Lateral relations are created so that the problems are solved at a lower level, thereby decentralising decision-making.

Rather than refer problems upward, task forces are formed that could help to solve problems. Specifications facilitate the creation of lateral relations as they form an arena for co-operation and communication for all those involved in development.

The above discussion illustrates that the use of specifications as support structures (by designers, for example) may help in reducing uncertainty, facilitating the decision-making process or simply ensuring better co-ordination. As stated by Womack and Jones (1994), in addition to co-ordination, the integration of actors within the OEM must be handled. They highlight the need for cross-functional teams where the members are under the authority of a transversal process management function. Clark and Fujimoto (1991) and Karlson (1994) all discuss the importance of integration and co-ordination, but limit it to internal actors and fail to explain the importance of co-ordination and integration between the internal and external actors. Helper (1991) details the importance of information exchange and commitment in an OEM supplier relation as 'rich information flow both endangers and requires a high degree of commitment to the relationship'.

It appears that both co-ordination between the OEM and suppliers and integration in their internal processes are important. Co-ordination requires support structures such as specifications. Also, co-ordination must be performed on an ongoing basis, as the OEM–supplier tasks are interdependent. Specifications could help in the dialogue process (communication between the participants) and improving communication leads to effective co-ordination between the OEMs and the suppliers on an ongoing basis. Specifications also help in integrating the actors from the OEM and supplier, as they require a joint effort in order for the specification to be articulated and turned into a final product. Integrated cross-functional teams at the OEMs may have to include actors from the supplier companies if the OEMs and the suppliers have to work together in an integrated manner, for instance, in making joint decisions. Let us investigate the specifications in more depth.

Specifications: an overview

Japan's main source of competitive advantage has been its ability to bring new high quality products rapidly to market in the global automotive industry (Ward *et al.*, 1995). Industry experts with whom initial interviews were conducted revealed that specifications could have been a factor contributing to the success of the Japanese. Two researchers in operations management (namely Everett and Swamidass)[11] attempted to assess operations management from a strategic perspective by using a specific method.[12] In order to do so, they reviewed the literature under the theme of 'The core content of manufacturing strategy includes cost, quality, flexibility and technology'. These authors first chose a representative sample of the current body of manufacturing strategy literature and identified the content variables in each of the writings. The authors conclude that although they have carefully examined the studies, the interpretation of the authors' intended content variable could be a potential source of error. Using concentric boxes, the most frequently mentioned variables are placed at the core and less frequently mentioned variables far away from the core. In this way, the most common themes can be identified. The less researched variables can also be identified.

The above discussion shows a structure when writing a literature review. In the research question on specifications the above structured approach will be followed. The main points in the structured approach are as follows:

- List the most representative sample of authors in the specification literature.
- Identify the message that these authors intend to convey.
- Note that there is bound to be error/inconsistency in the interpretation of the content variables.
- Identify the content variable most frequently mentioned.
- Draw concentric boxes to identify the most popular content variable and map it to the least popular concentric variable. This will also help identify the less researched and most researched variables.
- Comment on each of the content variables and their applicability to the research question. Identify possible drawbacks in the current literature so that the research questions can have a firm base in current literature.

The literature analysis on specifications begins with the list of authors and the content variables (see Table 1.1). After this, the concentric boxes are drawn to identify the most popular topic as opposed to the least popular topic. This is represented in Figure 1.2. The most important content variables[13] are listed in Stage 1, followed by Stage 2, Stage 3 and Stage 4. The literature review will be structured in the same way. First we will discuss Stage 1 and then continue sequentially until Stage 4.

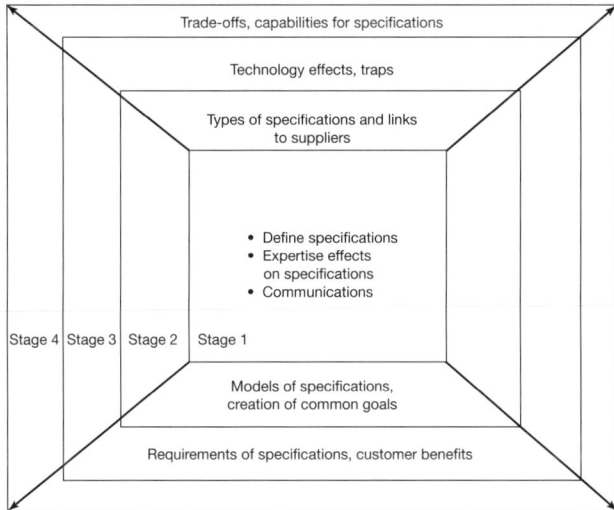

Figure 1.2 Content variables

Table 1.1 List of authors and content variables

	Define specifications	Types of specifications	Requirements of specifications	Models of specifications	Capabilities for specifications	Expertise effects on specifications	Customer benefits	Technology effects	Type of supplier	Trade-offs	Traps	Communications	Creation of common goal
Smith & Reinartsen	*												
Hollins & Pugh	*	*					*			*	*		*
Elliot	*												
Haslam		*											
Hollins & Hurst		*					*						
Roozenburg & Dorst	*		*										
Fine & Whitney			*			*		*					
Smith & Rhodes				*									
Iansiti				*									
Wheelwright & Clark					*							*	
Schein						*							
Schrader						*							
Clark						*							
Ward				*					*				
Karlson								*				*	
Aoshima													
Kamath & Liker									*				
Cusumano									*				
Rosenau											*		
Söderquist												*	
Clark & Fujimoto												*	
Karlsson et al.													*
Burnes & New													*
no. of times mentioned	4	3	2	3	1	4	2	2	3	1	2	4	3

Core elements: Stage 1

The core elements are those topics that have received the most attention in specification research. The topics include the meaning of a specification, the expertise effects on specifications and, finally, the communication of specifications. Many definitions of the term specification cause confusion and these different definitions will be discussed here. Different definitions of the term specification could lead to a misunderstanding of the role of the specification by both the buyer and the supplier. The modes in which the specifications are communicated will also be explored. Certain roles of the specification may require certain modes of communication. Finally, since specifications may be affected by the expertise present in an organisation, the expertise–specification link will be explored. The expertise present in an organisation could actually shape the way in which the desired specification is executed.

Define specifications

Specifications have been defined in a number of different ways. Smith and Reinartsen (1991) define them as the written description of products that are generated in advance to guide the development of the product. Hollins and Pugh (1990) define specifications as the systematic activity necessary from the identification of a market or user need to the selling of a product to satisfy that need. Elliot (1993), commenting on the process of defining the requirements in the early part of the design process, described it as being: 'to turn the abstract and (usually) ill-formed idea of the customer (his dream) into a concrete statement of requirements against which the supplier can tender and carry out detailed design (a specification)'. In Iansiti's (1995) interviews, an engineer described a specification as one that provided certain envelopes to stay within. Some of the parameters in the specification were fixed such as the size of the box, power outlets, etc., while the rest of the parameters could change.

The process of arriving at a specification has been well documented by Smith and Rhodes (1992). Each stage in the process of specifying leads to a straightforward compilation of information. Information on details is added and the content of the specification is progressively increased. A recent study by Söderquist (1997) indicated that specifications could contain data on the following:

- the scheduled order quantity for the finished product;
- design study lead time;
- quality demands;
- unit price for ordered quantity;
- a written functional description;
- competitive situation;
- internally generated budget and cost price, etc.

What was not mentioned, however, was whether the final specification or the transitional stages of the specification contained these data. This confirms

16 *Specifications: theoretical perspective*

Kaulio's (1996) contention that many researchers have not understood the complexity of specifications, their roles and transitional phases.

Smith and Rhodes (1992) illustrate the formation of the specification in a stage-by-stage approach including steps such as determine objectives, search and locate, obtain, sort and collate, synthesise and analyse and finally apply. As the stages are completed, the assimilation of information increases and so do knowledge and understanding. Smith and Rhodes comment that the market needs have to encapsulate the search in the following areas in order to satisfy the objectives:

- business and statistical departments;
- competitive and analogous products;
- patents;
- standards, codes, regulations and legislation;
- books, papers and reports;
- manufacturing facilities;
- specialists;
- buyers and users.

This information is fed into the specification, thereby increasing its content. The information from these areas may be enormous and Smith and Rhodes (1992) point out thirty-two primary elements such as:

- aesthetics;
- company constraints;
- competitors;
- customers;
- cost of the product, etc.

From the above discussion it is apparent that there are many parameters that can go into a specification. Söderquist (1997) mentions some of these parameters and Smith and Rhodes (1992) mention others. There could be many elements in a specification, hence, all attempts to create a definitive list of specification elements can be met with resistance by academics and practitioners alike, i.e., 'so what?' as there could be other elements. It appears from the above discussion that, instead of concentrating on the elements, it is more important to understand the factors that could be given to the suppliers based on their capabilities in order to promote mutual understanding between the buyer and the supplier. If there is so much information, then there is a need to analyse it, discard the irrelevant details, and thus concentrate on the important information (Smith and Rhodes, 1992). There is a diverging phase (Kaulio, 1996), where information is collected, and a converging phase, where there is consolidation or convergence of information. The information has to be sorted and collated in order to synthesise and analyse it, thereby undergoing a converging phase. There could be more diverging phases after the converging phase has commenced, as there may be particulars that need additional data. As the project grows, there is a need for more data in the converging phases so that the specifications can be updated and turned into a workable document. Specifications change over time and this point must be re-emphasised.

There are a number of different definitions of specification, which could also lead to confusion. This may be minimised by creating a common understanding of the specification parameters between the buyer and the supplier. The confusion could arise because the buyer and the supplier can interpret the same messages in different ways. There is a need to generate a common understanding of the elements that constitute a specification so that its role can be understood in the same manner between the buyer and the supplier.

Expertise effects on specifications

Kaulio (1996) observes that specifications change over time in relation to the user and are not static. Kaulio further points out that specifications are an arena for co-operation between the different actors in the design process. Therefore, it is important to examine the effects of expertise on the specifications. If the partners (the OEM and the supplier) do not reveal knowledge related to their domain of expertise, there could be a misfit (lack of clarity), or if the partners state requirements not in their area of expertise, there could be restrictiveness (Schrader and Göpfert 1994). According to Schein (1985), restrictiveness occurs when there is limited trust in the suppliers. Clark (1989) comments that the long tradition of OEMs doing everything in-house makes it all the more difficult to involve the suppliers and thus the OEM specifies the data to a very large extent.

According to Schrader *et al.* (1994) it is hard for the engineers to accept that the suppliers are experts due to the fact that the specifications are their requirements and thus they tend to break them down into great detail. If the problems occur in the engineer's sphere of responsibility (ibid.), then there could be negative personal consequences and as a result the engineers tend to do everything. There are other reasons for lack of clarity (ibid.), such as unclear tasks, changing situations, high cost of clarity and, finally, the engineers may wish to refrain from stating certain requirements that might be in conflict when individuals have different goals. The effects of lack of clarity could be that the solutions are of a poor quality or there may be changes in the product development process, etc. On the other hand, the effects of restrictiveness could be many, such as:

- the lack of motivation to seek better solutions;
- generation of early specifications based on preliminary problem analysis;
- no search for other solutions;
- delays as the customer demands specifications beyond their domain of expertise.

On many occasions, the design staff refuse to generate the specifications and put this responsibility onto the marketing staff. Perhaps they are trying to push the blame onto the marketing staff, in case problems arise. This means that there could be problems with the overall product as the whole product[14] is realised by iterating between the whole and 'parts of the whole' according to the practitioner tradition. The wholes and 'parts of the whole' are constructed by having clear specifications and by iterating between them. Though they can be agreed upon at the beginning of the process, the specifications are hard to visualise, so every attempt must be made to write the ideas down and then discuss them with the actors. This allows the specification to be used as a working document while also allowing the actors to co-operate.

Liker et al. (1995) comment that if the increased information complexity as a result of increased supplier collaboration is to be managed, then the OEMs will have to carefully think about the specifications that they give to the suppliers. Hence, the overall specification has to be broken down in such a way that the separate parts are integrated and add up to the overall specification. Integration of the different parts of the specification is necessary in order to have one document called the specification. This also means that the different constituents of the specifications will have to be integrated. This calls for collaboration and commitment on the part of the people working with the specifications. The observations from the above discussion are that both the role of specifications and the role of written contracts as a driver of specifications have potential for further research.

The specifications may have to be written for the whole product or can be written for parts of the product, as the existing specifications may suffice for the remaining parts. The specifications can be restricted due to certain legal demands and hence have to take many factors as given before the start of the specification writing process. The specifications can be affected by the cost. The converse is also true as the specifications can affect the cost. In other words, the quality of the specifications has a direct bearing on the costs that have been targeted for the part in question. Clark (1989) explains some of the above mentioned points with the help of the critical path analysis. The extent to which parts are developed in-house, as opposed to outsourcing the parts, is called 'scope'. This refers to the extent of involvement of the buyer in the specifications. Scope depends on the critical path and unless outsourcing can reduce lead time[15] in the critical path, it would make better sense to in-source the parts.

The suppliers therefore have to bring in additional capability to the project so that the lead time is reduced. The extent to which the specification formation can involve suppliers depends on the ability of the suppliers to reduce the lead time in the critical path. The critical path is the factor determining who generates the specification, the extent of carryovers in specifications, etc. The concept of carryovers from one project to another can be extended from one platform[16] to another. Between platforms, specifications are generally different, whereas within platforms, they are modified to a limited extent. Typical examples within a platform would be changes in the display dials, a small variation in the headrest of the seat, an extra cup holder, etc., whereas changes between platforms are in the overall architecture of a vehicle such as the chassis, wheel base, etc. The specification therefore depends on the type of project. Changes in the specification are directly proportional to the type of project. In other words, the more radically new the project, the greater the changes in the specification. In relating to the work of Smith and Rhodes (1992), it is quite apparent that the more radical the project is, the more time is spent collecting information about the project and consequently in the converging and diverging phases of collecting information.

Specification and communications

Good communication between the buyer and supplier, within the OEM and also within the supplier firm, is necessary for specifications. A review of communication patterns is necessary to clarify this. Wheelwright and Clark's (1993) model of communication fits well here as it presents different modes of communication such as those of early involvement, etc. According to Wheelwright and Clark, there are four modes of communication between the upstream and downstream, i.e., between the supplier and the buyer. There are also four dimensions of communication, namely the richness of media, the frequency of communication, the direction of communication and the timing of communication. The dimensions are on a scale from poor to good. The richness of media could be from sparse exchange of documents to a very interactive face-to-face exchange of information. The frequency could stretch from low and/or infrequent to a very high, frequent and interactive communication. The direction of communication can vary from one-way communication to a two-way dialogue between the parties. The timing of communication can stretch from late communication, such as after the design work has been completed, to a very early communication and, thus, early discussion of problems.

According to Wheelwright and Clark, the first mode of communication, is the serial or batch mode of interaction where the buyer does all the design work and transmits all the completed information to the supplier at one time. In effect, the buyer does not take into account the input from the seller and thereby might not benefit from the strengths of the supplier. Hence, as per the communication dimensions, the timing is late, the direction is one way, the frequency is low and the communication is sparse.

The second mode of communication is the early start in the dark where the suppliers start work on their own without any information from the buyer. The buyer informs the supplier in a one-shot transmission about the completed design. Though the buyer and supplier work in parallel, they do not share information and thus they may be working on totally different ideas, leading to a period of confusion when the one-shot information is communicated to the supplier. This confusion can increase the actual lead time of the process, though if the areas worked on by both the parties are complementary, the lead time can actually be reduced. This kind of communication occurs when the supplier feels that in order to survive, they need to get going early in the process.

In the third type, namely, early involvement, the buyer engages in active communication with the supplier, however, only after a substantial part of the design is done. There is sharing of information and joint problem-solving even before the design is completed and finalised by the buyer. The suppliers start their design work only after the buyers have finalised theirs. This joint solving tends to reduce delays, as there is a better understanding of the issues.

In the last type, namely, the integrated problem-solving mode, both the buyer and the supplier engage in discussions right from the beginning. The thoughts and ideas are shared from the start. In effect, there is integrated problem-solving.

Alexander (1985), signifying the importance of good communications, said: 'Innovative design does not sell itself but it depends on the creative communications skills and positive commitment of marketing staff working in conjunction with the designers to ensure the commercial success of a product.' The importance of communication is further emphasised by Clark and Fujimoto (1991), who suggest that there is an acute need to tear down barriers between different functions within an organisation such as purchasing, engineering, etc. Integration of functions in an organisation will lead to increased co-operation between the different actors. However, increased co-operation alone is not enough. Rich two-way communication is also a necessity for effective integrated problem- solving cycles (ibid.). Differences in skills, knowledge, education, experience and background can all contribute to misunderstandings, so in effect, better communication on its own would not help.

In order to be able to understand the other actors in the development process and ask the right questions, there is a need to understand the tacit knowledge possessed by the other actors (Karlson, 1994). Hence, the interpretation of information and an understanding of tacit knowledge are important factors in the product development integrative process as tacit knowledge is a reflection of the skill possessed by an individual (Söderquist, 1997). Since there are thousands of interfaces, components, etc., in an automobile, it is difficult for any one person to keep track of all the components at any given point in time. Many of the tasks have interfaces and interdependence may exist between different tasks. The interdependence between these tasks leads to co-ordination which is further defined by Mintzberg (in Karlson, 1994) as an activity that needs to be performed by any organisation if it is to run well. Communication and co-operation can be hampered if the actors have different professional affiliations (Karlson, 1994).

Karlson suggests that the complexity of tasks puts increased demands on co-ordination, which cannot be performed by generalists but by people with narrow or specialised skills. Integration of these specialists thus becomes a critical issue of concern. New product development consists of a complicated process with numerous inputs, which need to be co-ordinated and integrated, thus signifying the need to improve communications.

The above discussion indicates that the specifications are dependent on good communication. There are different communication modes as well as different categories of suppliers. One obvious question concerns what communication mode in the specification may be used with a particular type of supplier. Furthermore, if communication is a vital element in specification, then shouldn't the communication–supplier interface be mentioned as one parameter within the specification itself, so as to better articulate its role? Also, the form of communication has not been studied, i.e., whether a detailed specification or a drawing alone will be transmitted in these modes. Though it has been mentioned that one person alone cannot possess all knowledge, and that development tasks are inter-dependent, little has been said about how to achieve co-ordination. The specifications can be seen as performing the role of co-ordination by bring actors from different professional affiliations together in order to improve communication and the quality of the product.

Stage 2 elements

The topics that will be discussed here are in decreasing order of importance (in this research) as compared to the core elements. In this section, the different types of specifications will be examined in relation to their implications for the suppliers. In other words, the link between the categories of suppliers and the type of specification that they receive will be examined. This could also mean that a particular role of the specification could be to allocate the 'right' specification to the supplier based on their capabilities and capacities. The different types of suppliers will be explored, as the different kinds of specifications may necessitate different categories of suppliers. The different models of specifications will also be explored, as these models describe both the specification process and the way in which the written document called the specification is obtained. Finally, the creation of common goals between the buyer and the supplier to aid specification work will then be examined.

Types of specifications and links to suppliers

While there has been no detailed study on specifications, Haslam (1988) has identified five different types of specifications, even though it is not necessary for the complete specification to fit one of these types. This theoretical development can shed light on the different possibilities or types of specifications. The specifications can be closed, open, restricted, exclusive and negative. In the closed description, there is no need for any supplier input as the specification is complete in all respects. The closed specification offers a complete description of the item. In the open specification, the standards/functionality to be met are given to the supplier and the supplier is asked to supply appropriate samples. In the restricted specification, the supplier is asked to restrict him/herself to the use of certain items or sources, etc. In the exclusive specification, the use of certain goods or materials is prohibited. In the negative specification, items are written in a negative way, for example, instead of stating that an item should withstand a 13kg. weight, it would state that the item should withstand a force of not less than 13kg. The point is why apply a higher weight when it is not needed? While the different types of specifications can be used individually, a complex item like an automobile would require an integrated specification, i.e., a mixture of some of the above-defined categories. This is because the automobile manufacturer may employ different modes of collaboration such as total outsourcing, joint development, etc., with the supplier which would necessitate integrated specification.

Smith and Reinartsen (1991) discuss other types of specifications such as the weak specification. A specification could be weak (inconsistent, poorly structured, unachievable, etc.) if the marketing department works in isolation. In isolation they might generate inconsistent goals. If the engineers do not discuss these goals, the likely result will be a weak specification. Smith and Reinartsen state that the isolated work of marketing and the no-discussion policy of the engineers can lead to a product that is designed superbly, and yet, cost is twice the target value. This shows that conflicting goals need to be discussed from the beginning. According to Hollins and Hurst (1995), poor specifications can occur due to the following: omissions, misleading requirements, unclear accuracies, inconsistencies and impossible requirements.

The different types of specifications may confuse the OEM when it makes the important decision concerning the specification–supplier match. The explanation of the different types of specifications does not indicate the type of specification to be given to the different categories of suppliers. If this is not done and there is no match between the supplier and the specification, there could be problems, as the supplier will not be able to understand the specifications.

Based on their capabilities and capacities, suppliers can interpret specifications in different ways. Hence, it may be beneficial for the capabilities of the suppliers to be noted from the beginning of the project and specifications tailored accordingly. There are different authors who classify suppliers in a number of different ways. Kamath and Liker (1994) comment that not all first-tier suppliers are considered or treated equally. They classify the suppliers as partners, mature, child and contractual suppliers. Contractual suppliers are also known as commodity suppliers.

- Partners are at the top of the hierarchy; they develop entire sub-systems and are collaborative members during the setting of specifications.
- Mature suppliers have very small differences from the partners as they too design complex assembly but are given the critical specifications.
- Child suppliers design simple assemblies to the detailed specification of the assembler.
- Contractual suppliers are those who develop and manufacture standard products which can be ordered from a catalogue.

In order to acknowledge that suppliers have different capabilities and capacities Araujo *et al.* (1999) propose that companies need to have different types of interfaces with their suppliers. The type of interface used in a relationship will have direct consequences for the way the resources of the supplier are activated. This argument can also be extended to the type and quality of the interface used between engineering and purchasing within a firm. Araujo *et al.* propose four interfaces, namely, the standardised, the specified, the translation and the interactive:

- The standardised interface corresponds to contractual suppliers.
- The specified interface corresponds to child suppliers.
- The translation interface corresponds to mature suppliers.
- The interactive interface corresponds to partner suppliers.

Though Araujo *et al.* do not acknowledge the contributions of Kamath and Liker (1994), the characteristics of the interfaces described are exactly the same. For example, Araujo states that in a specified interface, the suppliers are given precise directions by the OEM. Kamath and Liker (1994) do not name the interface but state that child suppliers require detailed specifications from the OEM. A further example would be the translation interface where directions are given to the supplier based on the context and functionality required. This, according to Kamath and Liker, is a mature supplier who requires rough specifications from the OEM to commence work. The automotive industry has in particular tried to make use of partner suppliers and often called them systems suppliers (Nellore, 2001). But the term has been misunderstood, often driven by fear and rarely if ever implemented. Thus, the use of systems suppliers and a framework for their deployment in specification management are lacking.

Ward *et al.* (1995) define the suppliers' design relationship with Toyota on three levels, namely partnership, parental and mature. Toyota, according to Ward *et al.*, varies the supplier design responsibility according to the capabilities of the supplier:

- The first level of partnership (for example, with suppliers of alternators) is characterised by the situation where the suppliers do a lot of work before the OEM's specification and present a lot of concepts/alternatives to the OEM. This is similar to the partner suppliers proposed by Kamath and Liker (1994).
- Mature suppliers wait for the OEM to define their needs and then begin development.
- Parental suppliers have very little input and design to OEM specification. This corresponds to child suppliers as proposed by Kamath and Liker (1994).

Cusumano and Takeishi (1991) categorise the role of suppliers into three different modes with respect to product development.

- The first are those suppliers that develop parts on their own without any input from the OEM firms; these are referred to as suppliers of proprietary parts. These correspond to the partner suppliers as described by Kamath and Liker (1994).
- The second are those suppliers who do detailed engineering based on the functional specifications provided by the OEM firms or, in other words, black box parts. This corresponds to the mature suppliers as described by Kamath and Liker (1994).
- In the last category are the suppliers who produce according to the detailed specifications provided by the OEMs. These correspond to the child suppliers

in the Kamath and Liker (1994) typology. Cusumano and Takeishi (1991) and Ward et al. (1995) do not mention contractual suppliers.

The above discussed categorisation of suppliers points out the existence of four types of suppliers, namely, the partner, mature, child and contractual. If there are different suppliers with varying capacities and capabilities, then it may be necessary to create a match between the specifications given to them and their capacities and capabilities. This fact may be considered when communicating the specifications to the suppliers so that problems can be overcome in the specifications. The link could also be considered in the supplier network, as this network could contain suppliers of more than one category. As the supplier network is penetrated, the degree of knowledge[17] that can be contributed to the OEM by the suppliers is also reduced. Hence, the role of specifications that are awarded to the suppliers deep inside the network should be to provide as much information as possible. Specification writers may thus have to explore the different types of specifications while at the same time continuously evaluating the specification–supplier match.[18] This discussion pertains to effect of the network[19] of suppliers on the role of specifications.

Models of specifications

Smith and Rhodes (1992) comment that the need to understand and interpret market needs and to encapsulate them in the product design specification (PDS) is all the more important with intensified global competition. Smith and Rhodes investigate and develop an information-processing model that would be useful in generating a good and thorough specification. The stages of the model are as follows:

- Determine objectives such as the extent of search (locations) and the benefits expected (areas to be identified in competitive products).
- Search for and locate the manufacturers and distributors of competitive products.
- Obtain the information.
- Sort and collate the information.
- Synthesise and analyse the information and make deductions.
- Apply as an extraction of data from information areas relevant to each PDS element and decide on the information to be incorporated into each PDS element.

Roozenburg and Dorst (1991) also propose a framework of activities that need to be performed during the specification process. The first is to collect the goals and objectives, the second step is to analyse the objectives, and the last step is to formulate the requirements.

Most of the above models do not take the supplier into consideration. In other words, how would the specification change if there is outsourcing? Would the steps in the models change? Also, the models lack an explanation of how to deal with the different types of specifications. Would the steps change for the different types of specifications or would they remain the same? The above models can be seen as belonging to the scientific tradition, as they do not take into account the reflection side of specification work and also fail to comment on the divergence and convergence of information. Finally, these models have shortcomings, some of which have been discussed above.

Traditional arm's-length models of product development have been derived mostly by observations in the mature industries such as the automotive or appliance industry (Iansiti, 1995). This has also been pointed out by Mudambi and Helper (1998) who observe a model of close, but adversarial buyer–supplier relationships in the US auto industry. In other words, there is formal co-operation with non-co-operative behaviour with short-term profit maximisation being the goal of the buyer. These models emphasise a sequential approach and avoid unnecessary changes. In other words, they have a well-defined product concept and specifications. On the other hand, in uncertain environments the processes cannot be so rigid. Outsourcing could be seen as adding to uncertainty as there are independent suppliers involved. This means that in outsourced product development the conditions change. Iansiti gives the example of a company that embraces change. This represents a development that is characterised by flexibility and responsiveness. In the traditional model, the concept freeze is much earlier in the development process, whereas in the flexible model it is much later and nearer to the market introduction. Iansiti suggests that the flexible product development process can be a source of competitive advantage in environments where technological evolution and competitive requirements are largely unpredictable, for example, in software and telecommunications sectors.

A complementary perspective can be obtained from the research done by Ward *et al.* (1995) on Toyota's specification process. Toyota is a 'world-class company' and can help to identify important factors that have contributed to them being given this appellation. Ward *et al.* comment that Toyota delays decisions and provides hard specifications very late in the process in order to ensure that the wrong decisions are not taken. It is for the same reason that they work with an excessive number of inexpensive prototypes including digital/virtual prototypes. Toyota begins designing and building body-stamping dies before all the drawings are finished. Toyota provides ranges in the specifications and then narrows it down rationally. In other words, Toyota uses a set-based concurrent engineering approach. The difference between a set-based and a traditional concurrent approach (Liker *et al.*, 1996), is that in a set-based approach, a set of possibilities are narrowed down rationally, whereas in the case of a traditional concurrent approach (the point-based approach), there is only one possibility that is tested (both the traditional and set-based approach are executed with cross-functional teams) but the approach is still point-based. However, even the set-based approach has problems. According to Liker *et al.* (1996), in many cases the suppliers found the ambiguous targets frustrating and preferred more straightforward targets and only some suppliers could handle this ambiguity.

Toyota communicates a whole set of possibilities simultaneously and avoids changes that move out of the set (Ward *et al.*, 1995). As a result, they reduce the frequency of communications, eliminate the need for co-location, etc. The above discussion gives a good theoretical background. Toyota's approach, which will be referred to in the analysis and conclusion chapter can be summarised as follows:

- define a set of solutions at a system level;
- define a set of possible solutions for the various sub-systems;
- explore sub-system solutions in parallel;
- narrow down and converge to a single solution;
- do not change until absolutely necessary.

All the suppliers present Toyota with their latest developments and present between one and three concepts with suggestions about the most promising ones (Ward *et al.*, 1995). The presentations include comparisons with other designs, test data, and working prototypes. Toyota, on the other hand, gives the suppliers extensive suggestions on improvements. In every case, the presentations preceded any information or statements from Toyota about the new model, but the suppliers were able to proceed because of their long relationship with Toyota and their understanding of the market trends. In contrast, the US manufacturers develop a list of specifications in-house, ask the suppliers for proposals and then choose the lowest bidder, according to Ward *et al.* (1995). Before embarking on a project, Toyota gathers information from the suppliers, understands the possibilities of the products, etc. If the suppliers exceed their target, then it becomes the new specification, otherwise the supplier can show Toyota that the specification is not possible to attain and a new level (lower than the target level) of specification can be reached.

Sobek II *et al.* (1999) have recently identified principles that are at the core of set-based concurrent engineering practices. These principles are three-fold, namely, mapping the design space, integrating by intersection and establishing feasibility before commitment.

Map the design space

- Explore a set of design possibilities within the problem area.
- Each functional department explores the constraints on its systems and sub-systems, i.e., they explore what can and cannot be done.
- Explore trade-offs by designing and prototyping systems/sub-systems or simulate the functionality of these systems/sub-systems so that the best alternatives can be chosen.
- Communicate sets of possibilities through matrix reports that contain evaluation of all the alternatives.

Integrate by intersection

- Choose the solution that is acceptable to all. This will be visible through matrix reports that allow the intersection of feasible sets to be visible.
- Impose minimum constraints on the functional areas so that there is flexibility to choose the best alternative and make the best compromises.
- If a product is made that is conceptually robust, i.e., fits with all the available alternative solutions, then it should proceed without waiting for other designs to be ready. This can also help collapse development time.

Establish feasibility before commitment

- All the opportunities and constraints must be fully understood before commitment is made to a certain design.
- As the concept possibilities decrease, the amount of detail within the remaining possibilities should increase as designers work to further narrow down the possibilities.
- The designers are expected to stay within the committed sets, so as to allow the other team members to proceed without concern for change that can cause rework.
- Toyota manages uncertainty by managing the expectations at each of the process gates in the development process. For example, high uncertainty items like transmissions are decided at the vehicle concept stage gate (pre-start-up phase in the development process) so that the uncertainty is dealt with early on in the process.

Iansiti's (1995) discussion of the traditional and flexible product development processes appears to be at a more theoretical level. In organisations making complex products such as cars and aeroplanes, there could be a mixture of products requiring both traditional and flexible development processes. Thus it appears that specifications will have to consider both the parts that need a flexible development process and parts that need a more traditional development process. However, the models of specification in fact give a structure as to how the specification is created. This structure could be utilised in order to further develop the concept of how the role of the specifications can be managed for integrated outsourced development, as the models do not include suppliers and are made for insourcing. The lack of a specification model for outsourcing indicates the need for research into developing a model conceptualising the role of the specifications.

Creation of common goals

Reinartsen (1997) claims that the creation of a strategy is the key context in which specification work is done. The products developed and produced are a critical part of the strategy and, as such, the product choices must fit with the rest of the strategy. In other words, the product specifications must be in line with the strategy of the company which should be collating the needs of the different departments. Burnes and New (1997) also support this as they claim that buyer–supplier relationships at the strategic level are not always the same as at the operational level, thereby leading to supplier-developed products that are not planned. In other words, if the OEMs do not have the same understanding of the suppliers' contribution at all levels, then the supplier may be over- or under-utilised. Burnes and New through in-depth case studies in the Rover Group (automobile manufacturer) and TRW (Steering Systems Supplier) in the United Kingdom observed that buyer–supplier relationships are initiated at the strategic level but often played out at the operational level. Though this may lead to a partnership-style relationship at the operational level, the same cannot be said about the relationship at the strategic level as mistrust and animosity can set in at this level. Burnes and New stress that the buyer–supplier relationship can only survive if the strategic interests of both parties and the operational benefits of both parties are achieved.

The research programme initiated by A.T. Kearney and Manchester Business School showed similar results. They demonstrate that relationships at the operational level can be more open and collaborative than relationships at the strategic level since strategic integration requires that the buyer–supplier firms have complementary goals. Burnes and New (1997) emphasise that close working relationships at one level do not mean close relationships at other levels. Suppliers may have a close working relationship at one level and not at the other levels, which could lead to a lack of focus on the expectations from the supplier. Burnes and New state that it would be counterproductive to maintain close working relationships at all levels and at the same time also emphasise that strategic initiatives must be owned by the operational staff if they are to be successful. The above two statements appear to be confusing, as unless there is a common goal at each level with respect to the supplier, the strategic initiatives will never be accepted by the different levels. This is also corroborated by Bowen et al. (1994) who state that subjectivity in operational decision-making (in product development) can be reduced by the creation of an overarching vision. The vision, according to Bowen et al., focuses the organisation on the future, serves as a concrete foundation for the organisation and also as a focal point for current decision-making. In other words, if one is to benefit from the suppliers' involvement in product development, we need to have a common vision about our suppliers. Furthermore, it is important to develop the visions for suppliers else outsourced product development could be at risk. The existence of visions for suppliers would be the starting point for any specification work to be undertaken and as such can help focus the OEM on the suppliers' capabilities and capacities and thus involve the suppliers accordingly. We will begin with a review of visions.

Visions

In order to reduce subjectivity in operational decision-making and make the contribution to knowledge and capabilities from development projects more explicit, a guiding vision is imperative for efficient product development (Bowen *et al.*, 1994). They argue that a vision should focus on the future, serve as a concrete foundation for the organisation and as a focal point for current decision-making. An overall definition of a vision is the combination of the mission, the strategy and the culture of a company (Lipton, 1996). Visions emphasise what must be accomplished and why, but allow for individual interpretations of how to reach the goals (Bowen *et al.*, 1994). They identify three different kinds of guiding visions in product development: the line of business guiding vision, the project guiding vision, and the product concept:

- A *line of business vision* could be a statement such as 'to beat the major competitor', or 'to be a low cost supplier'. These can readily translate into innovation and capability development. In order to beat the major competitor or to be a low cost supplier, the company might be required to develop a new technology, certain organisational and/or individual skills, or a new information system, for example. Thus, these visions translate into what to do for the product development teams. As well as serving as guidelines for the product development teams, line of business guiding visions should be owned and understood by everybody.
- The *project guiding vision* guides the members as to what learning must take place in order to achieve the goals defined by the line of business vision; what to learn from the project so that follow-on projects will run smoothly and so as to enhance internal capabilities. This vision needs to integrate across functions and time, thus ensuring consistency and inter-functional learning. It will also lead to confidence-building so that with each decision everybody knows where they are going.
- The *product concept* links the line of business vision to the daily decisions made by the developers. It helps the developers capture the perception of what the product means to the customers. The product concept should be complete, i.e. capture all successful user experience; it should be constant, i.e. target a set of customers; and it should be visible to everybody in the organisation, i.e. it should unify the people in the organisation. We extend the product concept to all the individuals connected directly or indirectly with the development and thus rename it the individual vision. It is not only developers that can use the visions but, rather, all the individuals in the organisation.

According to Kotter (1996), it should be possible to present, describe and transmit a vision statement in less than five minutes, or else the company is in trouble. Furthermore, he argues that firms fail if they allow too much complacency, underestimate the power of visions, under-communicate the visions (for example, failing to get a message across to the entire organisation), or permit obstacles to block the vision. Bowen *et al.* (1994) argue that visions do not need to originate at the top of the corporate hierarchy, but can spring from creative minds anywhere in the organisation. If this is true, these signals must be captured, analysed, and developed which includes disseminating them to all concerned actors and integrating them in a company's organisational routines.

To sum up, visions should provide the link between strategy and operations by setting targets that ensure strategic development and competitive advantage, simultaneously guiding the plethora of operational decisions, and allowing for enhancement of skills, knowledge and capabilities. A guiding vision is a clear picture of an operational future, an organisational or project destination that serves as a referent and focal point for decision-making (Bowen *et al.*, 1994). Making parallels to learning theory (Kim, 1993), the visions thus play an important role in managing the creation, evolution, and modification of individual and collective mental models of product development work.

The changing role of suppliers in the automotive industry that is a consequence of outsourcing and black box engineering means important integration between buyers and suppliers in product development (Clark and Fujimoto, 1991; Karlson, 1994; Quinn and Hilmer, 1994). For example, supplier engineers can participate as guest engineers on project platforms (Gong, 1993), or engage in very frequent and broad-banded communication with their counterparts in customer firms. This development can be described as a form of quasi-vertical integration: ideal relationships should be characterised by longevity, closeness and exclusivity (Richardson, 1993). If suppliers are to be considered as extended families by the OEMs in order to use the competencies and capabilities of the suppliers, then visions may not only have to be vertically articulated within the company but also horizontally articulated between the buyer and the supplier. The interesting question that arises is how can the visions for suppliers be created and deployed? Visions, once developed, can be used to deploy the resources that exist within the buyer–supplier relationship or are common to both and thus can positively impact on outsourced product development. If resources are to be deployed, then capabilities and core capabilities are affected. But first, let us explore the expression 'visions for suppliers' in a little more depth. The way in which the different suppliers are to be treated might require a common set of shared meanings or, in other words, a common culture.

Culture

Culture governs how members of an organisation behave (Robbins, 2000). Organisational culture refers to a systems of shared meanings held by members that are key in distinguishing one organisation from another (Schein, 1985). In other words, if the OEMs want some of their partner suppliers to be an extension of their own organisation and develop complex parts, then the same shared meanings must be held by both the OEM and the partner suppliers. Reilly *et al.* (1991) suggest that there are seven elements that characterise an organisation culture:

- *Innovation and risk taking*: the degree to which the employees are encouraged to come up with new ideas and take risks.
- *Attention to detail*: the degree to which employees are expected to exhibit precision, analysis and attention to detail.
- *Outcome orientation*: the degree to which the management emphasises outcomes rather than the means to achieve the outcomes.
- *People orientation*: the degree to which the effect of outcomes on people is taken into consideration.
- *Team orientation*: the degree to which work is organised in teams rather than by individuals.
- *Aggressiveness*: the degree to which people are aggressive and competitive rather than easy going.
- *Stability*: the degree to which organisational activities emphasise the status quo as opposed to growth.

The above elements indicate the need to have a common understanding between the OEMs and the suppliers. For example, if the OEM wants to be innovative and risk taking and the supplier wants the opposite, then there will be problems if they are matched up. The OEM will never be able to get planned products from such a supplier. The same logic can be applied to the other elements. A further example would be that in integrated and complex projects (Söderquist and Nellore, 2000) there is a need for joint work between the OEM and the supplier. If the culture is different between the OEM and the supplier, then this may be difficult to achieve and thus, the complex product may not be realised.

Organisational culture is expected to represent a common perception held by the organisational members (Robbins, 2000) as culture is shared meaning. It is thus important that individuals with different backgrounds describe the organisational culture in similar terms. This becomes all the more important as without dominant cultures (where the core values are shared by a majority of the members of an organisation), there will be no uniform representation of appropriate/ inappropriate behaviour. For example, if Purchasing and Engineering do not share the same dominant values, then the suppliers might be treated in different ways, leading to confusion and problems. The OEMs need to present a single voice to the supplier and the supplier should have the capacities and capabilities to implement the single decision of that voice with total commitment. This means that there needs to be a match between the two cultures of the buyer and the supplier. A strong culture is characterised by the organisation's core values being intensely held and widely shared (Wiener, 1988). This is not only limited to OEMs but also to the supplier base so that the suppliers may have to be treated uniformly by the OEM. This is important given the fact that the suppliers should have the skills set in order to generate the planned products.

Culture is a liability when the shared values do not agree with those that will further an organisation's effectiveness (Robbins, 2000). Consistency of behaviour is an asset in a stable environment but can hinder an organisation's ability to respond to rapid changes. This makes it all the more important to continuously assess the culture, not only internally, but also in the supplier base as developmental activities are also carried out by the suppliers in outsourced product development.

Core capabilities

Bowen *et al.* (1994) emphasise the need for specific core capabilities in order to achieve the visions. Conversely, Söderquist (1997) found that visions intervene as decisive factors in the process of building core capabilities. All the different resources in a company, including visions, are potential inputs to the core capabilities. Hence, there is a reciprocal interdependence between visions and core capabilities.

According to Bowen *et al.* (1994), Grant (1991) and Stern (1992), capabilities are composed of basic resources (such as capital equipment, individual skills, and product and process technology), managerial systems (such as decision procedures and career development schemes), physical systems (such as information systems and technical support systems), and values (such as the status of different functional disciplines, or what is considered to be a priority). Core capabilities are those that are grounded in a firm's resources and differentiate the firm from its competitors (Lacity *et al.*, 1995). Through dynamic visions and learning processes the evolution of a company's core capabilities should be a perpetual process towards ever-new distinctive competitive advantage (Söderquist, 1997). Different projects – corresponding to different visions – may require different capabilities and hence there must be a match between the visions and existing or emerging capabilities (Bowen *et al.*, 1994).

A major problem, however, is that core capabilities can easily turn into core rigidities, for example, lower status for non-dominant disciplines could mean that the views of people working there are not listened to. Empowered and skilled people within such disciplines may then feel offended and leave the company. This might lead to a lack of particular skills needed in projects. Sometimes, outdated physical systems may actually create obstacles, for example, obsolete testing systems that are too slow. The management systems can lead to rigidities as well, for example, if there are no clear career paths for project leaders or project workers, skilled people may avoid these jobs and focus on a functional career within different technical disciplines. Bowen *et al.* (1994) propose that the right visions might prevent core capabilities from turning into core rigidities. The discussion on core capabilities is within an OEM and since we are concerned with outsourced product development it would be interesting to observe the effects of core capabilities on the relationship between an OEM and the supplier. Given the reciprocal dependence between core capabilities and visions, it would be appropriate to consider the joint effects of core capabilities and visions for suppliers on the OEM–supplier relationship.

Stage 3 elements

In stage 3, the topics to be discussed will be the requirements of specifications, the customer benefit connection with specifications, the effects of technology on specifications and the traps to be avoided in the specifications.

Requirements of specifications

Roozenburg and Dorst (1991) define the requirements of a good specification. According to them, a specification should possess five virtues. It should be *comprehensive*, i.e., there must be a clear understanding of the requirements and the information supplied by the normative statements[20] should be complete. It should be *operational*, i.e., the specification must have the same meaning for everyone in the design team. Also the requirements in the specification should be measurable in quantitative terms. The specifications should *not be redundant*. That means that there should be no double counting of the same properties in the design evaluations. The specifications should be *complete* in all respects and, finally, the specifications should have *minimum size*, as the evaluation of the design proposals becomes difficult with an increase in the number of criteria. Fine and Whitney (1996) have also studied the requirements for specifications in the aerospace industry where the specification process is also called systems engineering and referred to as a top-down design process. According to them, an important lesson from system engineering is that a good specification and decomposition lead to a good product design. In each stage of the system engineering process there are skills that are needed, such as the ability to determine the needs above (i.e. the customer), to break these needs up into supporting capabilities and specify these capabilities to the suppliers, who will then deliver them after the development. Not every item is totally decomposable, i.e., can be described without any interfaces, though the totally decomposable items are the best candidates for outsourcing.

It appears that there are many requirements on the specifications. The requirements will have to be considered when creating a specification or communicating one. Without imposing certain requirements on the specification, the specifications could turn out to be incomprehensible.[21] These requirements would be helpful when communicating the specification and the parameters that it contains so its role is articulated in a succinct manner. Currently, there is no ISO standard for writing a specification.

Customer (OEM) benefits and specifications

There must be a focus not only on the product, but also on the customer (OEM) benefits that the product is supposed to give (Smith and Reinartsen, 1991). It is important, during the specification writing, to focus on what the customer perceives as a benefit and then make the trade-offs. For example, in the specification writing for a printer, a consideration might be that the customer might

34 Specifications: theoretical perspective

want the printer to be compatible with their current office automation, which could have been supplied by other suppliers. If this is not done, i.e., a customer benefit is not focused on, then there could be losses.

Specifications are of vital importance, as they could affect the development process and the product as well, for example, a badly designed specification can delay the start of development and/or increase the time to start of production. According to Smith and Reinartsen (1991), many companies simply write specifications for the sake of writing them and never use them as working documents. People are more concerned with having a piece of paper called the specification. They use it as a tool to prove their innocence if things go wrong, instead of incorporating customer benefits and using the specification as a working document. Specifications are not the end but just the means to the end. Therefore, it is necessary not to delay the specification writing, even if all the required information is not available.

Technology effects on specifications

In order to understand the technological effects, the specification situation with respect to the computer industry will be examined at first. The history of IBM, DEC, etc., has been described by Fine (1998). During the early 1970s, the vertically integrated systems suppliers dominated the computer industry and IBM dominated virtually every aspect of the industry. They needed to be the best in all the sub-systems so as not to lose customers. In the late 1970s, IBM's personal computer division broke away from the tradition and used a modular architecture, i.e., the operating system came from Microsoft and the microprocessor from Intel, etc. This created a horizontal industry structure where there was sufficient competition within each system that made up the entire computer. With competition becoming cut-throat, Intel and Microsoft started penetrating other segments/systems, as the industry was no longer stable due to the competition. One question that arises is whether the extent of supplier involvement (vertical/horizontal industry) would affect the content of the specification.

The lesson for this research project is that the content of the specification should reflect the involvement of external parties, for example, a completely tight specification (as in a vertical industry) cannot be given to a supplier with a high knowledge content when outsourcing (as in a horizontal industry). This problem can be observed when large suppliers are over-managed, leading to chaos in the development process. The specifications need to reflect the industry and changing conditions. Apart from reflecting the industry, the specifications could also consider the amount of information that must be given to the supplier or obtained from the supplier in case of outsourcing, as systems/components do not work in isolation in the automobile. They need to work together and hence it is of utmost importance that these items be interfaced with each other. Therefore, when suppliers develop products,[22] the specifications should consider whether there should be a transfer of relevant technology to the supplier. There are basically two types of technological knowledge transfer, namely, components and systems knowledge transfer (Aoshima, 1993). Components can be further classified as independent and systems components. A simple component such as a wiper can be developed in isolation and does not have any effect on the development of other components. On the other hand, in order to assemble a HVAC (heating ventilation and air conditioning system) one would need knowledge about the other items that it needs to be interfaced with, as it is a dependent system. This is a systems knowledge transfer, which is in fact the more difficult of the two.

The product status helps the managers to understand and emphasise certain aspects of the specification over others, for example, when to have straight carryovers as opposed to developing completely new specifications/products all the time. The concept of product status is defined and used extensively by Hollins and Pugh (1990) as a tool to direct design managers. Hollins and Pugh describe two kinds of product status, namely, the static and the dynamic. Products are said to have a dynamic status when the design changes are of a radical nature and changes occur in the basic concept. Products are static in status when the changes are incremental and the basic concept is unchanged. It is important to remember that products can have static and dynamic status, i.e., the status can change. The key to managing the specifications is to correctly estimate the product status so that suitable design changes can be emphasised. This can also lead to the correct focus on design, marketing and production, for example, if the design is dynamic, then patents are more important than standards. Wasti and Liker (1999) point out that in the case of dynamic designs (which have high technological uncertainty), there is a positive association with the level of supplier involvement, i.e., the higher the technological uncertainty, the greater the level of supplier involvement. Knowledge of the product status will help companies to decide when to develop new technologies. Hollins and Pugh state that if the product specification is the best available within a certain technology, then the product design is unlikely to change[23] as is the case with restricted product design. Huge investments in machinery can make a product static as the investment is based on the estimation of a certain volume. A product will be static if it has a large number of interfaces and so will limitations on time to design, according to Hollins and Pugh, as the designer will be forced to use the existing tools. The concept of product status can have an impact on the relationship between the buyer and the supplier as can the type of specification allocated to the supplier.

The above discussion can also be related to the problems that companies face with respect to the role of the specification given to their suppliers when moving from total insourcing to outsourcing of various degrees. In outsourcing, the specifications cannot be same as those developed during insourcing. Awareness of this difference is important for both the buyer and the supplier when understanding the term specification in the same manner, and also in linking specification to the technology. In other words, there is a change in the technology transfer when there is a systems transfer as opposed to a component transfer. The concept of product status appears to be important when communicating the role of the specification otherwise, how would the OEMs know when the technology would change in systems or components that they outsource? The change in the role of the specification when moving from outsourcing to insourcing and vice versa is a potential problem area that may have to be dealt with when trying to manage the role of specifications.

Traps and specifications

Companies fall into a trap when developing a list of performance specifications for a new product. This is called the best of best specification trap (Rosenau, 1992). This problem is typical when a company's specifications are based on the single best features of the competitor. Thus, the new product design is driven by competition and not by market insight. Delays can be created in the product development process when there are rumours of competitive changes as the specifications will have to be changed. This problem can occur when the marketing people have a sales background. A sales person would want to sell a product cheaply in order to meet their quota whereas a marketing person would devise ways and means to sell the same product at a premium. When the reward is on profit and not on sales, the marketing people with a sales background are in a quandary. A marketing person with a sales background would try to generate a specification which equals the best among the competitors and then try to sell it for a price lower than the least proposed by the competitors. On the other hand, a person with a marketing background would try to generate a specification that tops all the others, includes competitive advantage features, is customer-driven and then try to get a price premium for it.

If specifications are written solely by marketing, then the features emphasised by them would be based on the present customer needs. On the other hand, the engineers would like to experiment with new technology and make new discoveries. Manufacturing people have to work out the bugs in the new product. A good specification can only be generated by the combination of these different kinds of knowledge. There should only be one document called the specification and it should be created by the joint labour between the different parties and there should be no separate specifications (such as one from each department), according to Smith and Reinartsen (1991). There needs to be joint participation in the writing of specifications, as no single person or department knows everything. Balance between the different trade-offs is the mark of a good specification.

Avoiding traps can help to achieve planned products. There are numerous traps as well as those suggested above. It is also necessary to deal with as many traps as possible so that they can be avoided. The above discussion points towards examining the different problems that are faced with regard to the role of specifications.

Stage 4 elements

The following discussion will centre on topics that have been given the least attention in the specification literature. These topics concern the capabilities that are required for specifications and the different trade-offs that could be made in the specifications. These elements thus form the outer core for the current literature organisation.

Capabilities and specifications

There are certain important capabilities required by the buyer and the supplier in the specifications (Wheelwright and Clark, 1993). They state that from the point of view of the buyer there are three major capabilities, namely, the ability to create downstream friendly solutions, quick problem-solving and error-free design. In the first case, there must be an attempt to take into consideration the limitations and capabilities of the supplier. However, excessive consideration for the supplier capabilities can lead to losses and hence there needs to be a trade-off. Time is money and errors can increase both time and cost. For a variety of reasons, it is crucial to have error-free designs, as this decreases the number of loops required to solve the problems. Errors detected at a late stage can require substantial changes for the suppliers and thus lead to increased costs. There should also be an emphasis on fast problem-solving. Problems arising from the supplier's end need to be resolved as soon as possible. For this reason, having short feedback loops can prove to be very beneficial.

The suppliers are also required to possess certain capabilities, namely, the ability to forecast criticisms from the buyer, manage risks and cope with unexpected changes, according to Wheelwright and Clark (1993). In the first case, the supplier must have the capability to understand the clues from the buyers, for example, to develop and propose solutions when they are worried about certain items in a design. The second is to manage risk, in other words, to balance the trade-off between the risk of design change and an early start. For example, the suppliers can design parts that are least likely to change and work less on areas that are most susceptible to change. The third ability is to react to unexpected changes and develop solutions faster. Different contingencies must be thought of, as speed is essential in integrated problem-solving. The supplier must have the ability to design fast solutions.

In integrated problem-solving, top management can play a facilitating role, (Wheelwright and Clark, 1993), for example, a visible display of problem-solving between the buyer's and supplier's top management teams can prove to be a guiding force for the rest of both organisations.

As stated earlier, the product development tasks cannot be performed by an individual/firm, but rather need to be divided between individuals and firms so that they use each other's expertise. It can be concluded from the above discussion that both suppliers and buyers need to possess certain capabilities to understand and interpret the specification. Doing this will allow a specification–supplier match. If there are no supplier capabilities and the specification cannot be managed with the existing in-house ones, then there are bound to be problems. Not having capabilities and knowing the reasons for this could be helpful in understanding the underlying problems in the role of specifications. This understanding

Trade-offs and specifications

Specifications are hard to write and, according to Smith and Reinartsen (1991), there are many reasons for this, such as the following:

- Often the crucial elements in a specification are hard to put into writing or into quantitative terms.
- Pure narrative statements are hard to understand and, as far as the engineers are concerned, not all information can be discovered before the design start.
- Information that should have been in the design is obtained after the design start.
- Difficulties may arise because of the interaction between various elements in the specification.

The interaction problems can be explained by giving an example[24] concerning the height and processing capabilities of a food processor. The designer will have to read between the lines to make the best trade-offs. He or she cannot simply rely on the single statement in the specification, but rather on the combination of values that suits the user even better. For example, the specification could read as follows: 'The machine should be taller as it will process food better.' There are many questions that arise from the above statement, for example, how tall should the machine be? What is better processing? etc. The designer has to read between the lines and have detailed discussions on the specifications in order to make the necessary trade-offs. If the specification writers concentrate more on things that they can describe easily or things that they understand instead of matters that are hard to describe or understand, then the specifications will be better. However, specification writers must force themselves to understand and describe the crucial elements as well.

It is apparent that specifications are the outcome of trade-offs between different factors or parameters. The specifications writers must not only describe the easy elements, but also the elements that are hard to visualise. This means that the specifications may have to consider these if they are to overcome the inherent problems. If problems are present, then ways and means have to be developed in order to overcome them.

Managing trade-offs is a difficult issue. The trade-offs have to suit the customer, otherwise the product may not sell. Trade-offs can be made in different spheres of the product, for example, in a car the trade-offs may encompass areas such as the electronics, the dashboard, etc. In particular, if a navigation system is to be installed in the car, then the dashboard may have to be in a slanting position. Some customers may not like it. However, a trade-off will have to be made between the slanting dashboard and the navigation display. This trade-off may require investigation by the wire harness supplier, as the wire harnesses may have problems in routing. What is being emphasised is that there are different departments that may have to make the trade-offs and hence there is a need for a common forum where all the possibilities can be written down and discussed. This provides an ideal setting if people are willing to change their attitude towards specifications and consider the specification to be a working document instead. Not making trade-offs in a rational manner will result in problems in the specifications. If trade-offs in the specification cause problems, then it may be helpful to observe the effects of these problems on the role of specifications and then find means to overcome them.

Conclusion

A wide range of factors have to be considered while dealing with the role of specifications. If the specifications are not generated with the necessary parameters and processes, then both the OEM and the suppliers have to bear the consequences of customer disenchantment with the product due to delays in product introduction, poor quality, expected innovation levels, etc. This could lead to losses both for the OEM and the suppliers and underlines the need for an integrated approach between them. Current research has shown gaps in understanding the definition of the term specification, lack of competence building in specification management, and poor specification flow management. At a higher level the visions to drive the specification process are also missing. Finally, applications of specifications in outsourcing, and structures for specification management such as systems supply including digital procurement are also missing. This book will examine these issues in the following chapters.

Notes

1 It does not mean that all suppliers in the lean era will be given system responsibility. The trend is to help all suppliers to reach the level where they can handle systems and sub-systems.
2 A specification in the craftsmanship era could have been as follows: make a steering wheel with the steering rod to fit in a hole of diameter 15 cms.
3 General Motors had drawings for most of the parts or at least specifications that were presumed to be complete in all respects. Source: interviews with six General Motors executives, in Detroit (March, 1998) based on observations of archival documents by the executives to maintain confidentiality. The big GM family at that time included its internal divisions such as Delphi and sourcing is the term used to reflect buying by the GM family and not purchases made between and from internal divisions.
4 GM was making losses in many of its divisions as a result of loose specifications. This was one of the reasons for the abrupt departure of Billy Durant (*History of General Motors*, Workbook Companion to the *The Chairman's Perspective: General Motors Yesterday, Today and Tomorrow*, November 1999, Detroit).
5 The term design is used to refer to product development.
6 Kaulio (1996) is the only reference that discusses the double nature of specifications. There is no other reference to the double nature of specifications.

7 'A good deal of information must be processed to co-ordinate the interdependent sub-tasks. As the degree of uncertainty increases, the amount of information processing during task execution increases.'
8 Uncertainty is defined as the difference between the amount of information available and the amount of information required in order to perform a given task (Galbraith, 1973).
9 The views expressed by Simon (1976) are very formal and mechanistic in nature. Karlson (1994) expanding on the limitations of Simon's model states that co-ordination is of little importance if the development personnel do not understand each other's language. In other words, there is a need for redundancy and the flow of tacit knowledge in the organisation to ensure development performance. Further, co-ordination does not imply only development, communication and acceptance of the plan, but also includes the joint implementation of the plan by the development personnel (Karlson, 1996).
10 These specifications will have to allow the input of the different personnel and hence, cannot be totally closed.
11 Adam, Jr. E.E. and Swamidass, P.M. (1989) 'Assessing operations management from a strategic perspective', *Journal of Management*, vol. 15, no. 2, pp. 181–203.
12 This method is bibliometric as it allows the reader to pose questions and reflect on the conclusions reached by each of the authors. The conclusions reached by each of the authors are not the absolute truth.
13 The topics have been ranked in order of importance only in terms of frequency of coverage by authors.
14 Whole product refers to the complete product like the auto. 'Parts of the whole' refer to the parts that constitute the whole product like the engines or wheels for an automobile.
15 Lead time is only one of the factors identified by Clark (1989).
16 A platform is representative of a particular category of cars that have common characteristics. A platform consists of a collection of assets that are shared by a set of products. They are components, processes, knowledge, people and relationships; see Robertson and Ulrich (1998).
17 The suppliers deep inside the network are those with whom the OEM has no direct contact. In line with the research conducted by Lamming (1993), the suppliers deep inside the network have no direct links with the OEM and, therefore, have no technological influence on the OEM.
18 Competition will exist only within a category and not between categories of suppliers. This is because the categories of suppliers cannot deal with all types of specifications and have certain limitations, as explained by Kamath and Liker (1994).
19 This denotes the link between the suppliers that have direct contact to the OEM (first tier suppliers) to all the sub, sub-sub suppliers, etc., of the first tier supplier.
20 Customers express their needs normatively.
21 Many OEMs want their suppliers to be ISO9000 accredited. The accreditation allows the suppliers to follow standards that facilitate common understanding and improvements in productivity.
22 Products could mean systems, components, etc.
23 This has its advantages and disadvantages. The advantages are that the staff can concentrate on areas that are changing and not on areas that are static. The disadvantages are that the technologies might change without the firm being aware of it, leading to competitive disadvantages for the firm.
24 This example has been taken from Smith and Reinartsen (1991).

2 Specifications
Do we really understand them?

In this chapter we will explore the meaning of the term specification. Those engaged in development work communicate requirements with the help of specifications. The development of a product such as an automobile is the result of the interaction of thousands of collaborators from different departments, including marketing, after-sales, engineering, manufacturing, etc. Thus, there are different types of specifications which communicate each department's distinct requirements; for example, the market segment specifications originating from the marketing department and the after-sales specifications originating from the after-sales department. These different specifications come together to form the overall product technical specifications, indicating the joint requirements of all the departments together for the complete final product. These specifications are either developed by the original equipment manufacturer, their suppliers, or both. In varying degrees, the OEMs and the suppliers co-operate in order to fulfil a set of needs. In other words, the suppliers are also involved in the specifications. However, in many development projects, we have observed that suppliers do not always satisfy the specifications. In fact, the product that is produced as a result of the development might be totally different from the intended product. Both the OEM and the suppliers blame each other for the failures and occasionally some of the suppliers are dismissed.

What is a specification problem?

Let us take an example to reveal the problems caused by non-respect of the specifications. A customer satisfaction enquiry revealed problems with the radio in a car model. Specifically, the customer could not listen to the music due to a continuous humming noise. The root cause of the noise was magnetic interference from wire harnesses above the radio. The automobile manufacturer determined that the supplier was at fault and tried to force the supplier to pay the damages. However, the specifications did not require the supplier to evaluate the effects of magnetic interference. Therefore, the automobile manufacturer had to foot the bill. The automobile manufacturer tried unsuccessfully to collect damages from the supplier. The problem was further compounded as more than a thousand radios had already been produced.

The above problem can be traced back to the fact that the supplier obtained only approximate parameters in the specifications from the OEM, calling for further development by the supplier itself. However, the supplier's capabilities and capacities were not suited to such an exercise; the supplier required well-defined, detailed specifications from the OEM. Problems like this are often due to buyers and suppliers interpreting the term 'specification' in different ways. There are, indeed, different types of suppliers and it is important that the specification parameters take this into account.

In the example cited, the problem with the magnetic interference occurred because the supplier did not understand the specifications. Why not? We conducted a survey to determine how suppliers define the term 'specification'.

The survey

We distributed a questionnaire to 400 suppliers asking them to respond to an open-ended question: 'What do you understand by the term specification?' The questionnaire was addressed to the Director of Engineering who was responsible for the OEM in the supplier companies. The responses (54 per cent returned completed) are shown as follows in Table 2.1.

Table 2.1 Meaning of a specification

ID	What do you understand by the term specification? Responses	% of suppliers mentioning
1	Requirements of the customer/user that the product has to fulfil.	56
2	A very careful description of a product or a process.	52
3	Technical descriptions of products and processes which may contain drawings.	50
4	Norms which specify several characteristics of the part or system to be fulfilled in order to guarantee its good functioning and, of course, to meet customer requirements.	45
5	The specifications are a preliminary product performance requirement that allow the product to meet and survive satisfactorily 'in use'.	42
6	Specifications are the description of a product and its properties as well as the methods of obtaining it. The methods could include details about the level of technology involved.	34
7	Specifications are the summary of all important data, limits, methods, performance and targets. Some of these parameters may be in the form of drawings.	32
8	Defines the product properties that are necessary or will be measured.	31
9	Specifications are technical regulations and drawings.	26
10	Specifications are the requirements to meet the function.	20
11	To manufacture in accordance with the customer requirement.	18
12	Specification is a vehicle for common understanding of requirements.	15
13	Any written communication is a specification.	14
14	Description of process operations and acceptance standards.	10

These different issues were discussed with product development managers and operational design staff in the case study suppliers. They shared the same understanding of the term specification and agreed upon the relevance of the issues. This further analysis resulted in a categorisation of problems presented in Table 2.2 in decreasing order of importance.

Exploring the identified parameters

Let us now analyse the categories developed in Table 2.2 in order to understand the features of a specification.

Communication

The specification is a document that is used to make a product. Changes are a part of the development process and thus specifications must reflect the changes. Hence, making all changes incorporated into the specification would lead to improved communications and a quality product, as all-important details regarding the product and its interfaces would be documented and not overlooked. However, communication efficiency can be hampered if there is redundancy in the specifications. In order to strengthen communication and avoid errors related to confusion, redundant statements need to be minimised. Roozenburg and Dorst (1991) support this by stating that people are less likely to read specifications that are very long. Communication can also be strengthened by adapting specifications to alternative formats for the different kinds of suppliers. Generally speaking, it is important to assess what formats, phrasings, or terms make the specification most clear for the relevant supplier.

Wheelwright and Clark (1993) point towards four modes of communication which have great significance in the relationship between specifications and the suppliers. Involving the suppliers, classifying them accordingly and utilising the appropriate modes of communication as defined by Wheelwright and Clark can facilitate communications (see Table 2.3).

The partner suppliers work with concepts and present these to the OEM even before the OEM decides to start work on a project. There is continuous

Table 2.2 Categorisation of definition areas

Category	Response ID
Communication	1, 2, 3, 4, 5, 6, 7, 8, 9, 10, 11, 12, 13, 14
Product requirements	1, 2, 4, 5, 6, 7, 8, 10
Functionality	2, 3, 4, 7, 10, 11, 13
Process requirements	2, 6, 7, 8, 10
Standards	1, 3, 7, 9, 14
Drawings	3, 7, 9
Customer requirements	1, 4
Level of technology	6

Table 2.3 Supplier–communication mode interface

Type of supplier	Communication mode
Partner	Integrated problem-solving
Mature	Early involvement
Transition phase from child to mature	Early start in the dark
Child	Serial interaction
Contractual	Serial interaction

interaction between the OEM and the supplier, both before and after the start of the project; thus, there is integrated problem-solving. The mature supplier needs rough specifications such as product requirements, customer requirements, and functionality descriptions to start work. Hence, there is a need for early involvement once the rough specifications have been determined. The child and contractual suppliers need a serial mode of interaction, as they do not contribute in any way to the product design but just manufacture to specifications. However, an early start-in-the-dark pattern can be used for long-time child suppliers in the process of becoming mature suppliers.

Specifications can be operational (used as a working document) in order to facilitate communication when dealing with suppliers, regardless of their category. The specifications can thus be communicated or written in such a way that they convey the same message to all concerned.

Once the specifications have been submitted, either by the suppliers or by the OEM (depending on who is responsible for generating the specification), they need to be discussed further in order to avoid misunderstandings. In most cases, face-to-face communication is best for solving problems. More discussions and early work should be achieved before the specifications are implemented. Multiple communication techniques can be used, such as written confirmations after a telephone conversation to clarify the matter, seminars to discuss the specifications, etc. Also, regular review meetings and liaison work are required to understand the capabilities, requirements, and limitations of each collaborator.

Product requirements

The product requirements can be separated into the general description of the product, which could be a narrative description to get a feeling for the product, and the technical description of the product to allow satisfactory 'in use' features. Specifications need not only mention the end product, but also the requirements of the ways and means of obtaining the end product. One of the most important requirements is to examine whether the product will work satisfactorily and that means that the product properties to be measured must be known in advance. In other words, *what is going to be measured* must be clearly stated. The targets that the product has to fulfil (cost, quality, lead time, etc.) are to be included in the technical description of the product. This corroborates what was pointed out by Roozenburg and Dorst (1991), namely, that the specifications should contain quantitative measurement indicators demonstrating that the requirements and benefits have been met to the extent needed by the customer. In summary, the argument being proposed is to enlarge the scope of the specification to include not only the final product, but also the process of arriving at the final product.

Functionality

Functionality refers here to the practical use of the product and not technical details. The specification may contain a list of these functionalities and the requirements needed in order to meet them. Often partner suppliers can be given a free hand in determining the requirements to achieve the functionality as stated by the OEM. An example of functionality would be when the OEM tells the supplier 'to have an audio system that corresponds to the brand image of the OEM and is of premium quality to the end user of the car'. The reason why the partner suppliers are given a free hand is that they have the required capability and capacity to understand functionality and its implications. Since child suppliers do not have these capabilities, they will have to be provided with specifications that are complete in all respects.

Process requirements

The specification can cover the process requirements that will be used for the manufacture of the product. It is possible that the suppliers chosen to deliver a certain product have processes that do not match the manufacturing needs of the product. Hence, the process requirements should be mentioned in the specifications, so as to check that the product can be produced in the manner required by the customer. For example, audio equipment suppliers should use automated diagnostics to check the printed circuit board. This allows for early rectification of errors and reduction of scrap and improvement of quality.

Standards

The specifications can include the standards that are to be followed. Smith and Rhodes (1992), who identify thirty-two different primary elements of a specification, also emphasise this. There are standards for components, for example, all edges located within the panel area in the car should have a radius of 2.5mm minimum in order to prevent injuries. There are standards for certain constituents within the components, for example, quicksilver cannot be used, and certain types of glues are not allowed. There are also legal standards, performance standards, and country standards. There are standards for the processes used for the manufacture of components, for example, the printed circuit board should be cleaned with citrus fluid, offering the best combination of purity and respect for the environment. Understanding and knowledge of all the different standards can help prevent late changes. All possible legal guidelines, dates for certification, and liability issues should be identified and a risk analysis undertaken in order to get the development process under way without hindrance. Standards are an important component of specifications and can be used in the dialogue with suppliers. While partner and mature suppliers are expected to be knowledgeable about the standards, all the other types of suppliers may require explicit communication of the standards in order to fulfil them.

Drawings

A specification may contain drawings, as many features in the specifications need pictorial explanations. Drawings often contain details that cannot be put into a written specification. It is important to remember that drawings are the outcomes of specifications and not vice versa. In the magnetic interface case cited earlier, the automobile manufacturer sustained huge losses in generating the drawings first and then writing ten to fifty pages of technical regulations to supplement them, as opposed to the top-down approach where the specifications lead to the drawings. The need for drawings and detailed quantitative information increases when one deals with child suppliers as opposed to partner suppliers. For partner and mature suppliers, drawings are not given and instead, the supplier is expected to develop their own drawings and quantitative requirements based on rough and essentially narrative specifications from the OEM. Figure 2.1 illustrates the continuum from narrative to quantitative specifications with respect to different suppliers.

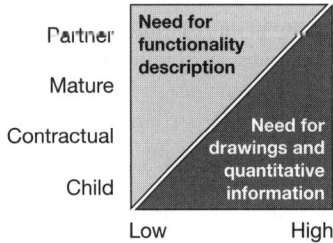

Figure 2.1 The continuum from narrative to quantitative specifications

Customer requirements

Customer requirements give the necessary impetus to create the product requirements, which in turn lead to the process requirements. Thus, specifications need to cover the latter as well. It is important that the creation of the product and process requirements occur in parallel with the identification of the customer requirements. When the OEM gives a specification to the supplier, the customer is the OEM and the requirements to be fulfilled are that of the OEM. In turn, the requirements of the OEM are generated from the needs of the final customers, i.e., the people who buy the final product. Suppliers would need to consider the benefits of the product they make not only for the OEM, but also for the final consumer, hence, there needs to be a customer-requirement–customer-benefit discussion where the specifications could be used as a working document. This also confirms Smith and Reinartsen's (1991) conclusion that usage of the specification as a working document could speed up the development process. This discussion shows the opportunities not only to satisfy the customer requirements, but also to provide additional benefits to the customer by pushing performance forward. For example, the customer requirement might be a telephone; the OEM can satisfy this requirement and also provide an additional benefit such as a microphone that allows interface with the customer's existing telephone. The supplier of the telephones to the OEM can satisfy the requirement of the OEM by providing a microphone and can also provide a benefit to the final customer by adapting the microphone interface to a number of different brands of telephones. The requirements and benefits stated in the specifications can be comprehensive, as indicated by Roozenburg and Dorst (1991), so that they are easily understandable and contain an overview of the product that the specification is ready to create.

Level of technology

The level of technology in terms of technological sophistication influences the interfaces between the different components and systems within a product. Thus, statements on the proposed functionality of a product must consider the level of technology involved, which is also confirmed by Aoshima (1993). If the technology can be developed for a component or system without knowledge of the interfaces, then the specifications need not show details about the interfaces. On the other hand, if the technology to be developed requires knowledge about the interfaces, then the specifications should ensure that the necessary details are taken into account. The capability level of the supplier is a significant factor in determining how the suppliers interpret the knowledge of the interfaces. Mature and partner suppliers would take the lead and start direct talks with the suppliers of interfacing components or systems. On the other hand, child suppliers would need drawings that include all possible considerations of the interfaces.

The specifications can consider whether the technology is static, i.e. remains the same compared to previous components, or dynamic, i.e. contains innovation, which Hollins and Pugh (1990) also indicate. With certain parts, there can be a combination of both. If this difference is understood, then the work can proceed faster, as the static parts can be adapted immediately, and resources allocated specifically to the dynamic ones.

Conclusion

The definition of a specification contains several parameters that could be fulfilled either by the OEM or the supplier or both, depending upon the type of supplier and the communication pattern used. What is important to note is that the suppliers should be given specifications based on their capabilities and capacities, for example, a child supplier can simply be given a drawing that contains all the parameters. The assumptions are thus clear and the OEM has carefully considered all the elements in the drawings. A partner supplier, on the other hand, is expected to create the drawings and work with functionalities. Referring to the theoretical definition of a specification by Smith and Reinartsen (1991) as 'a written description of products to guide the development process', I argue that guidance will be improved if the specifications satisfy the eight parameters discussed in the analysis. These parameters indicate that the specification process resembles the total design concept suggested by Hollins and Pugh (1990), as it represents the chain of activities from need identification to the satisfaction of the need. Poor or non-existing parameters can jeopardise cost, quality, and lead time. The integration of the elements is illustrated in Figure 2.2.

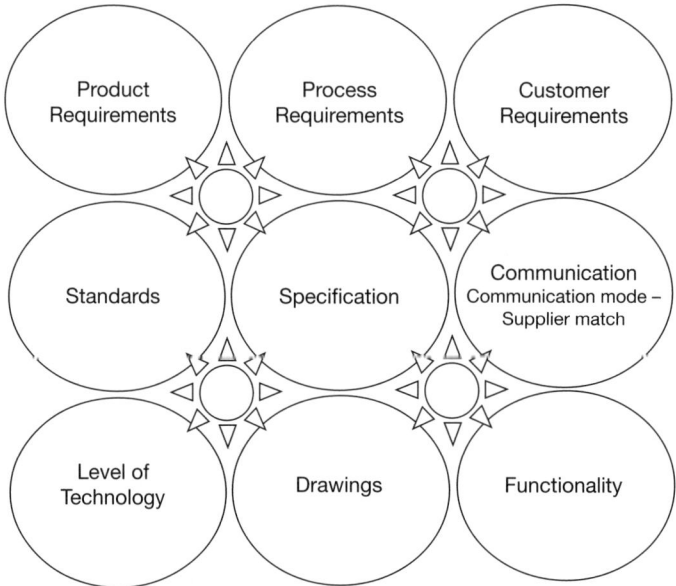

Figure 2.2 Contents of a specification

Case study

This particular case study concerns manufacturing of the armrest in the car model. The armrest fell under the 'interior' sub-system, so it was outsourced to one of the largest interior systems suppliers in the automotive industry. The interior systems supplier was to supply the complete seats in the car along with the carpets, i.e. the systems supplier was in charge of total interior design. The interior systems supplier was a mature supplier and needed rough specifications such as product requirements, customer requirements and functionality descriptions from the OEM before it could generate the products. A number of child suppliers work for the interior systems supplier and among them was an armrest supplier, who came from a different industry (plastics) where its major customer was the white goods industry (appliances, refrigerators, etc.). Hence, the child supplier did not understand the automotive industry demands such as plush finishes and, in particular, those in premium automobile interiors. The child supplier responsible for manufacturing the armrest to the design provided by the interior systems supplier provided an injection-moulded armrest, 'gated' (i.e. the point where the nozzle injecting hot plastic meets the armrest mould) at the centre, which was visible when opened. The armrest lacked the interior's refinement as was evidenced by numerous customer complaints. The seat supplier responsible was questioned and expressed regret that he had not informed the child supplier of the demands of the interior.

In order to better understand the problem, let us consider the key elements of the supply network as proposed by Harland (1996). They are *end customer, competitive priorities, supply network structure* and *supply infrastructure*. Figure 2.3 illustrates the case with respect to these parameters.

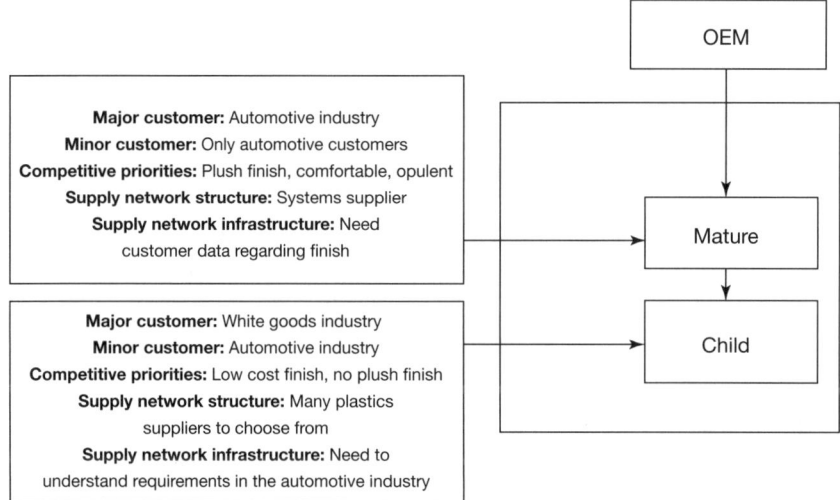

Figure 2.3 Supplier network depicting the development and manufacture of an armrest

The lack of knowledge about the car industry and its difference in terms of competitive priorities on the part of the child supplier were the main reasons for the problem. Moreover, there was a lack of understanding on the part of the interior supplier about how to deal with a large base of plastic suppliers not necessarily aligned with the auto industry.

Post-mortem

The specifications were examined. In spite of the fact that the seat supplier was a mature supplier and needed rough specifications (such as product requirements, customer requirements and functionality descriptions), only functionality specifications like 'make the interior suit our car' were communicated. The specifications submitted to the child supplier by the seat supplier were also checked. There was no mention of the OEM interior demands. In fact, the child supplier did not understand that the final customers of the OEM paid a very high price for premium cars and thus demanded a premium interior.

Applying the model

The model in Figure 2.2 helped us to reduce these problems. The seat supplier was also asked to follow the same model when communicating with its suppliers. The specification model was followed in the next car model of the OEM. The seat supplier was given a specification that gave details on the functionality, customer requirements, and product requirements. The right communication mode was used, i.e. the rough specifications were communicated after the automobile manufacturer had carefully articulated them. In this way, the seat supplier was better able to understand the demands for the automobile manufacturer's vehicle interior. The seat supplier communicated only a drawing to the child supplier. However, the drawing also indicated that the 'gating' could appear only at the corners but not at the centre of the armrest. In fact, the drawing encompassed all other parameters including customer requirements (smooth interior), product requirements (product dimensions), communications (late, after the drawings were complete and simulated), level of technology, standards (to the segment in which the OEM operates) and functionality (what the armrest is supposed to do). For this reason, the confusion and problems were reduced and eliminated to a large extent.

Reflection on the dimensions

The eight dimensions identified in Figure 2.2 have to be observed with reference to the complex context of the OEM and its entire supplier base (including the different levels of suppliers). The partner supplier is expected to satisfy each of the eight dimensions by proactively seeking information from the onset. The partner supplier must understand the OEM's business and aggressively seek information about these dimensions. The mature supplier would need the functionality description, product and customer requirements, which form the rough specifications, in order to perform its work. The remaining five dimensions have to be satisfied by the mature supplier. The child supplier gets a drawing and the rest of the parameters have to be articulated by the OEM and contained in the drawing.

Finally, the contractual supplier delivers a standard product. There is no need to exchange dimensional specifications between the OEM and the supplier. Firms in diverse industries employ a variety of suppliers. In learning how to manage them effectively, firms have to balance the type of specification with respect to the capabilities and capacities of the suppliers. The importance of the dimensions of the specifications varies with the type of supplier.

3 Visionary-driven outsourced development

Knowing that specifications have to be tailored to suit the capabilities and capacities of the suppliers is not enough. We have observed in many companies that in spite of having different tailored specifications for the suppliers, the wrong specification is often given to the suppliers. In other words, there is no clear vision for suppliers and organisations should develop this internally. A supplier vision of R&D contribution cannot be used for a nut and bolt supplier and detailed control parts with a small financial margin cannot be developed with the aim of proposing innovative solutions or contributing to the productivity of the customers in the development process. It is important to make expectations clear between the OEMs and the suppliers in outsourced product development. Developing visions for suppliers can play a role in helping OEMs realise this and thus use the core capabilities of the buyer–supplier firms accordingly. This chapter attempts to explore the impact of visions for suppliers in outsourced product development, the creation of visions for suppliers and finally, the interplay between visions for suppliers and the core capabilities of OEMs.

What is a visionary-driven outsourced development?

Consider a global automotive OEM operating in the luxury segment in the process of commencing to build a new generation car. The company has decided to offer an integrated navigation system on the vehicle to be marketed in as short a time as 12 months to attract customers into buying the car, as competition is very tough. The engineers have measured themselves against the tough goal set by the corporation and think that they have the capabilities to achieve it. They then write the specifications for the integrated navigation system and request purchasing from a leading supplier. Once the supplier has been selected, engineering gave the specification to the supplier and dictated the manner in which the integrated navigation system would be developed and manufactured. The supplier offered additional functionalities to overcome the inherent defects that they observed in the specification given by engineering. Purchasing refused to incorporate these changes due to the additional costs and engineering refused them as well on the grounds that they knew better than the supplier did. Two months before the deadline, engineering realised that the supplier was correct but by then it was too late. The project was delayed, which led to customer disappointment. This delay surprised the management of both the OEM and the supplier, as they had signed a memorandum of understanding extending full co-operation to each other. Faced with this complex problem, the OEM management asked several questions: why was the supplier not treated according to its capabilities and listened to as it was the leader in this field? Why did engineering think that it had the capabilities when it did not?

The above questions require that the characteristics of the supplier be clearly articulated within a company in order to utilise the supplier's capabilities and capacities to the full. The entire organisation will need to have the same view of the involvement of the supplier if the supplier contribution is to be realised, i.e. a common vision for supplier involvement. In spite of the research on supplier involvement, little evidence was found as far as the existence of visions for suppliers was concerned. Thus, a tool for reduction/elimination of subjectivity in decisions concerning suppliers is missing.

The questionnaire

Initial interviews at the OEM revealed that they had only one vision in the company and no specific visions for suppliers. We searched for internal documents that explicitly stated this vision of the firm. This was observed to be as follows: 'Proud staff winning through excited customers.'

A small group of five Vice Presidents were asked to break down the vision statement into the mission, strategy and culture that it represented. The group identified the mission to be 'to win', the strategy was identified to be 'exciting customers' and the culture was identified to be 'proud'. Even after breaking down the vision statement it was observed that there was no guidance on how to deal with suppliers.

One Vice President of the OEM explained that, 'The lack of clear visions on how to deal with the suppliers is perhaps the biggest challenge that the company has to deal with in its pursuit of early supplier involvement in the development process.' Based on these initial interviews, we decided to distribute a questionnaire to 400 employees selected at random. One open-ended question was asked, namely, 'What in your view is the vision of your Company that engages in outsourced product development?' The questionnaire was meant to explore and confirm the statement made by the Vice President regarding the visions for suppliers. Some 400 questionnaires were returned indicating a 100 per cent response rate, achieved thanks to a letter from the Vice President requesting the employees to fill in the questionnaires. The letter stated that the responses were important in order to improve relationships with the suppliers, which was necessary in order to achieve profitability and cost-cutting targets of the OEM. This particular automotive company was chosen for a number of reasons such as: the author was working as an assistant project leader and had access to data, the company is multinational and the company wanted to involve new suppliers.

Findings

The results of the questionnaires are presented in Table 3.1. The aim was to understand the perception of the vision for suppliers among a cross-section of employees from different departments. We did not attempt to understand the potential differences in the perceptions of the project vision between the different departments. Rather, we simply tabulated the perceptions to observe whether visions for suppliers were present.

Examination of Table 3.1 shows that the visions for the suppliers are not clear among the staff, even though outsourced product development was being engaged in. The vision of dealing with suppliers was not seen as important by the project staff as was the case with the corporate staff who created the corporate vision. One could state that the visions exist to guide the internal management and not external management (such as managing suppliers).

Effects of supplier visions on outsourced development

Let us explore the effects of visions on outsourced product development between buyers and suppliers through an example. There are three forms of integrated audio systems that are offered by the OEM to the final customers, which are in turn sourced from an audio system supplier:

- the radio;
- the radio along with the cassette player;
- the radio along with the cassette player and the compact disc player (CD player with place for one CD).

During validation testing, alternator noise was observed which was audible whenever the cassette player was switched on. The OEM engineers thought that it might be a problem with the audio system, but later discovered that it was a

Table 3.1 Employee-defined visions (items that scored at least 10%)

Features	(%)
Unique combination of performance handling and comfort with high quality standards	54
To do changes that one can trust	54
Premium quality, reliability, fun to drive	53
Stand apart from the crowd	45
To make the best possible quality	43
Qualify as a member of the premium segment	33
Performance, individuality	33
To give the customer a degree of satisfaction, thus giving the OEM good business	30
Trouble free ownership, value for money	26
To generate better financial figures for the company	16
To secure position in the premium market	10
Lower costs than competitors	10

54 Visionary-driven outsourced development

problem with the wire harnesses (the wires that carry signals). There were a lot of wire harnesses, supplied by the wire harness supplier, above the radio, which caused magnetic interference when the cassette player was switched on. The problem was not discovered in the early prototypes, but later in the pilot series with just two weeks left to build customer cars.

At a first glance, this problem might seem to relate only to the assemblers' way of integrating the system. However, it was in fact more complicated than that and directly related to visions. The wire harnesses are unique for every car as they depend upon the options desired by the customer. In order to understand the problem, the specifications for the audio system were looked into. The following issues were observed:

- No statements linking the interconnection between the audio system and the wire harnesses were found. In fact, for minimal magnetic interference, there should be as few wires as possible above the radio.
- The operating environment was not described in the specifications. Therefore, the OEM could not sue the supplier for failure to follow the specifications.
- It was also not pointed out what would happen if the problems were not solved, i.e. what the responsibilities of the OEM and the supplier, respectively, were.

The problem was observed to be related to the positioning of the supplier in the wrong category. The supplier required detailed specifications and was in fact given open specifications. The lack of vision for suppliers allowed the wrong positioning of the audio system supplier. To overcome this problem with the alternator noise, there were a number of options as illustrated in Figure 3.1.

The employees did not know what option to adopt. There was no vision to guide the development personnel and thus, the project, in dealing with the suppliers. As the OEM wanted to keep control over the integration, they did not want the wire harness supplier and the audio system supplier to collaborate. This increasingly complicated the problem. Further investigation revealed that the employees, in line with the vision of being proud, were behaving arrogantly with all the different categories of suppliers. They did not take into consideration the inputs from suppliers who were more knowledgeable than the OEM itself. The opposite was also true as they followed the suggestions of suppliers who were less knowledgeable than the OEM. Let us now examine how to develop the visions.

Creation of supplier visions

Past observations with other companies and the case study OEM allow us to corroborate Lipton's (1996) statement that visions are the sum of the mission, strategy and culture of the company. Creation of visions for suppliers would need to encompass them as well. We would like to clarify that it would be impossible to create visions for individual suppliers but it is feasible to create visions for supplier categories.

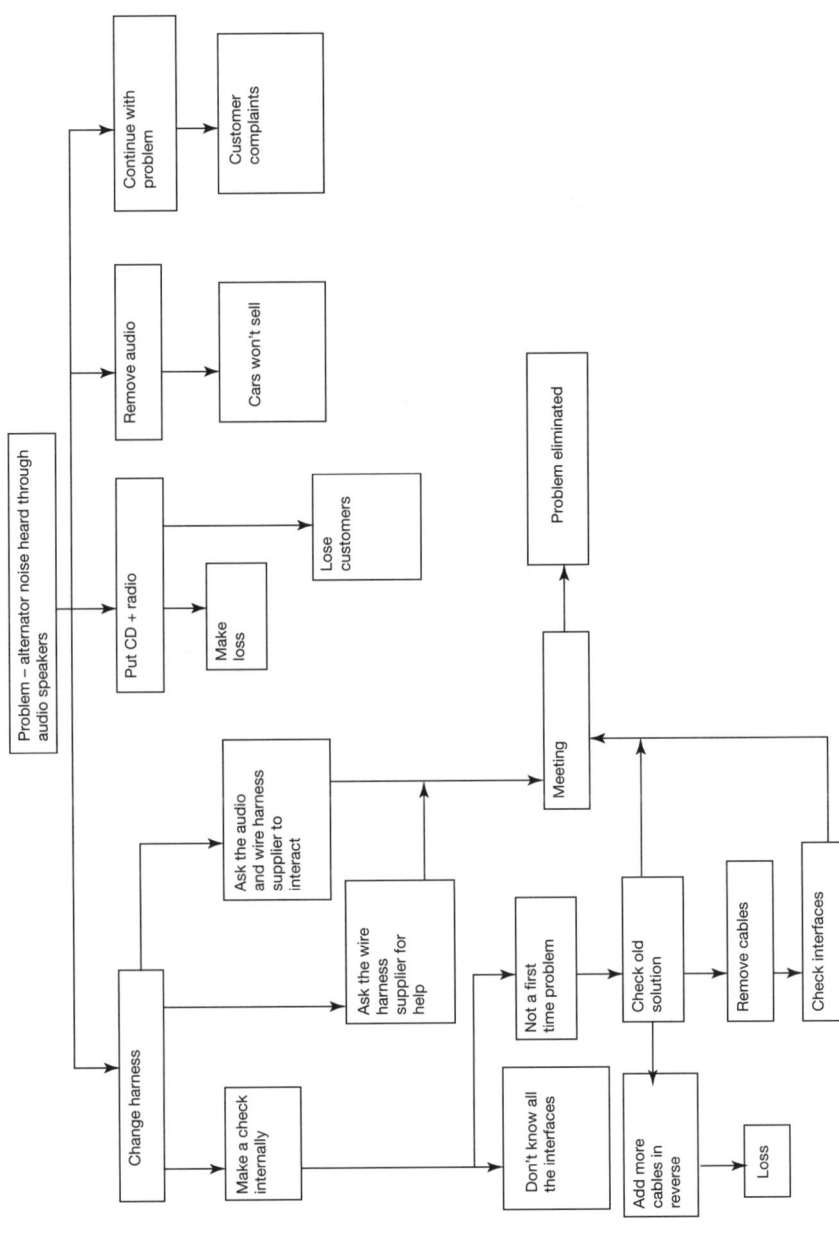

Figure 3.1 Solution options to fix alternator noise in the car

56 Visionary-driven outsourced development

In creating visions for suppliers, the components of the vision: mission, strategy and culture, will need to be reconciled between the OEM and its suppliers. This can be seen as a matching process (Figure 3.2).

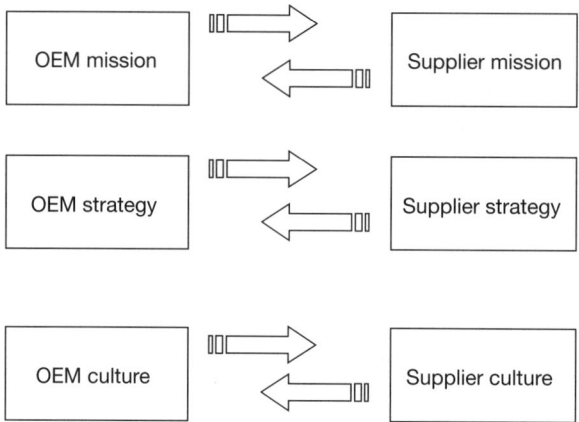

Figure 3.2 The matching process

The matching process entails reconciling diverse views between the OEM and the suppliers. One can argue that companies such as BMW or Saab Automobiles selling in the premium segment would hardly ever use a supplier whose mission is selling acceptable quality at high volumes. Therefore, even if BMW or Saab Automobiles have engaged in dealings with such a supplier, the mistake would lie in the supplier selection process. No importance should be given to reconciling diverse views with such a supplier. Interviews and observations at companies reveal that all companies, whether they operate in the premium segment or the low end of the market, engage with a wide variety of suppliers (in particular, all the four categories described by Kamath and Liker, 1994) depending on the degree of strategic vulnerability of the suppliers and the competitive advantage that the product generates in the marketplace. That means that even a company like BMW would engage in relations with a contractual supplier and, thus, needs to invest resources in reconciling the diverse views within a supplier category.

Let us elaborate on the matching process by considering the mission, the strategy and the culture components of the vision. Assume that the mission of the OEM is to sell at a premium price and thus sell a high-quality car. The mission of the supplier, on the other hand, can be to sell to volume producers with 'acceptable' quality. When these diverse views are reconciled, the joint mission could be to deliver a premium car to the customer with high-quality components and with maximum profitability in the value chain. The supplier would thus have to refocus his priorities.

Let us now consider the strategy component of the vision. In order to achieve its mission, the OEM strategy could be to have differentiated products whereas the supplier strategy could be cost leadership. Reconciling the differences, the common strategy to achieve the joint mission could be to focus on high performance and quality and thus focus on a particular market segment. Inadvertently, the customer base also becomes clear to the supplier.

In the case of culture, let us assume that it consists of the organisational design elements, namely, tasks, people, structure, rewards, information and decision-making (Hanna, 1988). Comparing the two cultures, the suppliers and the buyers will offer a lack of information regarding compatibility. The elements can be reconciled, e.g. proud people who think that the 'OEM is always right' can be removed from the project.

In summary, the joint mission is related to 'What do we want the supplier to do?' The joint strategy is related to 'How will the supplier execute the task and what will be the OEM contribution?' The culture issues are related to 'What are the characteristics of the supplier?', 'When will the supplier be involved?', 'What decisions can the supplier make?', 'How and when will information be distributed?', and 'What actions will be rewarded?' This is shown in Figure 3.3.

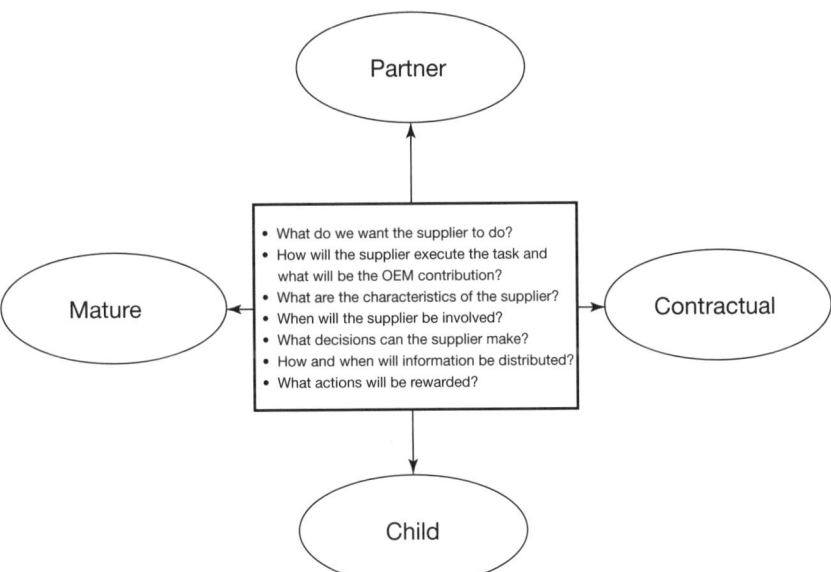

Figure 3.3 Creation of visions for suppliers

In outsourced development, i.e., when suppliers are involved, Bowen *et al.*'s (1994) concept of three visions needs to be expanded to include a fourth vision, namely, the vision for suppliers. The vision for suppliers also originates from the line of business guiding vision and from the input to the specifications (Figure 3.4).

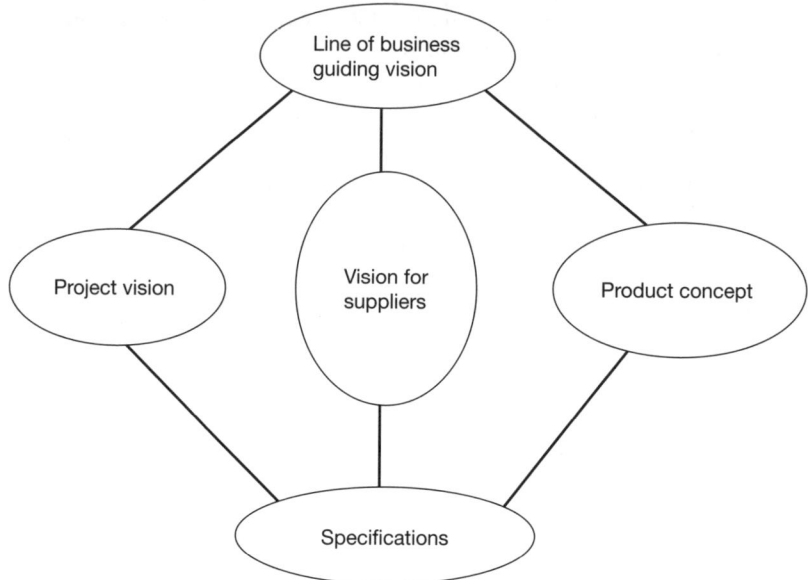

Figure 3.4 The vision for suppliers

Interplay between visions and core capabilities

Let us now explore the effects of supplier visions on the capabilities to use resources in order to improve the development process. In order to do so, we will use the core capability framework developed by Bowen *et al.* (1994). This framework consists of knowledge, managerial systems, physical systems, and values. We will use the example of the relationship between the OEM and a global seat supplier.

Towards the end of development, just before delivery of customer cars, problems were noticed with the seats; they were uncomfortable. In accordance with the supplier typology of Kamath and Liker (1994) the seat supplier qualified as a mature supplier. However, it was considered to be a partner supplier by other OEMs as it had an enormous capacity to innovate with numerous product concepts under development. The OEM considered itself to be the best in comfort and thus felt it necessary to give detailed specifications to the supplier. The values of the OEM reflect that it is the best in the industry. This value encouraged the OEM to forget that the supplier, by virtue of working with many different customers, had developed the latest state-of-the-art test methods. Moreover, a narrow perception within the OEM's engineering department concerning learning opportunities from suppliers led to the OEM dictating a slightly outdated test method to the supplier. The visions influencing the current state of capabilities in the buyer–supplier interface are displayed in Table 3.2.

This state of capabilities led to a future situation where the empowered people in the OEM did not want to listen to the supplier. In fact, the latest test methods

Table 3.2 Current state of capabilities

Dimensions of core capabilities	Current state of the capabilities within the auto OEM
Knowledge	Comfort knowledge (like ergonomics) is assumed to be the best practice within the OEM. Therefore, the supplier needs to be told the comfort specifications even though the seat can be outsourced. It does not matter that the supplier makes interior systems (including seats) for several major global automobile manufacturers.
Managerial systems	Continuous education is not encouraged within the OEM and the incentive system is poor. There are no apprentice programmes. Narrow outlook of staff at the OEM leads to control over minor details. The supplier's managerial systems are good as they have employed personnel with extensive educational and operational backgrounds and in fact, many of the auto OEM engineers.
Physical systems	Auto OEM feels that the thousands of hours that have been invested in the development of validation systems is good enough. This perspective does not allow the auto OEM engineers to proactively search for the latest in validation methods for comfort within the supplier base. This is in spite of the fact that the suppliers are familiar with the latest in validation systems in the automotive industry.
Values	The 'OEM is always right', and a 'We know everything' culture exists within the OEM. Product engineering is the dominant discipline and all the top jobs are offered to engineers. For example, the latest person to head a platform has an engineering background. Engineers hold a majority of the top management jobs.

were not used; the OEM was not even aware of them. The managerial systems in the OEM were not good, for example, non-technical employees (such as process owners) were often frustrated and afraid of losing their jobs. This meant that they tried to control minor details in the process of managing suppliers. Due to a fuzzy vision of how to integrate development with suppliers, the knowledge sought from the supplier was very limited; the OEM did not take into account the fact that the supplier had a world-class expertise in seating. The possible future state of capabilities as a result of the dysfunctions identified above is presented in Table 3.3.

The above case study demonstrates a number of critical factors, which are listed as follows:

- The values in the OEM were affected by the visions they had for the suppliers. Unclear visions on how to deal with suppliers could result in a situation where ideas from suppliers are not considered important.
- The values affected the physical systems dimensions. The 'we know everything' culture biased the OEM into not taking advantage of the physical systems of the supplier and instead relied on its internal outdated systems.
- The values affected the managerial systems. These systems turned the organisation into chaos. Only engineering jobs were encouraged and the

Table 3.3 Future state of capabilities if negative trend continues

Dimensions of core capabilities	Future state of capabilities within the auto OEM
Knowledge	Supplier input is not taken into account and multiple concepts are not encouraged and tested. This will lead to a slack in seating technology.
Managerial systems	Non-technical jobs are not encouraged. Faulty appraisals and empowerment systems can lead to loss of skilled employees and extremely costly power struggles.
Physical systems	The lack of technology scanning through suppliers will lead to outdated testing systems.
Values	The empowered people in the OEM do not want to listen to suppliers, thereby decreasing supplier credibility further. This leads to technical isolation in an engineering ivory tower.

uncertainty due to the large number of problems in the final product led to their concentrating on petty details.
- The value dimension affected the knowledge sought. The OEM staff, along with their engineering drive, always felt that the suppliers did not know anything. This led to unnecessary problems and changes during the development of the product.

The existence of visions for suppliers can help build the development of good values. These include faith in each other's abilities, trust, social responsibility towards fellow employees, and team working, depending upon the category of the supplier. Good physical systems can develop with the emergence of comprehensive data systems, exchange of data, world-wide project management systems, and technology sharing between customers and suppliers in view of improving technology synergy. Good managerial systems can be developed by the emergence of comprehensive training and development programmes or programmes to improve motivation. The knowledge aspect can be improved by understanding the capabilities of different actors and by developing broad-based inter-functional and inter-company values in project teams. There needs to be a clear match between the four dimensions of core capabilities, between the buyer and the supplier. If the visions for suppliers are not clear, i.e., if the place and role of each actor and the expectations based on a comprehensive understanding of the needs and capacities of one another are fuzzy, there will be problems of over- and under-management of suppliers.

Let us take another example to demonstrate the importance of visions. There can be different types of projects in an organisation (Cusumano and Takeishi, 1991) such as totally new design, a rapid transfer of functional solutions from other related projects so that there is joint development between projects, sequential design transfer where designs are transferred from unrelated completed projects, and design modifications within a specific project. The auto OEM tried to implement a sequential design transfer from an unrelated completed project in terms of carrying over the radio, cassette and CD player from one of its subsidiaries. In order to fix the carry-over in the new model, the auto OEM had to change the illumination intensity in the display panels of the audio system to ensure that it matched with the SID (Side Instrument Display). After the project started, there were numerous delays as follows:

- Two different suppliers produced the tape tuner combination and the CD changer. Neither of them matched the bus (signal carrier) protocol of the auto OEM.
- At the start of the project, the tape tuner supplier received a major order from one of the leading volume competitors and hence, did not spend much time in solving the bus protocol with the CD changer supplier. The subsidiary, however, continued to buy the same tape tuner as it matched with its bus protocol.
- During this time, the styling department and the marketing department at auto OEM realised that the styling of the audio system would not suit the interior design. The styling department was contemplating whether or not to change the appearance on the front of the tape tuner. This new front alone would have cost millions of dollars. There was a year of activity after which the project was scrapped. Overall, there was wastage of time, cost and resources.

This example demonstrates that the audio system supplier was assumed to be a partner supplier and expected to take care of the interfaces. Yet he was not, as he was a mature supplier. The level of knowledge in the specification writing was misunderstood. The managerial systems in the relationship were not tuned to improving the relationship, for example, the OEM did not work on incentives to be exchanged, work on the bus interface, etc. This meant that the OEM did not emphasise that the bus solving capabilities were the most important in the relationship. The physical systems did not encourage the relationship. There were no facilitating factors for communication such as a common information system. The values were problematic in this case, as the product emphasis was not on solving the problems. The problem clearly illustrates the need to match the visions for suppliers and the capabilities.

In conclusion, one can observe that the visions affect the culture of the company, which in turn affects the knowledge that the company seeks and wishes to retain. This has an effect on the managerial systems and the physical systems as well.

Conclusion

Our survey and in-depth case studies have identified the need for visions for suppliers in outsourced product development within the automotive industry. Non-identification of visions for suppliers was observed to be a factor negatively affecting the final product.

62 Visionary-driven outsourced development

We have observed the complexity of problems that may arise by not understanding the impact of different levels of visions for suppliers and the differences between the types of suppliers. The analysis indicated that in order to obtain a viable product, a complex web of interconnected factors must be considered. The most important implications from this chapter are described with reference to Figure 3.5, which essentially captures the conclusion.

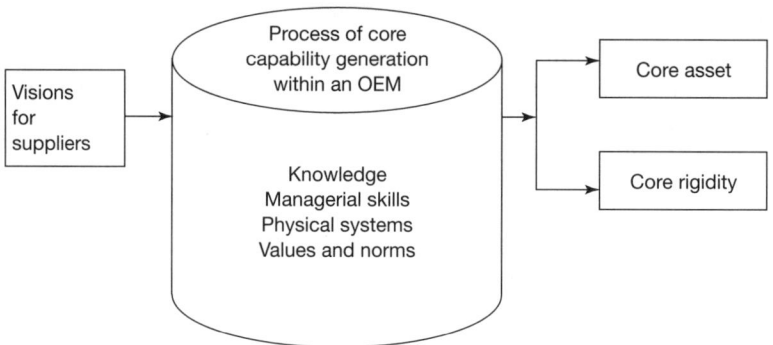

Figure 3.5 Integrated means of guidance-related capability and generation model

Visions for suppliers affect the core capabilities of an organisation, for example, as analysed in our case study, the relationship with suppliers. The output can either lead to a core rigidity/bad product or a core asset/viable product. Hence, in order to get a viable product, the link between core capabilities and visions for suppliers must be taken into consideration. Fuzzy visions spell trouble for companies. In the case of the seat supplier, the state of capabilities was heading towards a core rigidity in terms of designing and testing seating in-house using outdated techniques. With an appropriate vision for suppliers guiding the buyer–supplier relationship, considering the supplier as a partner supplier, and emphasising learning opportunities, the capabilities situation could lead to a core competence in integrated design of seats based on technology and competence sharing and synergies.

There are several important lessons to be taken from this study:

- Develop one vision for each category of suppliers and for companies following the Kamath and Liker (1994) typology – four categories of suppliers, thus there will be four visions for suppliers appropriately linked to the specifications.
- Managers must source only from suppliers that have the same vision as defined by the OEM for the different categories of suppliers and which fit well into the definition of the different categories. Differing visions between the buyer and the suppliers can lead to unrealistic expectations of each other and, thus, problems throughout the development process.

- Visions may be such that they can integrate the different types of suppliers/customers/products.
- The knowledge sought will depend on the values that a company has and, thus, it is of utmost importance that visions are checked at regular intervals. This will help to ensure that all changes in the environment are taken into consideration.

4 Redefining the role of product specifications

The specification process in new product development in the automotive industry is critical in reducing lead time, cost, and improving quality. However, this process has been little studied in spite of the rich literature on product development management. By means of a questionnaire survey of automotive suppliers, the research reported in this chapter first of all identifies the main problems perceived by suppliers in the specifications process in black box engineering. The results from the survey are grouped into five categories of problems; technical content, changes, cost, interpretation and understanding, and participation of suppliers in the specification process. A specification–supplier framework which can help both OEMs and suppliers improve and sustain specification management is proposed. It is concluded that the establishment of clear definitions and mutual agreement concerning the role of suppliers at the outset of every new development project would have a positive effect on the development process. Black box engineering redefines the role of specifications by encouraging the suppliers to become more proactive and to take an active part in specifying. More direct contact between operational design staff in OEMs and suppliers, and a changing attitude towards seeing changes as learning opportunities, might facilitate this transition.

Framework of problem areas in specifications

This section reports on the findings from the questionnaire. The objective was to understand what are the critical issues in the field of specifications from a supplier's point of view (the supplier can, in fact, be seen as the 'customer' of the specification). Some 350 suppliers returned the questionnaire answering the question about the problems that they thought were rampant in the specification process. Table 4.1 displays the significant problem areas identified by the suppliers; these were areas that scored at least 10 per cent from the suppliers studied.

These different issues were discussed with the product development managers and the operational design staff in the case study suppliers. They shared the same problems and agreed upon their relevance. This further analysis resulted in a categorisation of problems as presented in Table 4.2. Item 10 in Table 4.1, short lead time, is a transversal factor influencing all the above categories.

Table 4.1 Problem areas identified through the survey

ID	Problem area	% of suppliers mentioning
1	Specific requirements often lead to specific versions. There is not enough standardisation which increases cost.	10
2	Sometimes there is no cost optimisation.	32
3	Sometimes the specifications are too general and do not cover the requirements of the part in question.	23
4	The OEM does not give reasons for changes in specifications to the supplier.	35
5	Even when it is very urgent, some specifications are missing such as tolerances and dimensions.	15
6	There are problems in interpretation of specifications as well as in language translations.	49
7	Specifications keep changing all the time.	52
	Specifications are even changed after tooling and method of manufacture have been decided.	28
8	Sometimes the specifications are gold plated. There are a lot of opportunities to add more costs.	15
9	OEMs do not listen enough to the expertise of suppliers, for example, too much cost saving in the design might lead to poor functionality in several cases.	29
10	There are extremely short lead times.	22
11	There is a lot of over-specification which increases the cost, for example,	35
	the tolerances are too narrow	15
	some of the criteria are well beyond the life usage of the product.	20
12	New specifications are not discussed in the planning stage.	16

Table 4.2 Categorisation of problem areas

Category	Problem areas
Technical content – level of detail in requirements	1, 3, 5, 11
Changes of specifications	4, 7
Cost	2, 8
Interpretation and understanding	6
Participation of suppliers in the specification process	9, 12

Context and causal explanations of the identified problems

In the second part of the research, we tried to understand the problems identified through in-depth case studies. The aim was to analyse the context in which product specifications are developed and used, to identify the reasons for the problems, and to discuss their possible solutions in order to improve the specification process. As shown in Table 4.2 and as will be further analysed below, the problems with specifications are directly related to product development performance measurements in terms of quality, cost and lead time.

Technical content

Two main problems existed concerning the technical content of the product specification, i.e. the functional description consisting of written text and rough sketches, and technical data such as dimensions, tolerances, capacity, strength, temperature, vibration and chemical resistance. The first problem was that specifications sometimes were very general and vague and did not cover the requirements of the specific part or product in question. This was true in the case study supplier firms where design technicians sometimes complained that specifications were incomplete, something that considerably delayed and increased the cost of operational design work as they had to spend extra time and money trying to decipher the meaning of specifications.

However, behind the expression 'the specification is not complete' one can ask the question whether the specification ought to be more complete, i.e. if information has been left out by error at some stage in the elaboration or transmission of the specification, or if the specification was intended only as a guideline that the customer did not wish to specify further. This problem is clearly related to the move towards general guidelines and guiding visions rather than detailed instructions in the customer–supplier interface in product development – identified as black box engineering.

The present research provides a complementary picture of the process of specifying in black box engineering. Indeed, the study revealed a general problem for design engineers in determining in which category different specifications belong, but project members at the two supplier companies did not have any particular problem with developing new product solutions from only partially framed specifications. What was perceived as a problem was knowing when a design demand concerned a black box type of product or a more detail-controlled one. Several examples were quoted when a design problem was seen as pertaining to the first category, but where customer reaction to proposed solutions was negative, on the pretext that detailed specifications existed for the component. In such a case the OEMs clearly bore the responsibility for the misunderstanding. The most important reason for this problem, found in the study of the OEM, was that the OEM, after having sent out a request containing framing specifications, often got delayed in the further specification of the component in question. This is because of system integration difficulties related to modifications in other interfacing components. On the supplier side, a one-week silence from an OEM combined with a defined lead time in the initial draft specification resulted in a launch of a development project, thinking it was a question of a black box study.

The second problem concerning the technical content was related to over-specification. Often the correct tolerance level was not mentioned or very narrow tolerances were given. Too narrow tolerances can mean that a product cannot be made and thus unnecessary time will be wasted in changing the specifications and achieving a realistic tolerance level. In some cases the content, e.g. functional solution, material, dimensions of a specification can be 'extreme', i.e. very hard or even impossible to realise with existing technology. The main reason for this was the fact that there is often no time to involve internal or external experts when innovative propositions are developed. The result will be the birth of a very costly product or, worse, a specification that cannot be realised or a product with no operational use, for example, that cannot be integrated with other technologies in a system.

As illustrated above, the specifications are too detailed in some cases, and in others they are not detailed enough. Hence, the supplier risks not being able to make progress, losing precious development time and money. The main reason seems to be an information gap in the buyer–supplier interface concerning the exact capabilities of different suppliers.

Changes in specifications

According to the suppliers, there are too many changes in the specifications. Too many changes means rework, thus delaying the product development process. Changes could be due to a number of reasons such as mistakes, lack of harmony between various demands within the OEM's different technical centres and the need for interaction in the functional system, etc. Often the reasons behind changes in specifications are not given to suppliers, thus making it harder for them to adapt component characteristics, and to understand the implications that the changes might lead to in relation to the evolution of a system. A particular form of late change occurs if mistakes once noted have not been implemented in the specifications. Major delay and cost problems can be expected if the changes in the specifications are made after the supplier has set up tooling. This would mean that the supplier has to retool, thus increasing the cost. OEMs try to reduce the product development time. However, in doing so, they underestimate the usefulness of testing. If the case study OEM had invested in testing out prototypes thoroughly before suppliers engaged in serial tooling, then it could have reduced this risk and saved both time and money.

Even though the specification is often seen by design engineers in the supplier companies as one relatively *fixed* document, observation of the activities taking place between the initial receipt of a specification and the moment when it was considered completed, indicated that specifying in black box engineering is a *process* taking place at the *systemic level* of operational design work, i.e. involving project teams in customer and supplier firms as well as development teams in suppliers of interfacing components. It always requires further interaction with the customers, cross-functional consultations inside the supplier companies, and often also the advice of experts such as sales engineers or research staff. These observed tendencies have strong parallels with the recent research on the use and management of specifications reviewed above. They confirm Kaulio's (1996) proposal, also in the case of designing car components, that the specification is an arena for co-operation, and a series of documents that are generated by all the actors involved.

What actually happened in the successful black box engineering projects that were identified was that a set of different specifications was developed based on the initial framing guidelines transmitted by the customer. This practice resembled the practice at Toyota suppliers as described by Ward *et al.* (1995). This contained nothing revolutionary in itself; design technicians generally developed several product solutions and prototypes for every new development project, so the 'raw material' for such an action already existed. What was changing in both supplier companies under study was that these parallel solutions, in the form of blueprints, prototypes, different text documents, were successively presented to the customers. Traditionally, the different developed solutions were evaluated inside the supplier company and only the final chosen solution was presented to the customer.

Cost

Why are cost targets so difficult to agree upon between OEMs and suppliers? First of all, a trade-off was identified within the OEM. When the technical content is specified, engineers and marketing managers tend to think mostly in terms of technical performance – innovativeness, and setting new market standards. When purchasing managers set cost targets, they think principally of the overall project budget. The problem facing selected suppliers is then that there might be an important mismatch between technical content and cost target.

Second, there are issues related to the content problem discussed above. When black box specifications are given to suppliers, they are generally about 60–70 per cent complete and hence subject to change. As discussed earlier, the suppliers do not always understand this fact. They quote a price for this 60–70 per cent specification on the assumption that this is 100 per cent of the specification and thus demand compensation for every change proposed by the OEM. There are different opinions about specifications between the suppliers and the buyer. The OEM does not want suppliers to change their prices or ask for increased compensation for every change. On the supplier side, however, there is another interpretation to this. According to the suppliers, it is impossible to estimate the changes required at a very early stage and thus difficult to quote a price which includes the unforeseen changes as well. Sometimes the cost book price may also be wrong.

The third cost-related problem concerns the lack of cost optimisation and the opportunities to add more costs that affect both suppliers and OEMs. Often the specifications are written in such a way that it is very easy for the suppliers to add costs. The specifications leave large gaps for interpretation concerning materials, functions or levels of tolerances. If there is no time or relevant links available to check up on ambiguous or apparently missing information, suppliers might end up over-designing components, thus increasing cost both for them and the OEM. For example, the OEM had to incur a loss of 5 per cent due to the fact that a supplier used a particular material that was 10 per cent more expensive than originally planned by the OEM. The OEM refused to pay the 10 per cent increase and accepted only a 5 per cent increase, leading to a shrinking margin for the supplier and an increased cost for the OEM. Also, often the defined specifications are far beyond the usage of the product, thus adding on more cost.

Interpretation and understanding

Shrinking development lead times are a daily concern for development staff in both OEMs and suppliers. OEMs want to exercise any option that may help in reducing lead times. When a lead time is defined, the product specification is supposed to be complete, the supplier will know what to do, and no further changes will occur. However, as our study has shown, this is not necessarily the case. In reality, this means that within the framework of a theoretical minimum lead time, there will be delays in terms of modifications, wrong interpretations, and insufficient information exchange. The result is that suppliers often find themselves in a vicious circle of delays that increase incrementally from project to project and from customer to customer. The consequences are continuous rescheduling, insufficient prototype testing, and hard prioritising to please the largest customer or the one that puts the most pressure on.

Our observations of specifications sent out by the OEM and received by the suppliers show that sometimes the specification is full of words with little focus on purpose – it is thus difficult to understand. Language and translation problems can be other reasons for misinterpretation. Misunderstanding or mistranslation can mean that the critical aspects of the process can be misunderstood. If most of the specifications are not discussed early enough in the planning stage, there will be a lot of iterations towards the end of the product development process. There can be communication problems between the supplier and the buyer on specifications. In the worst case scenario, suppliers do not even read the specifications properly. Problems with interpretation and understanding arise not only between the buyer and supplier but also internally within the OEM or within the supplier's company. The different layers of specifications are created by different people, for example, the marketing specification, top level of specification, system specification and component specification. The people involved do not bother to read whether their requirements have been fulfilled or not in the requirements flowdown, which results in certain demands not being fulfilled. This realisation comes when the product is ready and it is too late to make any changes. If changes are made at this late stage, then there will be cost increases and increased time to market. The communication patterns are thus distorted due to lack of feedback between the different levels involved in the requirement flowdown.

Participation of suppliers in the specification process

Several of the problems in the product specification process were related to a lack of early and/or in-depth participation of suppliers in the development process. In spite of the discourse and development of tools and methods presented in the product development literature, our study indicates that this is extremely difficult to achieve in practice. An important result of the study is that the project organisation in all OEMs and direct suppliers today is insufficient to ensure rapidity and relevance in information exchange. For example, an initial question from a supplier design technician concerning an ambiguous issue in a product specification first has to pass via the project manager in the supplier company, then through the supplier's sales engineer, and finally through the function project manager in the OEM, before reaching the design technician concerned. This caused at least two problems in the studied supplier firms:

- The design technician in the OEM would not return information that was 100 per cent relevant in relation to the original request.
- Implicit elements in the initial message and in the answer might disappear.

It is important to emphasise that the problem of information transmission was not related to deliberate withholding of information, but to a distortion due to the fact that different actors did not perceive the question in the same way.

Another example where lack of supplier involvement causes problems is in the setting of overall technical targets for a system. If suppliers are not involved in this process, their solutions can easily jeopardise the overall performance of a system. An example of such an overall technical target is weight limits. A problem observed in the OEM was that weight requirements were rarely included in the specifications, thus suppliers sometimes increased weight, which could lead to overall weight problems. Even though weight is a very important requirement in the automotive industry, neither the OEM, nor the case study suppliers had a separate department or function looking into the weight issues and trying to reduce the weight throughout the car.

These different interface problems are intimately related to the question of how information is transmitted between customers and suppliers during product development. When the supplier is working on black box or their own proprietary development projects, there is a need for frequent information exchange for mutual adaptation and evolution of interfacing components. Field observations and the problems analysed above indicated that information exchange at the project level, as prescribed by organisational routines, was not enough to ensure optimal integrated development. Through the case studies, a specific way of communicating at the individual operational design engineer or technician level could be observed. This exchange of information with customers, by-passing formal routines, was very frequent and broad, i.e. concerned issues that at a first glance sometimes looked quite distant from the actual activity performed by the engineer or technician. Through this information exchange, accuracy in technical discussions was improved and lead time was reduced. Moreover, it allowed the participants on both sides of the interface to learn about new practices that could be transferred to other parallel projects.

Other important actors also come into the picture when designing black box parts, namely, suppliers responsible for interfacing components evolving at the same time. For the companies studied, their integration in the development process caused as many problems as that of integrating with customers. It seemed that the system co-ordinators did not fully master this complex integration process – that had emerged only recently – but that tends to become more and more important. In addition, the participating suppliers were normally less focused on their horizontal colleagues than on their vertical customers.

The research findings indicate that the systemic nature of design work should draw managerial attention to integration between participants in the design process. With an increasing number of interfacing actors, both external and internal, the need for efficient co-ordination also increases. Through the change in the industrial organisation towards more inter-company collaboration and concurrency in the development process, suppliers have been taught the need of integrating both internal operations and external inputs the 'hard way'. Integration has become the inevitable means to an end of remaining an expert supplier to the automobile manufacturers. However, at the same time that systemic work is a driver for integration, it is also a facilitator: people will turn towards more of an outward-looking perspective because they will understand the sense of communicating and informing because of their own need of information from others.

Implications for the specification process

We have examined the problems faced in the specification process by both suppliers and an OEM. In order to overcome the specification-related problems we propose a specification–supplier framework. There are no general rules for success as there are many factors such as the environment, the nature of the product, previous knowledge of the partners, etc. which can affect the relationship with the supplier. However, the framework that we propose can help companies to assess and reflect on their specification management and ultimately improve and sustain it. Finally, we would like to add that it is people who deal with each other in both the organisations. Hence there may be social, personal and political factors affecting the management of specifications. The proposed framework is presented in Figure 4.1. It comprises the items analysed above, and adds three factors, control and limitations that constitute direct governance links for the specification process, and prototypes that constitute the tangible artefacts exchanged between buyers and suppliers as a result of the specification process. The framework is not exhaustive but exploratory.

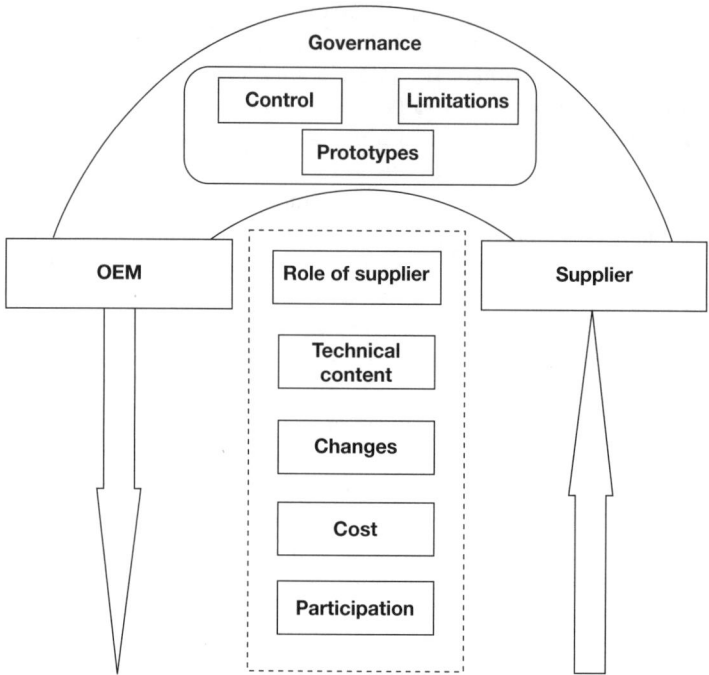

Figure 4.1 Specification–supplier framework

Figure 4.1 displays a set of factors and governance mechanisms that the OEM and the supplier may consider in order to improve the development process. The central box contains factors of high importance to regulate between the two parties and the upper box contains important mechanisms to govern the relationship as follows. Both the OEM and the supplier can decide as to the role to be played by the supplier. The technical content of the specification is a reflection of the capabilities and capacities of the supplier and thus would play an important role in the factors that can help improve development. Factors like cost, changes and participation on the part of the supplier can contribute to improved development. Control, limitations and prototypes form governance mechanisms that help to regulate the relationship between the OEM and the supplier.

Role of the supplier

First, the role of the supplier needs to be defined. Different types of suppliers have different roles and hence the content of the specifications would be different in each case. In this case we are interested in the role of black box suppliers, i.e. the suppliers who are given critical specifications that frame the component or systems requirements and call upon the suppliers' innovation and development capability. Confusion in the OEM about the capabilities and competencies of suppliers leads to their over- or under-management.

Our studies have identified tendencies that challenge the generally accepted tier model where first-tier system suppliers are given black box specifications, and second-tier sub-contractors are given detail-controlled ones. Triangulation, i.e. a relationship model where innovative expert suppliers participate directly in integrated development even though their components are delivered to a system supplier, might become an increasingly important alternative (see Figure 4.2). In this model, three actors will be directly involved in the specification process, which emphasises the need for precisely defining the roles of one another.

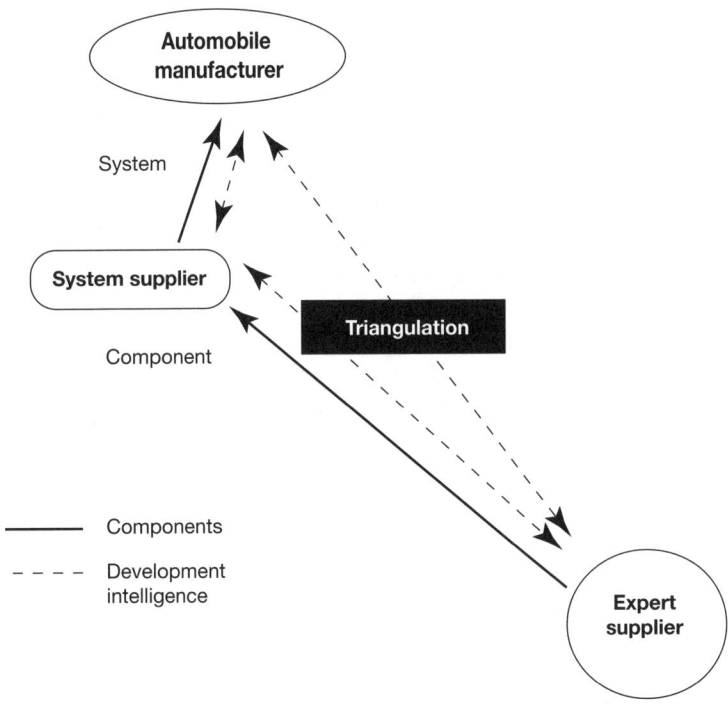

Figure 4.2 Triangulation

Technical content

Once the role of the supplier has been established, the content of the specifications needs to be clearly mentioned. If the supplier is a detailed parts supplier, then the completeness of the specification in all respects is a necessity. In the case of a black box supplier, the specifications may be written in such a way that they will be able to manoeuvre and use their engineering capabilities. In order to reduce the problems concerning level of details in requirements, clearer information from the OEM may be asked for. Black box engineering necessarily redefines the role of the specification. The data indicate that the specification process can become more interactive than traditionally was the case. Faced with an ambiguous situation, suppliers may find it necessary to become more proactive in their customer relationships in order to obtain the information they need to do their work correctly. Moreover, the experience of product development managers was that the more active the supplier was in searching for information on their own initiative, the greater were the chances of profiling the company as an expert supplier. If specifications were used for spontaneous discussions with the suppliers, for example, through Lotus notes/EDI etc., many of the content-related problems could be avoided.

The internal performance of the supplier company in terms of information transmission and a relevant understanding of transmitted information will also be informally assessed in black box engineering.

Changes

The studies of the OEM show that the product specifications as defined by the OEM's product development staff are already the result of a very large number of interactions and adjustments. Before involving suppliers, it is desirable that the OEM makes sure that all internal functions agree on the specification outline and that no contradictory messages are sent from different functions to different suppliers (or even to the same supplier!).

For particular components there should be a core specification valid for all OEMs in the same business. The core specifications may be the same for all the OEMs with only specific features or distinguishing characteristics specific to the OEMs.

There can be sequential freezing every time partial specifications of a component or system have been mutually agreed upon between the OEM and all interfacing suppliers. This would oblige comprehensive testing of prototypes and updating of specifications, allowing all actors to advance on the same line. At the supplier level, suppliers may be obliged to put in more development resources and adopt a more flexible development organisation with strong links to manufacturing. Also, they should have flexible schedules for design technicians, open-plan design departments allowing for intra-functional exchange of knowledge and information, and the chance to take initiatives for direct contact with operational design staff in customer firms to reduce information gaps.

In order to balance the trade-off between the perpetual change of specifications during the development process and the demand for short development lead times, it might be useful to divide the design process into two parts:

- the functional concept: this is the product technology that will solve the functional problem that the customer presents;
- the dimensional definition: this consists of the dimensions and the form of the component.

If suppliers were to learn to work with 'sets' of functional concepts in a first phase and only subsequently devote time to the dimensional definition, after intensive exchange of information with customers and interfacing suppliers concerning the functional concepts, they would be able to reduce development lead time and redundant work, and at the same time respond to the evolution of specifications in a flexible manner.

As well as offering the possibility of freezing hard specifications later, the observed use of the set-based approach could promote innovation. When working in this way, customers became informed of the broader spectrum of the supplier's design capabilities. This made it possible for the supplier to further interest them in the possibility of proposing solutions that went beyond the perfection of single component performance, for example, mini systems or different technology to resolve a specific functional problem. These observations confirmed a somewhat contradictory practice compared to the general perception of 'lean' product development. Suppliers were indeed involved early in the development process, but hard specifications tend to be fixed as late as possible to promote innovative solutions. Thus, instead of talking about early design involvement, the case studies suggest permanent design involvement and late component procurement for successful black box projects.

Cost

In order to balance the trade-off between technical/marketing requirements and cost targets, a good project integration in the OEMs can be developed. The level of specifications needs to relate not only to the market need but also to whether the customer is willing to pay for it or not.

The cost of components can be openly discussed with black box suppliers before fixing framing specifications. If the supplier is involved from the beginning in the cost discussions, then the estimates will be more realistic as the supplier would include the possible number of change loops in their cost estimates. Changes are a part of the specification process and if the supplier understands this, it can lead to the specifications being used as a tool to discuss the forthcoming product. Finally, the cost parameters must be clearly stated also in framing specifications to avoid 'free' interpretations that tend to promote more expensive materials and other types of over-designs, making costs increase.

Participation

In successful projects, the specification was found to be not only a support structure for technical problem-solving at an individual level, but a vehicle for inter-functional and inter-company collaboration. As such, it improved co-ordination in different interfaces and creativity in product technology through the exploration of several different ways of resolving problems.

A specific communication mode which we label 'permanently open communication channels' was found to provide the essential amount of interaction needed for a smooth joint specification process. Its properties can be summarised as:

- high frequency of information exchange;
- non project-tied information exchange;

- non sequence-tied information exchange;
- openness and frankness; problems are discussed in order to find solutions together and there is a margin of negotiation within the triangle of quality, cost, and lead time.

The above discussion emphasises the possible advantages if managerial focus can be on supporting the systemic nature of design work and simultaneously avoiding a too scientific way of managing product development. This is done by favouring a mode that sets creativity free and supports the natural working practices in product development of co-ordination, integration and learning between different participants and functions. It is through systemic work that core capabilities take form, product technology evolves, and inter-firm and intra-firm learning are connected. At the same time, the negative side of systemic work, namely, that everyone tends to be preoccupied with everything at all times, can be recognised and mastered.

Governance and artefacts

The factors that govern the relationship, identified from within the OEM, can be described as control, limitations and prototypes. Authors like Bowen *et al.* (1994) treat prototypes as a form of understanding mechanism. In line with the same logic, the element *understanding* will be treated under prototypes. If suppliers are clearly defined from the beginning, then control can be exercised accordingly. If the number of prototypes and the reasons behind the prototypes are defined from the beginning, the need for prototypes is understood. A clear understanding from the beginning enables a joint decision regarding the limitations and the areas of trade-offs. The suppliers and the OEM can better understand each other if the suppliers are encouraged to ask questions and the OEMs are encouraged to give information as and when necessary.

Control

There is a move by the OEM to increase the dependency on suppliers and thus encourage the suppliers to contribute more. However, if all the design work is given to suppliers, then no internal engineering knowledge will be left within the company in several technology fields. With every proposal for a new demand the OEM will be forced to run to its suppliers and thus will be over-dependent on them. To limit this problem, OEMs write the top, or overall level specifications for functional systems and keep the overall engineering capability within the production chain. However, currently, the case study OEM not only writes the system specifications but also defines demands on the specifications of detailed components. That is the domain of the system suppliers, if the move towards increased supplier contribution is true.

The case studies confirmed this move, but there was confusion as to what a system supplier actually is. Certain suppliers call themselves system suppliers, yet they are given component-level specifications and are not allowed to work on grey or black box specifications for the components to be incorporated in the system. Even if they are allowed to work on the system-level specifications, their input is hindered to a very large extent. An obvious reason for the confusion in supplier firms concerning the level of details in specification was that the suppliers' role was often far from clear within the OEM.

Limitations and trade-offs

The limitations of the specifications may be better understood if the OEM and the supplier work jointly on them. This is desirable so as to confirm that there are no unrealistic demands placed on each other. Limitations in this case mean the limitations of the demands and validation requirements put down in the specifications. Let us demonstrate this with an example. Comfort in a car is defined by temperature and air speed. The OEM can develop a comfort specification which includes the air speed at the window and at the floor of the car and also the blend curves that are to be satisfied in order to get the comfort as illustrated in Figure 4.3. This is given to the black box supplier for development. When the curves are received from the suppliers they could be different, and then the suppliers and the OEM can jointly work on the limitations and the trade-offs in the specifications.

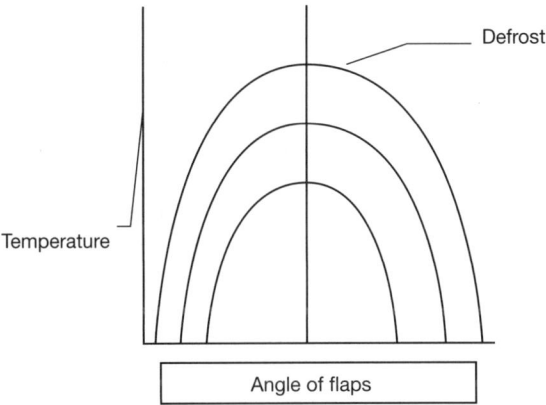

Figure 4.3 Comfort curve in an automobile

Often the suppliers do not read their specifications or understand them, for example, the fact that the curves depend on the market need. Fat people require a faster cool down and hence the blend curves will be different for fat people as compared to thin people. This provides an ideal opportunity to understand the limitations in the specifications and then make appropriate the trade-offs. There may be a tendency to hide problems and not correct problems at an early stage. The problems are sometimes not foreseen, or are hidden to protect people, etc.

78 *Role of product specifications*

An understanding of the limitations can help reduce the problems to a great extent, i.e. avoid unrealistic demands and expectations.

Prototypes

OEMs need to find ways of checking that what they ask for is provided. These validation requirements can be made clear through the validation specifications. A clear understanding of the needs for the different types of prototypes may prove beneficial, as all prototypes need not be complete in all respects. If this is not achieved, costs may increase. An understanding of the relationship between the test periods and cost may prove to be critical. The more a test procedure is delayed, the more will be the cost incurred due to different reasons such as tooling costs, etc. The different participants in the specification process need to read and check the requirements' flowdown. Seminars between the buyer and the supplier may be a useful means of reducing ambiguities and improving understanding. This helps co-ordination and is an open arena for co-operation.

Demonstrating the model

The model in Figure 4.1 can be demonstrated with the help of the air control example discussed above. Application of the model in a particular case does not prove it in all situations, but rather provides an example of how it could be used. With reference to Wheelwright and Clark's (1993) suggestion on the capabilities of the suppliers, it is obvious that not all suppliers will be able to forecast and propose solutions to the OEM as not all of them have the required capability. An understanding of the role of the supplier would help in recognising which suppliers could help in forecasting from the buyers' clues. Let us assume that the OEM recognised the supplier providing the climate control was a black box supplier. The specifications would need to reflect the capabilities of the supplier and hence would contain functional specifications such as customer satisfaction. Also the black box supplier will be more proactive, asking for information such as the level of comfort that the OEM is seeking. The changes would need to be thought of and can be estimated by working on sets of functional concepts, such as air flaps and the temperature. This would lead to an estimation of the costs as the costs depend on the number of changes. Articulation of the number of changes and the reasons behind the changes can lead to identification of many hidden costs gold plating the specification. Suppliers can participate in the specification process and thus exchange information such as the percentage of fat people, thin people, target people, etc., which is not necessarily project-related. Prototypes can be placed at strategic points in the OEM that can lead to rapid tests and comments. In fact, the climate control can be placed in the offices to test them. Identification of the role of the suppliers would permit control to be exercised, based on the capabilities of the suppliers and, in the case of limitations, as a governance factor. The different trade-offs like the rate of cool down can be used to guide the relationship between the OEM and the supplier.

Conclusion

In our survey of automotive suppliers and in-depth case studies of one OEM and two expert suppliers, we have identified specific problems related to the specifications process in black box engineering. The analysis of the context in which specifications are elaborated and the reasons for different problems illustrate the very complex web of interconnected factors that influence the performance of the specification process. The most important findings from the study are the following:

- Black box engineering redefines the role of specifications. Specifications cannot be regarded by suppliers as a fixed document, but instead as an open arena for technical adjustments.
- OEMs often give ambiguous specifications to suppliers because of internal functional conflicts, e.g. between marketing, engineering, and purchasing. A positive relationship between the level of specifications, market needs and the willingness of the customer to pay for the features was observed to be important.
- The proactiveness of the suppliers was observed to have a positive effect on the specification process. Several of the identified problems were related to wrong assumptions about the requirements in specifications due to a misunderstanding of the OEM's situation as a system integrator.
- Integrated component development starts at the specification stage. The involvement of operational design staff is pertinent and so is the necessity to allow them to have direct contact with their counterparts in the customer and supplier firms at this stage.
- Changes in specifications are unavoidable in any black box engineering project. This understanding on the part of the suppliers, coupled with the desire to work with several parallel sets of functional solutions that they can check with the customer before entering into detailed dimensional definitions, can reduce the time loss.
- Finally, changes in specifications do not deserve to be seen as a waste of time, money and engineering efforts. If product development managers in both suppliers and OEMs develop guiding visions that lead operational people to see engineering efforts as *learning opportunities*, this could create a significant competitive advantage.

Hauser and Clausing's (1988) model of the house of quality could be used to study the specification process. Depending upon the role of the supplier, customer attributes can be decided either by the OEM or by the OEM and the supplier jointly. In the particular case of black box engineering, customer attributes can be decided jointly. The content of the specification needs to reflect customer attributes and should be able to satisfy customer attributes though it is acknowledged that it is a compromise. The number of changes in the specification can reflect the compromises that are to be made in order to realise customer attributes. The cost would ultimately reflect the technical difficulty of achieving the technical solutions and the compromises to be made. Joint participation between the buyer and supplier would help in achieving realistic targets that are set by both. The governance mechanisms will help in guiding the house of quality. The house of quality example was not followed in the companies studied. Thus, the suppliers can be integrated into the house of quality, thereby understanding the various trade-offs, and the different customer attributes and the importance of delivering them.

5 Mapping the flow of specifications

The specification processes in new product development are essential in obtaining a high quality, low cost and well-interfaced product. However, despite the rich literature on product development, specification management has been given less attention. By means of two in-depth cases studies in one auto and one aircraft OEM, the research reported here identifies the specification processes in the case companies. Comparative studies of the specification processes in the two companies are conducted. A model of specification management is developed that identifies important steps from the conceiving of the idea to delivery and customer feedback. It is concluded that following the steps proposed in the model will lead to a high quality product.

The specification process at an auto OEM

The auto OEM and its suppliers have different opinions as to the significance of the specification. The auto OEM has different levels of specifications. The marketing department generates the market segment specifications (MSS) which is the starting point for further development of the specifications. It consists of market trends, own brand requirements, customer requirements, competitor analysis, supplier input and distributor requirements. The market segment specification along with the brand requirements subsequently generate:

- the initial vehicle technical specifications (IVTS), which is a preliminary specification regarding the architecture of the car;
- the vehicle technical specifications (VTS), which is the specification for the whole car;
- the sub-system technical specifications (SSTS), which is the sub-system level specification;
- the component technical specifications (CTS), which is the component-level specification.

Figure 5.1 illustrates the links between all these different specifications.

82 *Mapping the flow of specifications*

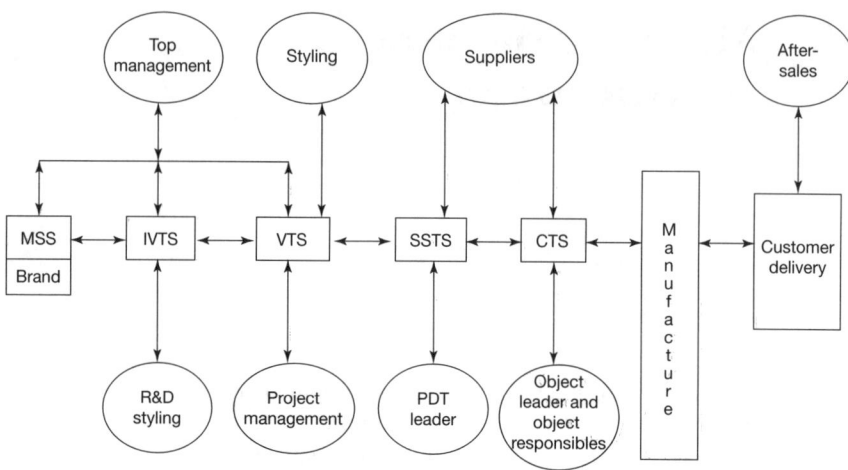

Figure 5.1 The specification process at an auto OEM

- The MSS is the point of departure for the specification process. It directly generates the IVTS with input from R&D and styling, and continuous input from top management.
- The VTS is generated from the IVTS. Here, project groups are formed and start to play an important role in the development process. Top management and styling still provide important inputs at this stage.
- The SSTS is generated from the VTS. These specifications are managed at the product development team leader (PDT) level. Suppliers are also invited to work on this level of specifications.
- Finally, the component technical specification (CTS) is generated from the SSTS. Object leaders and staff contribute here as well as suppliers.

We observe that there are different functions and management levels involved in the specification process. Project members work in a matrix organisation with the line management.

In the auto OEM, the entire car has been split up into six systems, namely, electronics, electrical, chassis, body, engine, and climate. This happens in the transition between the VTS and the SSTS. The systems are made up of objects, which in turn are made up of components. Figure 5.2 depicts the breakdown of the VTS into the sub-systems and objects.

The SSTS is generally the domain of the OEM but in certain cases the SSTS can be generated jointly by the OEM and the supplier. The CTS is made by the supplier but is subject to frequent interference by the OEM. Validation checks both by the buyer and the supplier are made at the VTS, SSTS and the CTS stages.

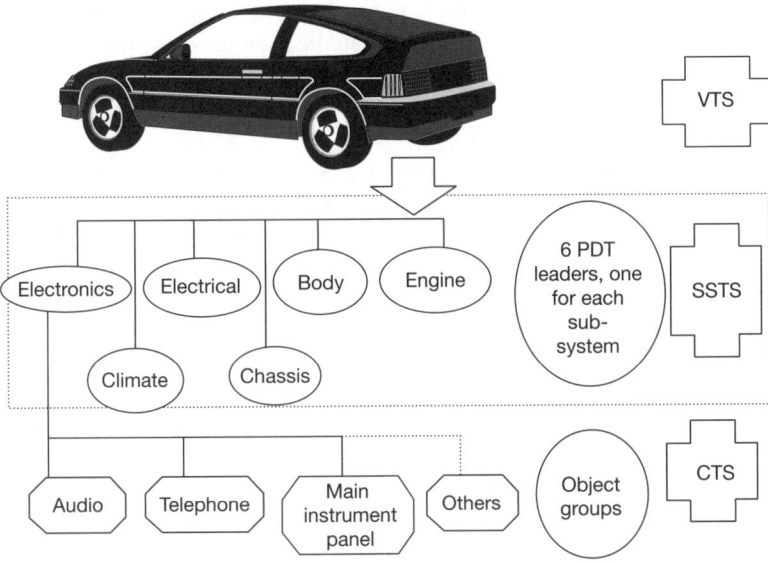

Figure 5.2 Breakdown of specifications

Role of different departments

Let us now describe the different departments involved in the specification process and the conditions involved in the specification process.

Role of top management in the specification process

Top management consists of the President and all the Vice Presidents of the OEM. These people are instrumental in defining the brand, which is the first step when starting a specification process. At the beginning of a project, top management asks for information from the marketing and engineering departments and decides which features to incorporate. For example, if the market wants a turbo engine and the OEM is the best in turbo engines (they employ a lot of consultants in order to benchmark price, quality, etc.), then top management may take a decision to incorporate a turbo engine. While the top management is involved in setting the total programme cost of the car, the individual costs for the objects are decided by the financial department in conjunction with the purchasing department. These costs have to be in line with the total programme cost.

Role of brand/marketing management

The brand management's role is to make the specifications in line with the image of the company, for example, the brand image of auto OEM is safety, hence, all safety features are emphasised. The rear seat belt warning sign is a safety feature.

If this feature is removed during a trade-off decision, then two issues are obvious. Either safety is not the brand of the company, or the brand vision is not clear within the organisation. The brand is important in order to get the price premium and also to be close to the customer. In elaborating the brand strategy, the auto OEM focuses on five important dimensions:

- Product category: Which product category is the focus of the OEM? Is it sports cars, family cars, leisure cars or executive/conservative cars?
- Needs: What are the needs in each product category? The needs could be safety, security, high performance, superior quality, aesthetics, etc.
- Heritage: Why are we making the product the way we do? For example, Volvo produces cars that have an image of providing extreme safety for the family.
- Expression: How do you express yourself to the customer? For example, BMW do not have humans in their advertisements. Humans spell imperfection whereas machines project perfection.
- User identity: The user identity needs to be projected. For example, a particular car could be projected for single business people, another for DINKS (Double Income, No Kids), a third for young families, etc.

The marketing department provides input from customer demands. However, these demands are not always interpreted correctly. Brand identification is a part of the marketing department's remit. There are frequent changes in the MSS and especially towards the end of the development process, which according to the marketing department is an outcome of the frequent changes in customer demands. A major problem is that the marketing department does not always check whether their demands are being fulfilled or not in the product development process due to a shortage of staff. Marketing is not able to staff all the object groups.

Role of R&D

This department is instrumental in developing the initial vehicle technical specifications. They also develop the product profile and interact with the marketing department in order to translate the market requirements into technical requirements. Many people in the organisation are not aware that the R&D department generates the initial VTS. The R&D department is instrumental in designing the geometry of the car and is responsible for deciding the various hard points in the car like the distance between the eyes of the driver and the front windshield of the car, the size of the car, bonnet height, ground clearance, dimensions of the wheels, i.e. all the measurements that are passed on to the styling department for further analysis and design work, such as reduction of noise in the car, reduction of fuel consumption, etc.

It is always necessary to ask the suppliers to make products that fit their existing production or manufacturing processes. According to sources at the OEM, this is not always done. If the products are in tune with the existing processes, then it is possible to get better quality. Hence it is necessary to avoid many unique designs that cannot be made by existing processes.

The R&D department is divided into the following sections: engine concepts, chassis-drive train concepts, simulation/computation and the platform or vehicle architecture concept. All these different sections propose vehicle characteristics for the different car lines. After the concept is initiated, the R&D representative works with project management and checks whether the car fulfils the characteristics that were originally decided. There is no manufacturing input to the R&D.

It can be observed that concepts are developed for only certain items that are considered strategic by the auto OEM. The non-strategic activities are based on standardised technologies, for example, the brake systems, etc., while the strategic activities are based on non-standardised technologies.

Role of after-sales/service

The after-sales/service department go through the design of the entire car and divide it into smaller sections with the intention of making 'design for reparability and serviceability'. Their requirements also need to be included in the specifications. It is their responsibility to ensure that the design of the car allows easy after-sales service and maintenance. They identify the 'wear and tear units' so as to have an optimism level of spare parts. For example, if there is a problem with a component in the gearbox, then it should be possible to simply remove it rather than take out the whole gearbox. The after-sales people work together with the different object groups and jointly explore mock-ups and prototypes. The later the after-sales staff are involved in the design process, the fewer are the possibilities for change. Table 5.1 shows some examples of the different after-sales requirements on the different specifications.

The car is a compromise. Let us illustrate this by two examples. Production wanted the door hinges welded to the body, while the after-sales staff wanted the door to be bolted to the body so that the door would be adjustable. However, this would have meant extra staff on the shop floor to adjust the doors while the bolts are being fixed. The second example concerns an opening in the dickey of the car through which the fuel pump could be reached, removed and changed. This feature existed on the older models of auto OEM. However, the stamping

Table 5.1 After-sales requirements on specifications

System	Condition
VTS	The car should run for 30,000 kms without any maintenance. The car should be able to operate with a particular oil.
SSTS	There should be easy access for the refrigerant to be used in the air conditioning unit. The tools carried by the car should be sufficient for operations within the car.
CTS	There should be standardised bolts so that all the bolts can be fastened or unfastened with the existing tools in the car.

operations to ensure the opening cost money, hence, it was abandoned in the new model. Now the whole fuel tank has to be removed in order to replace the fuel pump, which means that it takes more than one hour to remove and replace the fuel pump as compared to a few minutes when the fuel pump was accessible through the dickey. The above examples indicate that the specifications need to consider the customer requirements of easy accessibility, serviceability and reparability during the making of the car.

Role of manufacturing

The manufacturing engineers are responsible for the process while the line assembly is responsible for actually building the product. Often when the specifications do not meet customer requirements, product engineering make changes to the specifications in a non-standardised manner which adds to manpower, scrap, cost, etc. Product engineering staff are focused on new products and do not wish to solve the problems with existing products. Poor quality of the specifications may result in a defective product, as the manufacturing process may not be suitable, the tooling may not match. When the specifications do not match the tolerance levels on the tools, then defects are manufactured. If the role of manufacturing is downgraded, then the role of production becomes even more downgraded as they will always have to make compromises.

The project organisation: project manager

There is one project manager for each new development project. The project manager has two basic roles, namely, to be a leader, and to be a programme support executive, i.e. managing the core project team giving support to others involved in the product development process. As a support function the project manager is responsible for implementing the product development process that the company follows. Project management responsibility also involves planning structures, gates (dates where pre-determined attributes are checked and decisions made to either continue or delay the project until completion of the pre-determined activities), quality checks, and so on. For each particular car line, there is one project manager.

Different project managers run projects in different ways, for example, a project manager with a technical background may be more inclined to discuss details than a project manager with a commercial background. Experience, interest in project management, opportunities to grow and personal working styles can differentiate project managers. Certain project managers can be very bossy and interfere in minor details such as the shape of screws, while some can be very broad-minded, empower personnel and believe in their ability to perform. Still others are oriented towards the rigorous planning of every single project activity and prefer to manage their work to a large extent from their desk in an analytical, almost scientific way. Some are more relationship-oriented and practise a management-by-walking-around approach.

There is no need for a project manager to have very detailed technical expertise, but there is an acute need to ensure that the right people with the right skills are present within the project to do the job. The role of the project manager is not to design the car but to lead the project to success by managing the competencies of his or her team and the constraints of the project.

The project organisation: PDT leader and object group

There are six product development team (PDT) leaders corresponding to the six sub-systems: electrical, electronics, chassis, body, engine and climate. They all report to the project manager. The PDT leaders are in charge of several objects in their particular areas. For each object there is an object group with an object leader in charge of one single object. An object can be defined as a collection of components which are integrated together by a group of dedicated cross-functional people from marketing, purchasing, finance, production and after-sales, i.e. the object group. For example, the sub-system electronics contains the following objects: radio, telephone, main instrument panel and side instrument panel. The object audio system will contain the radio, amplifiers, loudspeakers, antennas and CD changer. The number of objects will be decided by the resources and time that the auto OEM can afford.

While the object group does all the technical work, the PDT leaders follow up on quality, timing, cost, and priority of the different jobs. The project manager follows up each and every object in the car through reporting from the PDT leaders. If there is a problem with the radio, the object group will approach either the PDT leader or the project manager directly who will then reach a decision on whether or not to accept changes in order to solve the problems, for example, changes in the composition of the radio, its performance, cost or timing. This will, in turn, be conveyed to top management who will decide on streamlining the start of production, for example, carrying on testing the full prototypes without the radio if it is not ready.

Intervening conditions

The following factors were identified as affecting the specification process. They can be seen as conditions in the specification process.

Directives

In order to understand the flow of information let us consider the specifications at the CTS level. Let us take the example of an object, the radio, in order to facilitate the understanding (an entire system may involve thousands of components and interfaces). The radio object leader issues an object directive from the programme management, which contains a description of what is expected from the object. The object directive consists of many elements:

- the risks involved with the object;
- a table for the financial side of the business;

- weight expectations;
- development cost;
- date for the start of production;
- supplier investment in tooling;
- material cost in each car;
- prototype cost;
- number of hours from the OEM and external consultants.

Financial figures are generally for eight years and the costs are expected to decrease during this period by certain rates. Based on the different figures, the total cost for each year can be found. It is in the interest of the object leader to keep the suppliers within the budgeted costs. However, for any change, the programme management has to give approval.

From the object directive, the object leader together with the object group develops a list of parts that are to be used in the radio, based on their previous experience. These lists of parts are further developed into drawings. The people who develop the drawings and parts vary from object to object. In most cases, the auto OEM staff deals with the drawings and parts at the component and sub system level, even though the suppliers are supposed to do this, depending on their capabilities. Suppliers are called in very late, e.g. when the parts do not work. The suppliers are then required to make modifications in the original drawings of the auto OEM and to develop new ones, which is tantamount to back loading in the development process.

A new car model is always a compromise. This means that all the changes to the specifications cannot be solved before the customer gets the product – so-called running changes. Risk analysis is a tool used in the compromise decisions by the auto OEM.

Risk analysis

The vehicle technical specifications, sub system technical specifications and the component technical specifications are the flowdown from the whole car to the components. These specifications have validation plans, namely, the vehicle validation plan, the sub-system validation plan, and the component validation plan. The problems that are found after the validations are completed, are classified into three categories:

1. A – These are very serious problems that could lead to customer complaints.
2. B – With the existence of these problems, production staff will have difficulties in ensuring the quality of the work. In the case of blind assembly, the operator fitting a part under the car does not know whether the part has been fitted correctly or not, as there is no feedback. This can be overcome by the operator hearing a click every time he or she puts the part under the car.
3. C – These problems are minor and hard for the customer to notice, for example, loose clips holding the cables in the car or if the indicator (left

or right) misses a tick in the 'tick-tack' sequence once every thousand times of use.

It is important to note that the problems may move from one category to another i.e. an A problem could become a B or C. If an A problem has been solved in engineering but not validated or corrected, it could become a B or C problem. There is a chart/logbook that records all the problems (A, B and C) at any given week as shown in Figure 5.3. In Figure 5.3, the number of problems in each category is clearly visible at any moment in time. It also shows whether the amount of problems is decreasing, constant, or spiralling upwards.

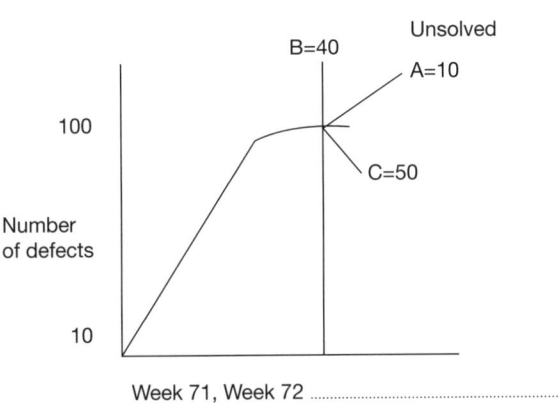

Figure 5.3 Risk analysis

After this, the problems (A, B and C) are displayed on a bottleneck analysis flow chart (Figure 5.4). This flow chart attempts to discover the sequence of the bottlenecks in the development process in order to solve them. Under normal conditions all major problems (A) should be solved. As illustrated in Figure 5.4, A constitutes the majority of the problems.

Only a certain number of problems in each category are allowed at each gate in the product development process. A logbook records the day the problem was discovered, the estimated solving time and the time taken for the problem to be solved. At each gate, a risk evaluation is undertaken and a new date when to solve the problems is decided on. There could be recommendations to delay the start of production if there are too many problems. The whole risk is to be considered when deciding upon which problems to solve and how to solve them.

Legal demands

Legal demands are very important as different markets have their own particular demands, such as emission requirements. Cars can be recalled if they do not fulfil the legal demands of the countries where they are sold. Yet the legal demands are

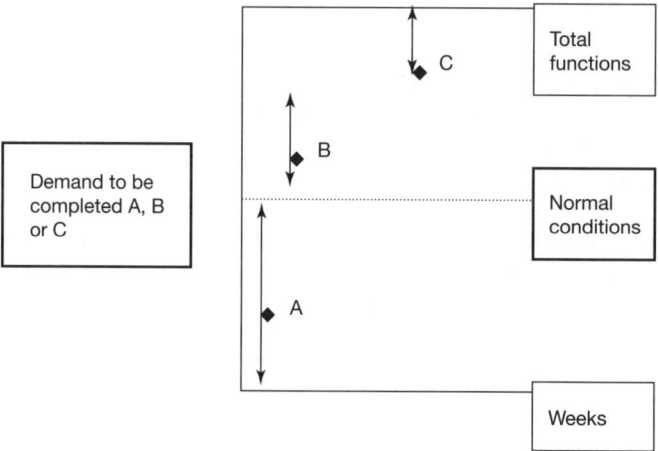

Figure 5.4 Bottleneck analysis

often ignored in the product development process, even though they have fixed guidelines and due dates for certification. During the elaboration of specifications the importance of legal dates is not kept in mind and the same is the case with liability issues where a customer can sue the OEM. However, all liability issues cannot be considered as many of them are difficult to judge. The OEM has to make a risk assessment and allow the product through. Legal requirements not only cover current regulations but also need to cover forthcoming regulations. For example, if a certain regulation is to come in force in the next three years then, the OEM should be able to decide whether the current design can cover it or not.

The specification process in the aircraft OEM

The aircraft OEM organises the specification process as illustrated in Figure 5.5. Once the discussions with the customer are complete through an iterative process, the top level of specifications is generated. This top level of specification is broken down into all the necessary requirements, also called compliance cards. These compliance cards are distributed to the different material groups like safety, air frame, etc. The compliance cards are further split up into the system level and component level specifications. These material groups, typically around fifty, are grouped under seven divisions, namely, airframe, system development, tactical, general, maintenance, support and flight control systems. The aircraft company follows a specification model as illustrated in Figure 5.6.

The company divides the product development into three phases, namely, development, manufacturing and support. The top half of the process model is the creation of documentation and the lower half is production/testing. In the development phase, temporary specifications are created, tested with simulators and after verification the temporary specifications are corrected. These

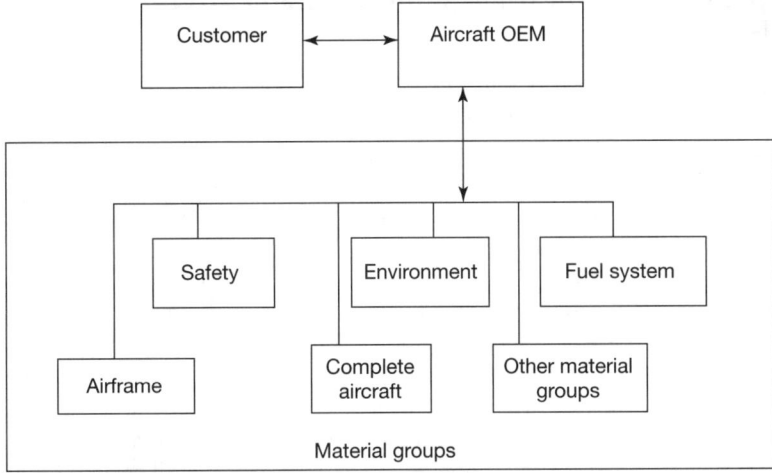

Figure 5.5 Material groups in the aircraft OEM

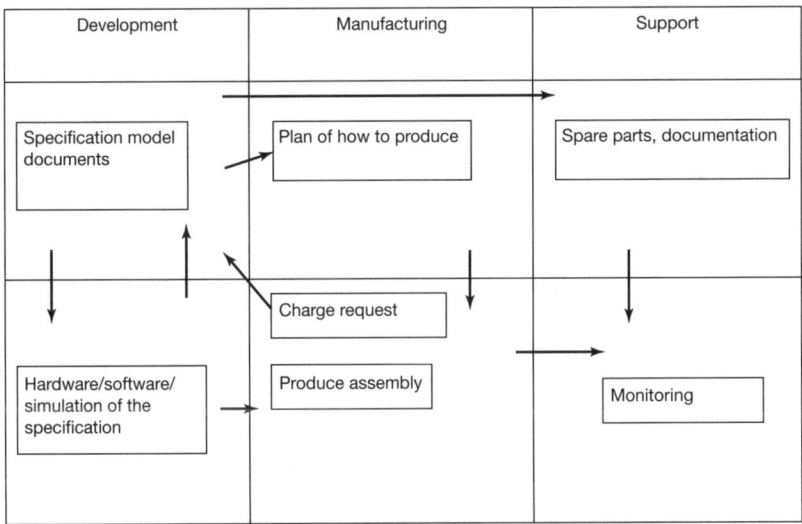

Figure 5.6 A process model for specifications in the aircraft OEM

documents are then used to decide how the product will be manufactured, and used as a basis for developing the assembly tooling. However, the assembly may create problems, which might need changes in the original specifications. The simulations and tests can also provide data for the assembly process (the lower half of manufacturing in Figure 5.6). After this the product is constantly monitored through written documentation, in-flight instruments and support documentation. This is also called the life cycle management process at the aircraft OEM.

Comparative specifications in the auto and aircraft OEMs

The specification process at the auto OEM will now be compared with the specification process at the aircraft OEM. This will serve two purposes, first, it will allow us to cross-check whether important factors have been missed out in the specification process at auto OEM and also add to current best practice, namely, that of the aircraft OEM. It will also allow for discussion as certain practices thought to be 'best' may really not be so.

There is only one version of specifications in the auto OEM as compared to two versions of specification in aircraft OEM – the customer requirement specification and the product requirement specification. The product specification is to be used internally within the aircraft OEM to develop the product, whereas the customer specification is used by the customers to verify the product. The product specification can be different from the customer specification as the aircraft OEM can make higher demands than those required by the customer. The auto OEM, on the other hand, has one version of a specification, which is the same as the customer requirement, i.e. the MSS, comparable to the customer requirement specification. The ability to develop internally achievable specifications, different from what the customer expects, allows internal talent to grow and the organisation to be one step ahead of the competitors.

Apart from product requirements and customer requirements, the aircraft OEM uses other data such as airworthiness requirements, and data requirements. The data requirements are requirements already verified from previous projects. This allows for previously critical demands to be re-articulated and not forgotten. Often demands that cannot be achieved at a given moment are forgotten, thus leading to the product being different from what was originally planned. If the original demands are conserved, possibly they can be introduced as running changes when the technology permits their introduction.

The aircraft OEM uses compliance cards where each and every requirement is put on a card. The compliance cards are decomposed step by step and thus allow the engineers to remember the requirements to be fulfilled. The auto OEM does not have such a mechanism to follow up on requirements. This leads to requirements being forgotten in the auto OEM. However, the aircraft OEM uses a manual procedure to follow up the compliance cards whereas computerisation of these cards would allow easy retrieval and follow up.

The requirements are simulated both in the aircraft and auto OEM through validation loops, i.e. each level of the specification, namely, the VTS, SSTS and CTS has a corresponding validation plan, VVP (vehicle validation plan), SSVP (sub-system validation plan) and CVP (component validation plan). In the auto OEM, the supplier uses the CTS to generate or produce the product and puts it through various tests. The OEM in turn checks the product through its own validation such as in prototyping and then decides on the condition of the product. The different types of specifications confirm the proposals by Kaulio (1996) that specifications change over time. It also confirms the views of Smith and Reinartsen

(1991), that specifications are created through a joint effort of the different people involved in the specification process. However, what was not mentioned by either Smith and Reinartsen (1991) or Kaulio (1996) is that the different types of specifications are related to each other and there is a step-by-step decomposition of the specifications from a higher to a lower level, i.e. the MSS to the IVTS to the VTS to the SSTS and to the CTS.

Model of product development by specifications

An attempt will be made to create a specification model as a result of the comparison between the aircraft and auto OEMs. The market segment specification is created at first (Figure 5.7). The input to the MSS will come from the previously verified requirements (IVTS), market trends, own brand requirements, competitors, customer requirements, suppliers, distributor requirements and the legal demands. When creating the MSS, inputs are continuously monitored and feed back is given from the MSS while it is taking shape.

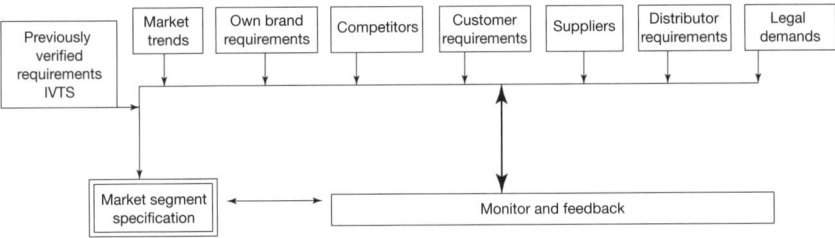

Figure 5.7 Elaboration of the MSS

Then the VTS is created. It is split up into the customer specification and the compliance cards (internal product specification) as the internal company goals may be higher than what the customer expects. These compliance cards are used to generate the SSTS and in turn the CTS. Each compliance card is a requirement and all the requirements in the VTS have to be identified. The compliance cards may have references to drawings and could contain the details of the other compliance cards that they are interfaced with. The compliance cards could contain references to the SSTS and the CTS. If all the compliance cards are computerised, then at a simple touch of a button, all the requirements, interfaces, and all the system level and component level requirements will be instantly available. It would then be very easy to check whether all the requirements have been fulfilled or not. Figure 5.8 illustrates the generation of these different levels of specifications.

Next, validation plans are generated. The CVP is generated from the CTS. The SSTS is used to generate the SSVP. Finally, the VVP is generated from the VTS. In case of problems during validations, a risk analysis followed by a bottleneck analysis is undertaken and the input fed to the necessary stage in the specification process.

94 *Mapping the flow of specifications*

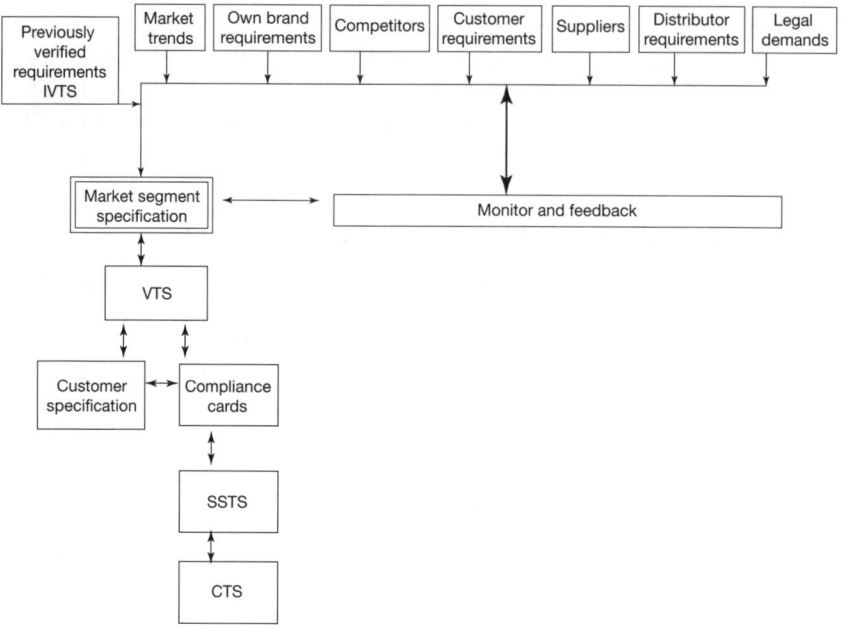

Figure 5.8 Generation of specifications

A final product is a compromise and not all problems can be solved or need to be solved. There are many problems that the customers will not notice, for example, the tick-tack sequence in the indicator as discussed before. Hence, all the problems need to be collected together and the risk associated with the problems is determined by assigning them priority numbers such as A, B or C. Then, depending on the priorities through bottleneck analysis, the A problems followed by the B and C problems are sent to either the VTS or the SSTS or the CTS stage for rectification. Problems are sent to the VTS level when it may be hard to determine where the problem exactly lies. Again, the validation loop is repeated with further problems being sent through the priority analysis stage as well. All changes and solutions generated are to be written back into the specifications so that the demands are not forgotten. Figure 5.9 illustrates the validation steps, the problem analysis and feedback where also suppliers play an important role.

Dependent on the decision of the core team to certify the VTS as be ready for manufacture, the VTS is sent to the manufacturing stage. The manufacturing process might prove that some designs cannot be manufactured and hence these will have to return to the VTS level for inspection and breakdown to the necessary level. This is needed because only the VTS documents have the complete interfaces of the car. Once again, the validation loop is repeated. Once the manufacturing has been cleared by the core team, customer products can begin to be manufactured.

There needs to be a group of people dealing only with the whole car/product. There are certain requirements that may not fit into any of the sub-systems and

Mapping the flow of specifications 95

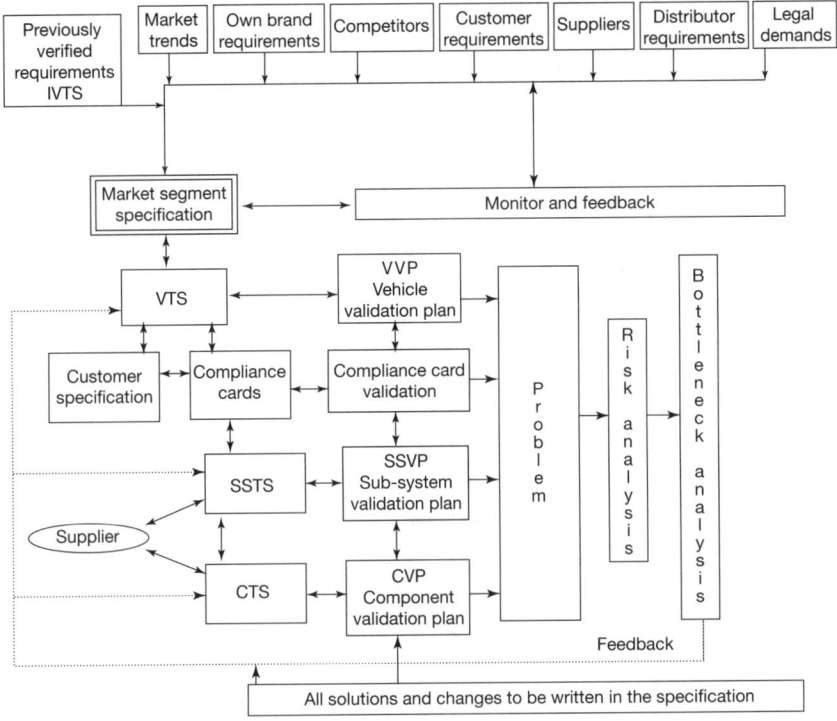

Figure 5.9 Validations, problem analysis and feedback

hence require such a group. For example, for the aircraft to fly at a certain height, there is a certain requirement on the air frame that it should withstand G forces, requirements on the survival of the pilot which in turn places demands on the oxygen masks, etc. This group would be the best to deal with issues that arise at the VTS level or those that cannot be sorted out at the CTS/SSTS level.

After the product has been manufactured it is continuously monitored and feedback is provided to the specification process, for example, input is provided to the market segment specification with regards to the customer satisfaction/experience. Figure 5.10 shows the complete proposed specification model.

The supplier can be involved during the SSTS phase or the CTS phase. Depending on the type of supplier, testing can be undertaken by the supplier, else the OEM will have to do the same. The specification could be written in such a way that the supplier has the power to manoeuvre and the OEM need not control details. All changes in the specification and reasons for them deserve to be included in the specification so that the same mistakes are not made again and again.

96 *Mapping the flow of specifications*

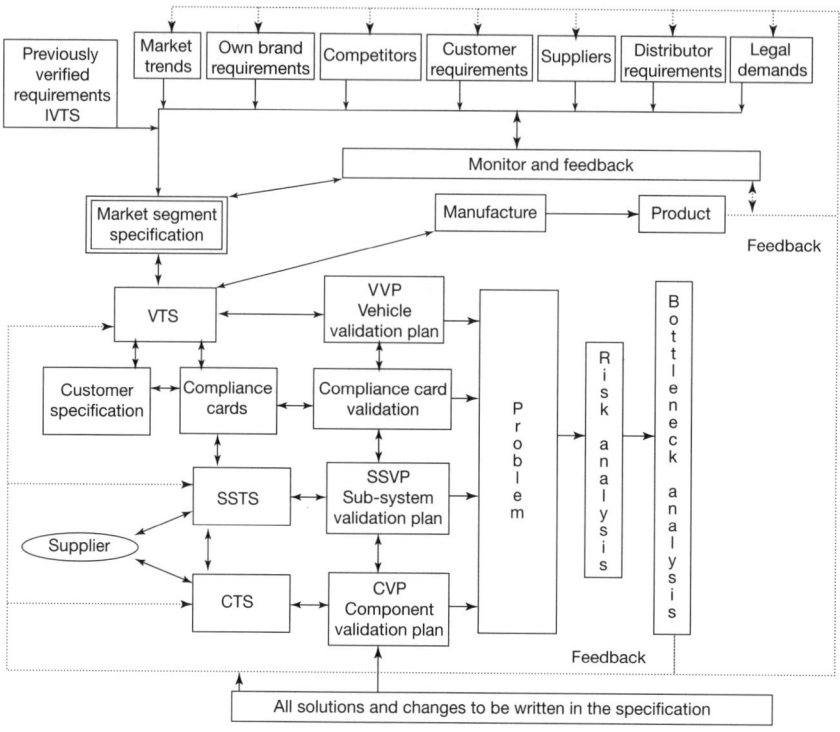

Figure 5.10 Proposed specification model

Conclusion

Specifications are a central element in product development management. We have suggested that the product development process can be seen as a flow of specifications and that this highlights the need for improved communication between all the actors involved – external and internal. The specification perspective emphasises rigour in all interfaces, anticipation and feedback in process steps, and a validation imperative.

Our in-depth and comparative study in two large OEMs has detailed the complex steps in product development, and explained the role of different critical functions. We have laid out a specification model by integrating the approaches in the two OEMs and taking into account the main problems encountered. Our main recommendations are as follows:

- Ensure broad input into the overall specification, including direct customer, distributor, and supplier feedback, and previously verified requirements stemming from analysis of previous development projects.
- Create a customer specification and see it as a lowest level imperative. In parallel, create compliance cards (internal product specifications) setting internal innovative goals in order to create a positive value gap for customers.

- Ensure validation plans at each specification level.
- Identify priorities through risk and bottleneck analysis.
- Ensure feedback at all levels of the specification process, and ensure memorising of all solutions and changes.

6 Applications of specifications in outsourcing

Building on Quinn and Hilmer

This chapter will explain how specifications can be used in outsourcing by expanding on an important outsourcing model developed by Quinn and Hilmer (1994). Outsourcing is one of the top priorities on the strategic agenda of original equipment manufacturers (OEMs) in many industries. The decision to outsource an activity as opposed to doing it in-house and the development of a part or parts system is one of the most complex decisions facing today's industrial managers. Several models have been developed in order to aid this process. This chapter analyses some of these models, and proposes an extension based on the role that specifications might play in outsourcing decisions. Based on how the specification is generated and on the nature of the data it contains, it can be of significant help in outsourcing decisions. A procurement matrix is developed in which guidance for outsourcing decisions is provided in terms of specification generator, type of supplier, and contract relationship.

An example of the problem

Consider a global automotive OEM in the process of defining a new car that should possess the following characteristics: innovative, fashionable, and attractive. The project team propose that the vehicle's key differentiating characteristics would be in its interiors, more precisely in the flooring, the seats, and the interior colours. Concerning the flooring, the team propose that there would be no carpets but a specially constructed flooring material. This innovative flooring material would be developed and sourced from a leading interior global supplier since the OEM had no specific capability in the related material and process technologies. Faced with this problem, the development team asked several questions: What kind of relationship needs to be established with the supplier? Does the supplier have the capabilities of developing and delivering a component/system that is critical to the sales of the proposed vehicle? As the OEM does not have the capabilities to write the specifications, what should be the characteristics of the specification?

The above questions require that the make/buy decision be carefully analysed. It is not a simple matter of just asking the vendor to deliver a product, but this is a process involving thinking about supply management (type of relationships with the supplier, capabilities of the supplier, etc.) and specifications (capability to write specifications, characteristics of the specifications required, etc.). Two of the major 'make-or-buy' models, incorporating more than one dominating decision-making parameter, are those by Quinn and Hilmer (1994) and Venkatesan (1992). These models have been developed in different industries and differ in detail as far as their descriptions of what can be outsourced/insourced is concerned. The model by Quinn and Hilmer best summarises the entire make-or-buy spectrum based on two dimensions: the degree of strategic vulnerability (SV) in outsourcing an activity, and the potential for competitive advantage (PCA). Quinn and Hilmer (1994, p. 21) propose a matrix where three scenarios are developed. However, the remaining categories identified by the matrix are not analysed. Moreover, neither of these models have connected supply management and specifications to the make-or-buy decision. Let us illustrate with an example. Specifications can be essentially qualitative (narrative), or essentially quantitative (encoded), or contain a mix of both qualitative and quantitative data (mixed). Narrative specifications would essentially appear to be linked to competitive advantages as they might provide an opportunity to convey tacit knowledge. But does this mean that narrative specifications should be used for in-house development only? The models of make/buy decisions fail to answer this. In order to understand these and related problems, we will analyse the above mentioned models, and try to establish the link between supply management and specifications.

Strategic outsourcing – what do we know?

Product development is like solving a huge equation system, it consists of thousands or even tens of thousands of tasks that must be woven into a complex network of relationships between individuals, groups and firms (Clark and Fujimoto, 1991; Schrader and Göpfert, 1994). Outsourcing the development of activities to suppliers creates a strategic, tactical and operational challenge, as both the OEMs and the suppliers need to take advantage of each other's domain of expertise (Lamming, 1993; Schrader and Göpfert, 1994). Inspired by the automotive industry, more and more firms in the entire manufacturing industry are opting for the outsourcing strategy. However, this does not mean that all activities traditionally performed in-house need to be outsourced. A careful assessment of a firm's assets and resources must precede any outsourcing decision so that only those activities for which the firm do not have any special capabilities or those for which the firm do not have a strategic need are outsourced (Black and Boal, 1994). Outsourcing is the consequence of the adoption of a resource-based strategy (Wernerfelt, 1984; Prahalad and Hamel, 1990) where firms concentrate on their set of core competencies through which they can provide unique value for the customers and outsource the rest of the activities. For clarification, we will use the word *activity* when discussing 'making' or 'buying', i.e. insourcing or outsourcing, regardless of whether the object of the discussion is an activity, such as design or testing, or a tangible product/part/parts system, such as a tool, a glass mirror or an engine.

Not all collaborations between the suppliers and the OEMs are successful; collaboration might have both positive and negative effects. The understanding of these effects can help in better outsourcing decisions, and also help to design and improve existing tools to manage collaboration with suppliers. Let us take a closer look at these effects as they have been discussed in the literature.

Positive and negative effects of collaborations

Some of the benefits of collaboration include the following:

- Spreading and sharing the costs and risks of product development, and of business in general (Ellram, 1991; Lamming, 1993).
- Reduced costs by using the cost reduction imperative as a driver for product innovation. The suppliers' cost base is also generally lower than that of OEMs. Open books allow checking the cost structure of suppliers, and successively reduced or at least stabilised supply prices can be obtained (Ellram, 1991; Lamming, 1993).
- With technological divergence, one company cannot exploit all the promising opportunities and the more alliances it can pool, the more likely are the chances of a successful outcome. Access to technological expertise (core capabilities) and exploiting of technological synergies are central in this context (Blonder and Pritzl, 1992).
- Reduced development lead time through simultaneous development of components and systems that are on the critical path (Clark, 1989).

To sum up, strategic outsourcing can give a company 'the full utilisation of external suppliers' investments, the innovations and specialised professional capabilities that would be prohibitively expensive or even impossible to duplicate internally' (Quinn and Hilmer, 1994). Early involvement and strong collaborative ties with suppliers as integrated partners have become more or less a rule in the automotive development process (Schilling and Hill, 1998), and many organisations such as Ford, Renault, Honda, and Fiat are rethinking and developing their internal functions in order to adopt efficient ways of dealing with the suppliers and their involvement. Similar development has helped many companies to slash development times by as much as 30 to 50 per cent (Bruce et al., 1995; Asmus and Griffin, 1993).

However, not all collaborations are successful. The following risks and negative aspects can be identified:

- If the objectives or expectations are not met, or the collaboration is unsuccessful for reasons such as domination of one party, incompatibility in culture and management, or opportunistic behaviour of either party, the collaboration can be very costly and represent an important strategic risk to the survival of either party (Harrigan, 1986).
- There might be high transaction costs associated with the time and effort

needed to manage these collaborations. Three types of costs must be closely monitored (Richardson, 1993): set-up costs (including search costs and supplier development costs, e.g. training and technology transfer); trading costs (including ongoing costs for co-ordinating exchanges as they occur (e.g. ordering, scheduling of delivery, and contract enforcement); and competitiveness cost (cost of lost sales or internal costs resulting from poor or unreliable supplier quality, etc.).

- Care must be taken to harmonise the different cultures of the collaborators and regular reviews must be undertaken to monitor the progress of the collaboration (Womack *et al.*, 1990). This takes time and effort.
- Most alliances are unstable as alliances are directly related to the trust between the collaborating parties (Porter, 1990). Trust is something that is subjective and cannot be measured, hence the problem of instability.
- Given the degree of communication and openness required at various levels within a collaboration, it can be difficult to keep confidentiality about core capabilities, which are the source of the company's competitive advantage (Gugler, 1992). This is a particularly delicate problem especially when suppliers are dealing with several competing OEMs.

In view of the risks associated with the decision to outsource, managers must be cautious when deciding whether to outsource or insource. In other words, not only the advantages of collaboration (which translate into a buy decision) but also the disadvantages (which translate into a make decision) need to be examined. In order to articulate the make/buy decision, several authors like Quinn and Hilmer (1994), Olsen and Ellram (1997) and Venkatesan (1992) have developed models that allow the make/buy decision to be based on multiple criteria, thereby compensating for the disadvantages of collaboration. Let us discuss these models one after the other.

Quinn and Hilmer's outsourcing models

Quinn and Hilmer (1994) link many of the parameters that form both advantages and disadvantages in collaborations, and develop two dimensions to classify the many different activities (development/production of components or products, service or support activities) that a firm deals with, namely *the potential for competitive edge* and *the degree of strategic vulnerability*. The different activities, that require different types of relationships with the suppliers, are classified into three groups (Figure 6.1).

It is to be noted that Quinn and Hilmer talk about activities in general without making an explicit difference between parts and intangibles. This corresponds to the perspective chosen, as explained in the introduction. Quinn and Hilmer's model suggests that activities with a high potential for competitive edge and a high degree of strategic vulnerability should be realised in-house. Moderate strategic vulnerability and moderate potential for competitive edge represent activities that call for a range of relationships like short-term contracts, call options, long-term contracts, retainer, joint development, partial ownership or full ownership in

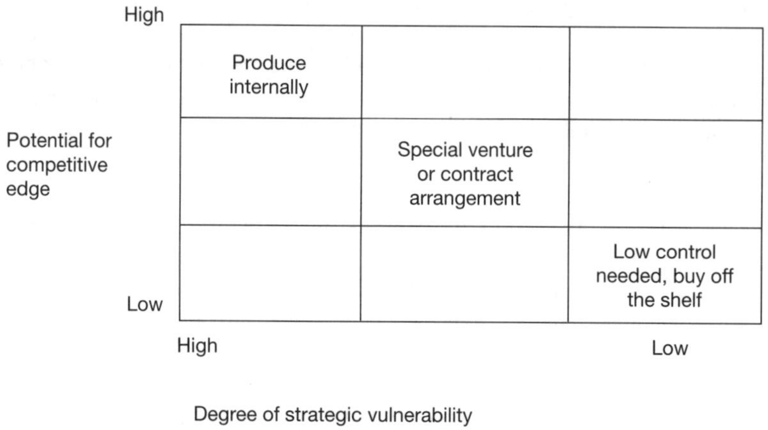

Figure 6.1 Strategic sourcing, adopted from Quinn and Hilmer (1994)

relation to the suppliers. Finally, activities with low vulnerability and low potential for competitive edge call for arm's-length relationships with the suppliers.

A careful analysis of the model reveals that it considers only three possibilities out of a total of nine. This leads us to ask whether there are no activities that are high in terms of strategic vulnerability and yet low on the competitive edge scale, or conversely, that are high on the competitive edge dimension and yet low in terms of strategic vulnerability. This question can be extended to all the six possibilities that Quinn and Hilmer have not considered.

Venkatesan's outsourcing model

This model indicates that there are two types of products, namely, core i.e. those that are strictly produced in-house, because they are critical for the performance of the end product and the OEM is distinctively good at making them, and non-core, i.e. those that are produced with the help of the suppliers, because they are less critical and the OEM lacks the expertise to produce them efficiently. The core products of Venkatesan (1992) correspond to the in-house products of Quinn and Hilmer as both the core and in-house products are produced internally without any supplier involvement. However, Venkatesan (1992) does not specify the type of relationships that could be used when engaging suppliers for the non-core products.

Olsen and Ellram's outsourcing model

Olsen and Ellram's (1997) model does not discuss the outsourcing decision. It focuses on products where the decision to outsource has already been taken. However, it provides an interesting analysis of the types of relationships that could be used in the collaborative mode, corresponding to the intermediate situation in Quinn and Hilmer's model.

According to Olsen and Ellram, parts that are outsourced can fall into four different categories: strategic, bottleneck, leverage and non-critical. These products are classified based on the difficulty of managing the purchasing situation and the importance of the project to the OEMs. Strategic products are very important and extremely difficult to manage. Non-critical products are at the other extreme and thus are low in importance and are easy to manage. Bottleneck products are difficult to manage and their importance is low. Finally, leverage products are easy to manage and their importance is high. All the identified product categories with the exception of the non-critical products require some form of collaboration. This is because the non-critical products to be developed are either based on the complete specifications of the OEM or bought as a standard product from a catalogue requiring no collaboration between the suppliers and the OEMs (Kamath and Liker, 1994).

Outsourcing models – a discussion

The three models discussed above can be summarised as shown in Table 6.1. There is a clear correspondence between the categories for classifying activities proposed in the different models. Venkatesan does not specify the collaborative mode, while Olsen and Ellram proceed to an in-depth analysis of this situation.

In summary, Quinn and Hilmer's model provides the best vision of the continuum from in-house to adversarial relations. The model proposed by Quinn and Hilmer has indicated a wide range of sourcing options. Simply stated, the products, which fall into these sourcing options, are different in terms of complexity. This places varying requirements on the capabilities and capacities of the suppliers. In other words, different types of suppliers must exist in order to deliver the varying complexity of products.

A tour of the case companies

Outsourcing decisions were top priorities on the two OEM case studies' strategic agendas. Both companies work with specifications that are developed and executed either internally (insourced) or externally (outsourced), in the latter case with the

Table 6.1 A comparison of the different outsourcing models

Make or buy	Outsourcing models		
	Venkatesan	Quinn and Hilmer	Olsen and Ellram
Vertical integration	Core	Strategic control	–
Collaboration	–	Moderate control	Strategic Bottleneck Leverage
Arm's-length supplier relations	Non-core	Low control	Non-critical

104 *Outsourcing: specification applications*

help of a wide range of supplier relationships. We asked the procurement and R&D managers in the two companies to identify three main activities in each of the categories – high, medium or low competitive advantage and high, medium or low strategic vulnerability. The managers were asked to think of both tangibles and intangibles. We compared their responses and went back to them in order to obtain a consensus. The responses were also cross-referred between the two companies so that the identified activities to a large extent were common. Through this procedure, seven activities were identified in both companies (Tables 6.2 and 6.3).

Once the activities were defined, we identified, through further interviews and participant observation, the associated category and type of specification. The data collected at the auto OEM are shown in Tables 6.2 and 6.3 and the data collected at the truck OEM are shown in Table 6.4.

Table 6.2 Activities in the auto OEM classified according to competitive advantage

ID no.	Activity	Competitive advantage	Strategic vulnerability	Type of specification	Content of specification
1	Styling of the car	High	High	Specifications generated and activities realised internally.	Essentially qualitative data
2	Brackets	High	Low	Specifications generated wholly by the OEM and then executed by the supplier.	Essentially quantitative data
3	Engine	High	Medium	Initial specifications developed either by the OEM or by the supplier, then co-developed by the party not generating the initial specification. Finally, realised by the supplier.	A mix of qualitative and quantitative data
4	Interior trims	Medium	Low	Specifications generated wholly by the OEM and then executed by the supplier.	Essentially quantitative data
5	Chassis	Medium	Medium	Initial specifications developed either by the OEM or by the supplier, then co-developed by the party not generating the initial specification. Finally, realised by the supplier.	A mix of qualitative and quantitative data
6	Hand-held tools	Low	Low	Specifications generated wholly by the supplier.	Essentially quantitative data
7	Door knobs	Low	Medium	Initial specifications developed either by the OEM or by the supplier, then co-developed by the party not generating the initial specification. Finally, realised by the supplier.	A mix of qualitative and quantitative data

Table 6.3 Activities in the auto OEM classified according to strategic vulnerability

ID no.	Activity	Strategic vulnerability	Competitive advantage	Type of specification	Content of specification
1	Styling of the car	High	High	Specifications generated and activities realised internally.	Essentially qualitative data
3	Engine	Medium	High	Initial specifications developed either by the OEM or by the supplier, then co-developed by the party not generating the initial specification. Finally, realised by the supplier.	A mix of qualitative and quantitative data
5	Chassis	Medium	Medium	As above	As above
7	Door knobs	Medium	Low	As above	As above
2	Brackets	Low	High	Specifications generated wholly by the OEM and then executed by the supplier.	Essentially quantitative data
4	Interior trims	Low	Medium	As above	As above
6	Hand-held tools	Low	Low	Specifications generated wholly by the supplier.	As above

Table 6.2 shows that competitive advantage is not a discriminating criterion as far as type or content of specifications are concerned. We therefore regrouped the activities following the strategic vulnerability, in order to observe whether this dimension would discriminate between the specification types and the specification contents. The results are shown in Table 6.3.

Table 6.3 illustrates a relationship between the strategic vulnerability and the type and content of the specification. In order to elaborate on the hypotheses made concerning the content of the specification and the outsourcing decision, four new categories were identified based on the content of the specification:

- The first category is one where the specifications are essentially qualitative in terms of content. These specifications are developed internally and the activity is also realised internally. The corresponding activities are high both on the strategic vulnerability and the competitive advantage dimensions.
- The second category of specifications are those that contain a well-balanced mix of qualitative and quantitative data. They are initially developed either by the OEM, or by the supplier, and then co-developed by the party not generating the initial specifications. The corresponding activities are ranked medium on the strategic vulnerability dimension, while they range from high to low in terms of competitive advantage.
- The third category is representative of those specifications that are essentially

Table 6.4 Activities in the truck OEM classified according to strategic vulnerability

ID no.	Activity	Strategic vulnerability	Competitive advantage	Type of specification	Content of specification
1	Styling	High	Medium	Initial specifications developed either by the OEM or by the supplier, then co-developed by the party not generating the initial specification. Finally, realised by the supplier.	Essentially qualitative data
2	Audio-system validation	High	Low	As above	As above
3	Engine	Medium	High	Specifications generated and activities realised internally.	A mix of qualitative and quantitative data
4	Chassis	Medium	Medium	Initial specifications developed either by the OEM or by the supplier, then co-developed by the party not generating the initial specification. Finally, realised by the supplier.	As above
5	Glass mirrors	Medium	Low	As above	As above
6	Brackets	Low	High	Specifications generated wholly by the OEM and then executed by the supplier.	Essentially quantitative data
7	Hand-held tools	Low	Low	Specifications generated wholly by the supplier.	As above

quantitative in terms of content. These specifications are developed wholly by the OEM, then the corresponding activity is realised by the supplier to the exact specifications of the OEM. A variant is when the suppliers generate the specifications wholly by themselves and propose the activity off-the-shelf. In this category, the activities are ranked low on the strategic vulnerability dimension. At the same time, these activities range between high and low on the competitive advantage dimension.

These results seem to confirm the hypotheses that qualitative specifications are insourced, quantitative specifications are outsourced without co-development, while mixed specifications are subject to co-development.

Let us now turn to the data collected in the truck OEM, which is displayed in Table 6.4. The managers in the truck OEM identified similar activities, with the exception of interior trims and doorknobs, where purchasing and R&D managers had diverging opinions in terms of classification on the two dimensions: vulnerability/advantage. These activities were therefore not retained. Instead, the managers in the truck OEM proposed two activities, namely, the validation of the audio-system and glass mirrors. These two activities were not clearly positioned in the auto OEM. Moreover, the type of specifications used for engine and styling differs in the two companies.

In order to test whether the previous conclusions were valid also for the truck OEM, we used the same classification as in Table 6.3. When applying the four categories developed from the data collected in the auto OEM to the data collected in the truck OEM, both similarities and differences can be found:

- When looking at the first category, high strategic vulnerability does not exclude co-development in the truck OEM. Here, suppliers were called in to work on activities where the specifications were essentially qualitative in terms of content.
- Concerning the second category – mixed specifications – two types of specifications were used in the truck OEM, namely, specifications generated and executed internally and specifications initially developed either by the OEM, or by the supplier, and then co-developed by the party not generating the initial specifications.
- In terms of similarities, the third category is identical.

The results from the data show that neither the competitive advantage nor the type of specification are discriminating variables in terms of outsourcing decisions. Moreover, the content of the specifications was not used as a discriminating variable in the truck OEM.

Search for common themes and dissimilarities

Let us now analyse the results in search of explanations for the identified similarities and differences. The aim of the analysis is also to assess to what extent the type and content of specifications can guide outsourcing decisions.

Essentially qualitative specifications

The more narrative a specification, the harder it becomes to articulate it and thus to imitate it. Engaging suppliers with this type of specification would mean divulging essential and highly tacit capabilities leading to high strategic vulnerability. In the case of narrative specifications, complexity is high, the simulation difficult and the evaluation subjective. The essentially qualitative specifications previously identified are compared in Table 6.5.

In the auto OEM, this kind of specification concerns styling. Styling is also ranked high in terms of competitive advantage and this leads the auto OEM to insource the entire styling work. This concurs with the conclusions made by Quinn and Hilmer.

Table 6.5 Comparison of essentially qualitative specifications

OEM	Category of specification	Examples	Degree of strategic vulnerability	Competitive advantage
Auto	Specifications generated and activities realised internally.	Styling of the car	High	High
Truck	Initial specifications developed either by the OEM or by the supplier, then co-developed by the party not generating the initial specification. Finally, realised by the supplier.	Styling of the truck	High	Medium
	Idem	Audio-system validation	High	Low

However, in the truck OEM, essentially qualitative specifications are used in collaboration with suppliers in the same manner as with the mixed specification discussed previously. Concerning styling, the explanation is that the truck OEM judges styling to be medium on the competitive advantage dimension. Customers' sensitivity to styling is not as important in the truck business as it is in the car business. Thus, the styling is insourced in the auto OEM and outsourced in the truck OEM. Furthermore, the styling of the car cannot be easily modified, whereas the shape of the truck can be altered to suit variances in components or equipment.

The audio-system check, i.e. testing the performance of the radio, cassette, CD player, booster and loudspeakers, is considered to be low on the competitive advantage dimension in spite of an essentially qualitative specification. This explains in the same manner as above the decision to outsource this activity.

The comparison of the above examples with the supplier categories suggests the presence of partner suppliers. Partner suppliers have to be responsible for executing essentially normative specifications, as the degree of strategic vulnerability on the suppliers is extremely high.

Mixed specifications

Mixed specifications contain rough or more detailed envelopes for both qualitative and quantitative information and data needed to realise the activity in question. Either the supplier or the OEM can initiate the generation of these envelopes. In the next step, the specification is co-developed together with the party not generating the initial envelopes. The aim is to reach an optimum solution where customer requirements are satisfied through leveraging supplier capabilities and product performance. Finally, the activities are realised by the supplier.

Examination of the data from the case companies indicates that the mixed specifications concern activities that range from high to low on the competitive advantage dimension, while the degree of strategic vulnerability is medium in all cases (Table 6.6).

Table 6.6 Comparison of the mixed specifications

OEM	Category of specification	Examples	Degree of strategic vulnerability	Competitive advantage
Auto	Initial specifications developed either by the OEM or by the supplier, then co-developed by the party not generating the initial specification. Finally, realised by the supplier.	Engine	Medium	High
	As above	Chassis	Medium	Medium
	As above	Door knobs	Medium	Low
Truck	Initial specifications developed either by the OEM or by the supplier, then co-developed by the party not generating the initial specification. Finally, realised by the supplier.	Engine	Medium	High
	As above	Chassis	Medium	Medium
	As above	Glass mirrors	Medium	Low

Chassis are medium on the competitive advantage dimension in both companies. Engines rate high on the competitive advantage dimension in both companies and finally, glass mirrors and doorknobs fare low on the competitive advantage dimension in the truck and auto OEM, respectively. There is supplier input in mixed specifications though the extent of involvement may vary.

Given the supplier involvement and the complexity of the activities, mature suppliers seem most suited to fit this situation. Mature suppliers have been defined as able to work on or themselves generate rough specifications and then continue collaborative development work with OEMs.

Essentially quantitative specifications

Two categories of specifications fall into this group: where specifications are generated wholly by the supplier, and where specifications are generated wholly by the OEM and then executed by the supplier. Since the corresponding activities are low on the strategic vulnerability dimension, they can be specified in a essentially quantitative manner. The essentially quantitative specifications previously identified are compared in Table 6.7.

The category 'supplier generated specifications' corresponds to the conclusions made by Quinn and Hilmer that products low on the strategic vulnerability dimension and also on the competitive advantage dimension are sourced to supplier specifications or simply bought off the shelf.

However, essentially quantitative specifications are not always low on the competitive advantage dimension. As seen in Table 6.7, they can also be high and medium. In both OEMs, brackets were considered high in the competitive

110 *Outsourcing: specification applications*

Table 6.7 Comparison of essentially quantitative specifications

OEM	Category of specification	Examples	Degree of strategic vulnerability	Competitive advantage
Auto	Specifications generated wholly by the OEM and then executed by the supplier	Brackets	Low	High
	Idem	Interior trims	Low	Medium
	Specifications generated wholly by the supplier	Hand-held tools	Low	Low
Truck	Specifications generated wholly by the OEM and then executed by the supplier	Brackets	Low	High
	Specifications generated wholly by the supplier	Hand-held tools	Low	Low

advantage dimension. This pushed the OEMs to write the entire specifications in-house and simply let the suppliers execute, i.e. manufacture, according to the specifications. Concerning interior trims in the auto OEM, the same situation occurred, indicating that the company uses only off-the-shelf parts where competitive advantage is undoubtedly low.

Referring back to the different categories of suppliers it can be observed that child and contractual suppliers fit into the categories of suppliers with whom the OEMs feels the least vulnerable.

Building on the Quinn and Hilmer model

The analysis has identified activities that represent all the categories in the Quinn and Hilmer (1994) model. We therefore propose an enlargement of their model comprising the additional six categories, and also a discussion of specification generation and supplier types according to the previous analysis. We call this model the procurement matrix (see Table 6.8). The three scenarios indicated by Quinn and Hilmer are shown in bold.

Our study shows that there are activities that fit in all the possible boxes in the model proposed by Quinn and Hilmer. We have also identified an additional distinctive criterion based on the content of the specification in terms of the degree of qualitative or quantitative information. Let us look at Table 6.8 and comment on the scenarios omitted by Quinn and Hilmer:

- In the high strategic vulnerability dimension, where specifications are essentially qualitative, two additional options exist, namely, those where the suppliers generate the rough specification and then work with the OEM or when the supplier generates the entire specification. Audio-system validation

Table 6.8 The procurement matrix

POTENTIAL FOR COMPETITIVE EDGE					
	HIGH	• Specification generator • Type of supplier • Examples	• OEM • No supplier • Styling	• OEM-supplier generate specifications together • Mature • Engines	• OEM generates detailed specification • Child supplier • Brackets
	MEDIUM	• Specification generator • Type of supplier • Examples	• Supplier generates rough specification which is then worked on by the OEM • Partner • Styling	• OEM generates rough specification which is then worked on by the supplier • Mature • Chassis	• OEM generates detailed specification • Child supplier • Interior trims
	LOW	• Specification generator • Type of supplier • Examples	• Supplier generates specification • Partner • Audio-system validation	• Supplier generates rough specification which is then worked on by the OEM • Mature supplier • Door knobs, glass mirrors	• Supplier generates the specification • Contractual supplier • Hand held tools
			HIGH	MEDIUM	LOW
			Essentially qualitative specification	Mix [qualitative and quantitative] specification	Purely quantitative specification
			DEGREE OF STRATEGIC VULNERABILITY		

is an example of the latter category while styling is an example of the former category. When styling is classified as high on the competitive advantage dimension, it is made internally, corresponding to Quinn and Hilmer's first category, while if styling is classified as medium on the competitive advantage dimension, it could be outsourced to supplier specification which is later worked on together by both the OEM and the supplier.

- In the medium strategic vulnerability dimension, two additional options exist, namely, when the OEM and the supplier generate the specifications together, such as in the case of engines where the potential for competitive advantage is high and, second, when the potential for competitive advantage is low as in door knobs and glass mirrors.
- Finally, the two additional scenarios in terms of low strategic vulnerability are those where the OEM generates an essentially quantitative specification executed by the supplier, and where competitive advantage is high or medium (brackets and interior trims). Brackets that are an integral part of the braking system represent a high potential for competitive advantage. Both in

a truck and in a car the brackets must be stable, irrespective of the way the customer drives the vehicle. Brackets also come under public safety regulations. Regarding the example of interior trims in the above figure, the OEM detail controls the specifications given the impact on the comfort levels experienced by the passengers.

The complexity and subjectivity in the outsourcing decision as well as the difficulty of simulating solutions were found to decrease when the specifications move from being essentially qualitative to essentially quantitative. Conversely, the resources required and the level of detail were found to increase.

Exploring the range of relationships for the six scenarios complementing Quinn and Hilmer's model

Quinn and Hilmer have indicated a number of possible relationships between the suppliers and the OEM when the degree of strategic vulnerability and the competitive advantage are medium. Since we have expanded the number of possible scenarios in the model from three to nine, it would be appropriate to comment on the relationship modes for all the different scenarios. Though Quinn and Hilmer did not indicate the required relationship for low competitive advantage and low strategic vulnerability, we will attempt to propose relationships for not only this scenario but also the remaining scenarios that Quinn and Hilmer do not discuss.

In the case of low strategic vulnerability and competitive advantage, suppliers can be engaged through short-term contracts and through contract orders whenever there is standardisation of parts within the industry. Low strategic vulnerability products are predominantly catered for by child suppliers. The same applies for products falling in the medium competitive advantage and low strategic vulnerability dimensions. This is because there is no initiative for the OEMs to offer longer-term contracts, as the competitive advantage is not high. The presence of long-term contracts becomes predominant as the competitive advantage is high while strategic vulnerability remains low.

In the case of medium strategic vulnerability, the presence of mature suppliers is predominant. In the case where the competitive advantage is low, the suppliers work on long-term contracts. The long-term contracts can be supplemented by retainers (where the suppliers are given incentives that are more than what the long-term contract can offer) whenever the purchasing situation is particularly difficult, for example, few qualified suppliers. Retainers are present along with joint development as a relationship mode when the competitive advantage dimension changes to medium. However, when the competitive advantage dimension changes to high, the type of relationship changes to full or at least partial ownership. This was observed in the truck OEM. The truck OEM formed a joint venture with another firm specialising in engine development/manufacture to manufacture fuel injection systems for its engines. The truck OEM had controlling ownership of the joint venture company.

Table 6.9 The procurement matrix complemented by contract relationships

POTENTIAL FOR COMPETITIVE EDGE		HIGH	MEDIUM	LOW
	HIGH	• Specification generator • Type of supplier • Examples • Contract relationships	• OEM • No supplier • Styling • Not applicable	• OEM-supplier generate specifications together • Mature • Engines • Full or partial ownership	• OEM generates detailed specification • Child supplier • Brackets • Long-term contracts
	MEDIUM	• Specification generator • Type of supplier • Examples • Contract relationships	• Supplier generates rough specification which is then worked on by the OEM • Partner • Styling • Joint development Partial ownership	• OEM generates rough specification which is then worked on by the supplier • Mature • Chassis • Joint development Retainers	• OEM generates detailed specification • Child supplier • Interior trims • Short-term contracts Contract orders
	LOW	• Specification generator • Type of supplier • Examples • Contract relationships	• Supplier generates specification • Partner • Audio-system validation • Joint development	• Supplier generates rough specification which is then worked on by the OEM • Mature supplier • Door knobs, glass mirrors • Long-term contracts, Retainers	• Supplier generates the specification • Contractual supplier • Hand held tools • Short-term contracts Contract orders
		HIGH	MEDIUM	LOW
		Essentially qualitative specification	Mix [qualitative and quantitative] specification	Purely quantitative specification
		DEGREE OF STRATEGIC VULNERABILITY		

In the case of high strategic vulnerability, partner suppliers are engaged. When the competitive advantage is low, joint development is encouraged, as the OEM must try to exercise some control over the specifications. As the competitive advantage rises to a medium level, partial ownership complements joint development relationships. This was observed at the truck OEM where a small stake in the styling supplier firm was present. Table 6.9 complements Table 6.8 showing the different contractual relationships.

Conclusion

Emphasising the role of specifications in making outsourcing decisions is an attempt to aid managers and senior staff working in the area of procurement and its management. These managers need as many tools as possible to support their decision-making. The procurement matrix can help companies to leverage their resources by carefully placing all the different types of products into one of the boxes in the procurement matrix. This will allow a match between the type of the supplier required, the product in question, the generator of the specification and the nature of the specification, in addition to assessment in terms of potential for competitive advantage and strategic vulnerability. Furthermore, this will also allow a match between the above-described parameters and the type of relationship that is preferred. This genuinely strategic framework uses the entire variety of strategic options available, and by analysing the positioning of its activities onto the procurement matrix, companies can overcome many of the risks associated with outsourcing. The procurement matrix, building on the model of Quinn and Hilmer (1994) can help in building long-lasting relationships with the suppliers, in improving return on capital, in allocating internal resources, and in enhancing the decision-making process in terms of strategic outsourcing decisions.

By simply changing the resource allocation in order to change the nature of the specifications from quantitative to mixed to qualitative or vice versa, the involvement of the suppliers, the decision to outsource and the product to be outsourced can be changed.

7 Applications of specifications in outsourcing

Portfolio approaches

In this chapter the applications of specifications will be elaborated on with examples from the 'world-class' Toyota Motor Corporation. Portfolio models have been used in strategic planning and marketing, but their application to the field of purchasing has been limited. This seems, however, to be changing, as procurement management has become more strategic. A major risk when applying portfolio models to purchasing can be that the implications for suppliers and/or operational staff are scarcely considered. The study reported here explores existing portfolio models in purchasing, which classify purchases into different product categories. By means of in-depth interviews, we attempt, first of all, to link these product categories to different types of suppliers, and, second, to link the product categories and the supplier types to the specification process, i.e. the specification types and the specification originators. We argue that product categories must be matched by distinctive suppliers that have the required capabilities and capacities to satisfy specific product demands. The connection between the portfolio models and the specification process will help original equipment manufacturers (OEMs) and suppliers to improve their relationship. Also, the understanding of who generates the specifications for different product categories can help both the OEM and the suppliers to better understand each other's involvement in terms of capabilities and timeliness in the development process. Based on these arguments, we further analyse and extend the supplier relationships and the action plans for managing different procurement situations proposed in the portfolio models.

A theoretical understanding of portfolio models

Portfolio models have their foundation in Markowitz's (1952) pioneering portfolio theory for the management of equity investments. Since then, portfolio models have been widely used in strategic planning essentially at the strategic business unit level. There exists a vast range of portfolio models which, until the emergence of the resource-based approach (Prahalad and Hamel, 1990), were among the most frequently used tools in strategic management, including technology management. The Boston matrix, where businesses are positioned in terms of market growth rate and relative market share, is certainly one of the best known

(Porter, 1980). General Electric pioneered another matrix, which is more marketing oriented. In the portfolio model presented by General Electric, each business is rated in terms of market attractiveness and competitive position (Day, 1986). A third very popular matrix, again oriented towards strategic management, is Porter's (1980) model of generic strategies. Porter proposes three generic strategies – differentiation, cost leadership, and focus – depending on positioning in terms of strategic advantage and strategic target.

Portfolio models have been criticised both for their general structure, in which the different dimensions are only approximate estimations of the parameters that are supposed to be measured, and for their limited applicability in specific fields such as marketing and purchasing (Capon *et al.*, 1997; Turnbull, 1990). In spite of the criticism of portfolio models, we agree with Olsen and Ellram (1997) who contend that they are an excellent way of organising information and can be used to classify resources and suppliers in procurement management. If regarded as indicators of how to deal with different suppliers, and of a number of possible action plans, portfolio models can be a useful asset for supply management decision-makers. In fact, they are starting to gain ground both in research and practice. We have observed purchasing managers and top-level managers actually implementing these portfolio models straight into their purchasing strategies.

Previous research on portfolio models in purchasing is presented and summarised in Table 7.1. It is important to note that the contributions presented in Table 7.1 are related to situations where the decision to outsource has already been made. This is also the focus of this chapter; we will discuss the applicability of these portfolio models and propose an extension in the context of outsourced product development, once the decision to outsource has been made.

Observations of the models displayed in Table 7.1 show that they have three steps in common, though the steps are termed differently by the authors. The three steps are as follows:

- analysis of the products and their classification;
- analysis of the supplier relationships required to deliver the products;
- action plans in order to match the product requirements with the supplier relationships.

We will now explore the models presented in Table 7.1 in more detail, referring to the three stages as the portfolio model or portfolio approach as all the authors basically use the same steps.

Analysis of portfolio approaches to purchasing

The Olsen and Ellram (1997) model classifies products into four groups, namely, leverage, non-critical, strategic and bottleneck. This classification is the first of the three steps in their model. The classification is based on two dimensions: the difficulty of the purchasing situation and the strategic importance of the purchase (Figure 7.1). The rationale behind the two dimensions is experience. They are

Table 7.1 Portfolio approaches in purchasing

	Olsen and Ellram (1997)	Kraljic (1983)	Bensaou (1999)
Step 1	Classify products with respect to two dimensions varying from low (L or L') to High (H or H') • Factors describing the difficulty of managing the purchase situation (L to H) • Factors influencing the importance of the purchase (L' to H') Where the following terminology is used: LL' = Non-critical Products LH' = Leverage Products HL' = Bottleneck Products HH' = Strategic Products	Classify products with respect to two dimensions varying from low (L or L') to High (H or H') • importance of the purchase (L to H) • complexity of the supply market (L' to H') Where the following terminology is used: LL' = Non-critical Products (Purchasing Management) LH' = Bottleneck Products (Sourcing Management) HL' = Leverage Products (Materials Management) HH' = Strategic Products (Supply Management)	Classify products with respect to two dimensions varying from low (L or L') to High (H or H') • buyer's specific investments (L to H) • supplier's specific investments (L' to H') Where the following terminology is used: LL' = Market Exchange LH' = Captive Supplier HL' = Captive Buyer HH' = Strategic Partnership
Step 2	Analyse the supplier relationships for the above mentioned product categories with respect to two dimensions; • Strength of the relationship between the buyer – supplier varying from Low to Average to High • Relative supplier attractiveness varying from Low to Medium to High	Map the supplier strength versus the buyer strength for each of the products identified above in a 3 × 3 matrix with the following dimensions: • supply strength market (varying from Low-L to Medium-M to High-H) • buyer strength (varying from Low-L' to Medium-M' to High-H')	Identify contextual profiles in terms of product, market and supplier characteristics for the four distinctive relationships.
Step 3	Develop action plans to match the product requirements with the desired supplier relationships	Develop action plans as follows: • Buyer should diversify in cases of L'H, L'M, M'H • Buyer should Exploit in cases of L'L, M'L, H'M • Buyer should follow a balanced relationship in cases of L'L, M'M, H'H	Design management profiles for each of the contextual profiles in order to take action.

operational in the sense that they reflect the way in which purchasing and engineering staff are accustomed to think about purchasing situations. The positioning in terms of difficulty of the purchasing situation will depend on a ranking of different items such as product novelty and complexity, supply market characteristics, and environmental characteristics, e.g. risk and uncertainty. As for the second dimension – the strategic importance of the purchase – the positioning will depend on competence factors, economic factors and image factors such as brand and safety. This first normative step represents an ideal situation in the sense that specific management situations correspond to the distinctive groups. A risk in this step is the subjectivity in the assignment of weights to different factors in order to proceed with the classification.

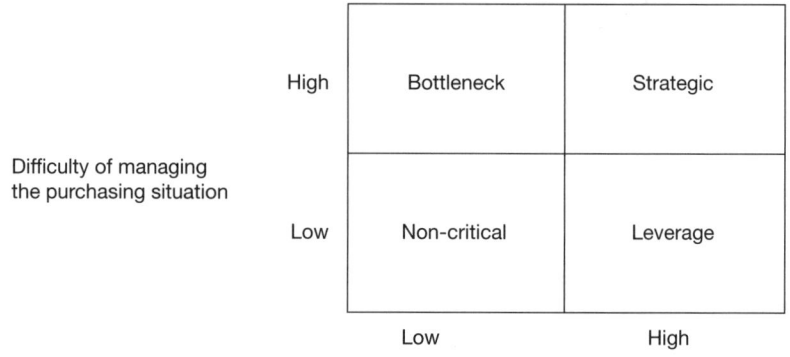

Figure 7.1 The Olsen and Ellram portfolio model

At first glance, the two dimensions might seem to be strongly positively related. That is, the greater the difficulty of managing the purchasing situation, the higher the strategic importance of the purchase. However, based on our practical experience, we have found that bottleneck and leverage situations occur as frequently as the non-critical and strategic ones. For example, tyres normally pertain to non-critical components, but in the high-end or niche segments, specific dimensions or tyre performance are required. When the auto OEM in our study (operating in a high-end segment) ordered a different dimension tyre, few suppliers were willing to supply it, turning the tyre purchase into a bottleneck situation. The pace with which dominant suppliers are taking over non-dominant suppliers through mergers and acquisitions, might also increase the occurrence and importance of bottleneck situations. This is because oligopolistic situations emerge, as in the case of seating suppliers to the automotive industry. There are two dominant seating suppliers, namely Johnson Controls and Lear Corporation. Lear Corporation has lately been on a buying spree, acquiring, among many others, Borealis, an important seating supplier located in Sweden.

Let us also illustrate a leverage situation. There are many foam suppliers available on a global basis, which would indicate that the difficulty of managing this purchasing situation is low. However, the auto OEM has positioned seats in its brand image. This means that the composition of the foam, the patterns in the foam creation process and the final level of comfort provided will allow end customers to identify with the brand of the car. Thus, the strategic importance of the foam purchase is very high, leading to a leverage situation.

In this text, we will refer to the product categories (strategic, bottleneck, leverage and non-critical) in the portfolio model as component categories because the purchasing and development problem we are dealing with is that of components. The word 'product' will refer to the final vehicle.

The first model in Olsen and Ellram's approach is operationalised by drawing a second portfolio model (adopted from Fiocca, 1982) of relative supplier attractiveness and strength of the relationship. This second descriptive step in the Olsen and Ellram model refers to a company's current supplier relationships in order to determine the way supply is managed. The positioning in terms of supplier attractiveness will depend on financial factors, performance (delivery, quality, price), technology and innovation, and organisational, cultural and strategic factors. The positioning in terms of strength of the relationship will depend on economic factors, exchange relationships, co-operation and distance between the buyer and supplier (social, cultural, technological, and geographical distance).

Let us understand these models through examples. Strategic components are those that are very difficult to manage and that also are a strategically important purchase to the OEM. An example would be the cockpit system, which integrates several different materials, electronics and important design elements. The supplier of strategic components should be highly attractive and have a strong relationship with the OEM. The second portfolio model helps to reaffirm this. Here, the strength of the relationship and the relative supplier attractiveness are adjusted, based on whether the supplier supplies strategic, non-critical, bottleneck or leverage components. For example, non-critical suppliers do not require any particular relationship with the OEM and, seen from the point of view of the latter, would be less attractive, as their contribution to innovation would be minor or negligible.

In the third step, Olsen and Ellram propose strategies and action plans for different categories:

- In the case of low attractiveness, the strategy could be to change supplier if the relationship is weak. With a strong relationship, it could be recommended to develop these suppliers' capabilities.
- With high attractiveness and strong relationships, the strategy could be to reallocate resources among different activities in order to maintain a strong relationship and to continue to encourage the supplier to develop state-of-the-art performance, thus maintaining attractiveness.
- Low-to-average strength of relationship and high or moderate attractiveness imply long-term resource allocation in order to strengthen the relationship.

In the short term, the OEM can show willingness to improve the relationship by improving communication, for example.

The merit of this three-step approach is that it provides a more detailed analysis compared to the classical portfolio models. It also develops recommendations for managing different types of supplier relationships. However, in our opinion, the portfolio model is still too superficial because it fails to take into account the link between engineering, purchasing and suppliers within the dynamic process of product development. In particular, the role of specifications is ignored in all four component categories in the portfolio model. Specifications are the language of the engineers on both sides of the buyer–supplier interface and the drivers of any development project. Also, there can be different types of specifications within a portfolio category where either the OEM or the supplier is the specification generator.

Let us briefly review the works of Kraljic (1983) and Bensaou (1999) in order to analyse whether they have addressed the shortcomings of the model proposed by Olsen and Ellram. Kraljic starts his model with the same basic step as Olsen and Ellram, i.e. classify components into four groups. The labels applied to these groups are different than those used by Olsen and Ellram; Kraljic integrates a management dimension in the first step and talks about the four groups as purchasing management, sourcing management, materials management, and supply management. The essence of the classification is similar, however, as the dimensions of both the models are identical. In other words, purchasing management corresponds to non-critical components, sourcing management corresponds to bottleneck components, materials management corresponds to leverage components and supply management corresponds to strategic components.

The next step in Kraljic's model consists in mapping the buyer's strength versus the suppliers' strengths. This essentially corresponds to analysing the supplier relationships based on performance, innovation, organisation, culture, relationships, and co-operation as proposed by Olsen and Ellram. In this step, Kraljic's model makes an additional contribution by emphasising that it is important to analyse the OEM strengths along with the supplier strengths. This will help OEMs to assess areas of opportunities or vulnerability, assess supply risks, and derive basic strategic thrusts for the attributes characterising the strengths. The final step is to develop action plans connecting the supplier relationship analysis with the component categories, as is the case with the model proposed by Olsen and Ellram. The model, however, fails to take into account the relationship between engineering, purchasing and the suppliers in the dynamic process of product development. As with Olsen and Ellram's model the role of specifications is ignored in all the four component categories.

Bensaou proposes a portfolio model, which is very rich in terms of the external and internal aspects of supplier relationships. The first step in his portfolio model consists in classifying supplier relationships into four categories based on buyers' specific investments, on the one hand, and suppliers' specific investments on the other. The rationale for using these criteria was their identification as discriminating factors in clustering four specific categories (see Table 7.1) of supplier relationships in a sample of 447 purchasing situations in three US and eleven Japanese car manufacturers. This rationale, though solid in terms of empirical validity, seems distant from the working language and operational concerns of purchasing and engineering staff.

Step two consists of identifying contextual profiles in terms of product, i.e., component, market and supplier characteristics for the four distinctive relationships (market exchange, captive buyer, captive supplier and strategic partnership). Compared to the component characteristics in the previously analysed models, the components exchanged in the market exchange situation correspond to non-critical products, those exchanged in strategic partnership correspond to strategic products.

For the remaining categories (captive buyer and captive supplier), the correspondence is not immediate. Components exchanged in a captive buyer situation can correspond to leverage components (high strategic importance for the buyer, thus their investments are high). At the same time, Bensaou argues that automobile manufacturers heavily depend on suppliers in this category, something that corresponds to a bottleneck situation. Components exchanged in a captive supplier situation can correspond to bottleneck components (low strategic importance for the buyer, thus their investments are low). At the same time, Bensaou argues that suppliers in this category have low bargaining power, which is more appropriate for the leverage situation. These contradictions are related to the different classification categories and show the importance of several approaches when analysing buyer–supplier relationships.

The third and final step relates to the design of management profiles for each of the contextual profiles in order to balance relationship requirements and relationship capabilities. High requirements–high capabilities and low requirements–low capabilities are paths to success. Conversely managers must avoid over- or under-managing relationships.

Bensaou's portfolio model is richer in content compared to the previously analysed models. For example, there is a description of supplier profiles, however, without elaborating specific supplier categories. Some product development-related reflections are also made as follows:

- In the market exchange case he states that suppliers manufacture to buyers' specifications in a situation where there is little interaction.
- The captive buyer situation calls for 'broad-band' communication in design.
- The strategic partnership situation is based on standardised rules and procedures such as electronic data interchange and schemes for exchange of guest engineers.

However, there is no consequent, in-depth analysis of specification flows or of the relationships between engineering, purchasing and the suppliers.

The discussion of models discussed above clearly reveals a common pattern with three steps in portfolio models. Olsen and Ellram's model incorporates terms that

122 *Outsourcing: portfolio approaches*

are easily understood by procurement staff. Some of the terms used by Krajlic, and the initial dimensions used by Bensau (based on specific investments), appeared to be confusing to the interviewees and hence, we adopted the terminology used by Olsen and Ellram. Furthermore, the contradictions within Bensaou's model make it difficult for a company to divide components into distinct categories. This was observed in the interviews, i.e., the validity of this argument is limited to our case study, even though it might apply to other cases as well.

Specification generators and the link to the component categories

During our interviews in Toyota, the auto and truck OEMs, we observed that there are three types of situations possible between the OEMs and the suppliers as far as the specification generation is concerned (Figure 7.2). These situations are as follows:

- *Situation 1*: here, the OEM generates the specifications on its own without any interference from the suppliers. Such components are known as detail-controlled parts (Clark and Fujimoto, 1991; Ellison, 1995).
- *Situation 2*: here, the OEM purchases parts that are a result of the supplier-generated specifications, which have been subject to no OEM interference. Such components are known as supplier proprietary parts.

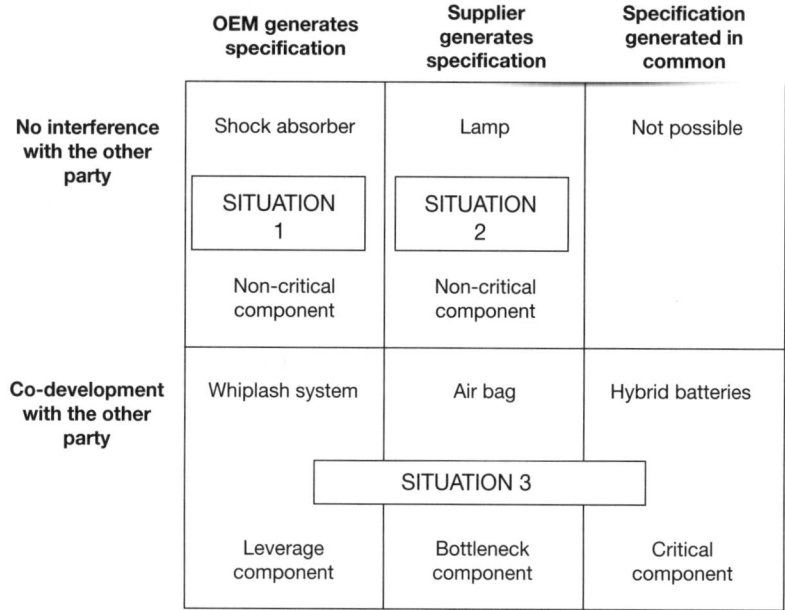

Figure 7.2 The specification generators

- *Situation 3*: here, the suppliers and the OEM engage in a range of relationships with each other, thereby generating components/specifications in an integrated manner. The range of relationships in this last type of interaction is collectively combined under the heading of co-development.

The four component types from the portfolio models were confirmed as relevant and are integrated in Figure 7.2.

The three situations between the OEM and the suppliers lead to five possible scenarios, which are illustrated by examples from Toyota Motor Corporation, collected during the field study. The examples from Toyota, which we consider as a best practice benchmark in this area, indicate that Toyota engages in a wide variety of relationships with its suppliers, thus:

- Shock absorbers are manufactured based on specifications developed by the OEM and simply executed by the supplier.
- Lamps, which are highly standardised items (except for headlights), were confined entirely to the suppliers, both in terms of specification generation and development. Lamps were uniform in the sense that they were entirely developed by the suppliers in all three OEMs.
- In the case of the whiplash system, the OEM dictates the specifications and the supplier uses co-development in order to jointly create the part, following the initial specification of the OEM.
- In certain cases, the suppliers are asked to generate the specifications and the OEM can engage in co-development with the supplier to fully meet the specifications by making changes in the interfaces, for example. This is how air bags are developed at Toyota.
- Total co-development, where the specifications were jointly generated and development was integrated between the buyer and suppliers, was possible in the case of hybrid car batteries. While it was apparent that the specifications were co-developed at Toyota for such critical components, there were no instances in the auto and truck OEM of collaborative specifications, even in the so-called strategic components. There was a tendency to over-manage suppliers throughout the specification process in the auto and truck OEMs. In general, co-development is prevalent for parts that may become sources of competitive differentiation or for brand new items coming out on the market.

To sum up, this shows that for non-critical components, the specifications are generated either by the supplier or by the OEM with no interference from the party not generating the specification. The specifications for leverage components are generated by the OEM with co-development from the supplier. The specifications for bottleneck components are generated by the supplier with co-development by the OEM. Finally, the specifications for strategic components are generated jointly by the OEM and the supplier.

It also becomes clear that for each component category, certain guidelines on how the OEM and the supplier are expected to contribute to the generation of the specification may be requested. In other words, even though supplier classifications exist, the OEM may wish to handle the specification issue differently. For example, for strategic reasons, an OEM may not want to allow a supplier classified as partner to enter into a collaborative specification setting if the supplier also supplies a competitor. On the other hand, the buying company might wish to intervene in almost all the specifications of certain systems. For example, the auto OEM in our study detail-controlled the specifications of the passive entry system in the car, even though it lacked knowledge in this area and the supplier was the most competent. Such under- and over-management of suppliers are corporate culture issues and hard to influence just by having categories of suppliers. The fact remains that even within a certain supplier category, the OEM may want to handle the specification issue differently. By knowing the different specification combinations that the OEM and the supplier could possibly engage in, a clear message can be sent to both the buying and selling organisations.

The analysis indicates that it is not enough to develop only categories of suppliers as suggested by Kamath and Liker. We also need to link the categories of the suppliers to the specification generators. It should be further noted that there are numerous combinations and it is not the aim here to discuss their total number but rather present the fact that each of them might deserve a particular type of specification.

The overall link – connecting link with the specification types and the supplier categories

We have stated that it is not enough to classify suppliers into different categories, nor does a component classification suffice. We also need to understand the specification relationship between the buyer and the suppliers. Thus, we will attempt to link the four categories of components in the portfolio models (strategic, non-critical, leverage and bottleneck) and the generator of the specifications to the supplier types and in this process, also develop a link to the different types of specifications. In order to do so, we classified twenty components in the auto OEM, Toyota and the truck OEM into the four component categories as identified by the portfolio models. Then we attempted to identify, within each component category, what kind of supplier was used and what type of specification was required. These two steps were validated by a focus group of engineers and purchasers in the two OEMs and through the interviews at Toyota Motor Corporation, respectively. The following parameters were found to apply (Table 7.2).

Non-critical items with a low innovation level (such as lamps, clips, bands, etc.) do not require partnership; hence they can be procured from any supplier. If specifications for these items were to follow an industry standard, their management could be simplified. Toyota appears to have fully understood the implications of having standard specifications for non-critical items. Suppliers of such parts to Toyota are not expected to be knowledgeable about innovation though they can be innovative if they want to move from delivering non-critical to

Table 7.2 The specification–portfolio link

Component	Specification generator	Supplier types	Specification types	Type of specification relation between OEM and the supplier
Non-critical	Supplier or OEM	Child or Contractual	Standard or closed specification from the OEM	Only the specification generator is active.
Leverage	OEM	Mature but the rough specification is developed by the OEM	Restrictive OEM => supplier, but turns to collaborative	Supplier co-develops with the OEM after the rough specifications have been generated by the OEM.
Bottleneck	Supplier	Mature but the rough specification is developed by the supplier	Restrictive supplier => OEM, but turns to collaborative	OEM co-develops with the supplier after the rough specifications have been generated by the supplier.
Strategic	OEM and Supplier	Partner	Collaborative	Direct and integrated. Both the OEM and the supplier co-develop with each other.

more important components. In the auto and truck OEMs, we found specialised drawings even for bands and clips. Thus, contrary to Toyota, they paid extra for these components. Further interviews with suppliers also indicated the same. The auto and truck OEM officials had not fully understood the link between different component categories and specification types. In one instance, for example, the auto OEM dealt with a supplier of strategic parts (sub-assemblies). The supplier was charging the OEM extra, and further investigation revealed that the supplier also had specialised drawings for non-critical items contained in the sub-assemblies. If the OEM had tried to use standardised specifications for the non-critical parts, cost could have been reduced, according to the supplier. However, communication and trust were lacking in the relationship, which led to the continuance of a non-optimal situation.

Once the use of standardised specifications for non-critical items has been more widely adopted, OEMs may have to instruct direct suppliers to use industry-standard specifications throughout the different tiers in the entire supplier pyramid. The above discussion argues that suppliers should follow a standard specification when developing non-critical parts. However, non-critical parts can also be those for which the OEM has developed a complete specification that the supplier is simply expected to execute. In this case, the onus is on the OEMs to follow an industry standard. In both cases, the supplier is not expected to contribute in any particular way in terms of innovation. This essentially points towards using child and contractual suppliers in these situations, as indicated by Kamath and Liker.

As with non-critical items, leverage components have many suppliers. If black box engineering is applied, i.e. the specifications are first of all developed internally by the OEM to a rough state restricting main parameters (function, cost, quality, system fit), the supplier base could be fully tapped and leverage exerted on existing suppliers. After handing the rough specification to the supplier, the latter would undertake further development and ultimate sealing. Toyota follows this approach in the case of leverage suppliers. Rough specifications are given to a large number of suppliers in order to exert leverage should the need arise. These suppliers need to be capable of developing a component based on the rough specifications from the OEM through a small-scale R&D division. The suppliers of leverage components are competing against many other suppliers for delivery of similar components. Hence, in order to differentiate between a number of suppliers of leverage components, there must be some distinctive knowledge residing within these supplier firms. According to officials at Toyota, there is no industry-standard specification for leverage components. Hence, the differentiating criteria will be the 'extra' that the supplier can add to the restricted specification of the OEM. An important difference between suppliers of non-critical components and those supplying leverage components is that the former can offer no add-ons. Relating the above discussion to the typology of Kamath and Liker, it can be observed that the suppliers of leverage components are mature suppliers. The specifications are rough when given to the supplier and restricted since the envelopes are already determined by the OEM. They become collaborative after the hand-over to the supplier so that the 'extra' can be added.

In the case of bottleneck components, the reduced number of capable suppliers makes it necessary to have collaborative agreements with them. This situation calls for continuous assessment of the component system. This implies that the OEM has to act in a collaborative way right from the beginning. The relatively low strategic importance of the purchase means that the OEM can allow the supplier to develop the specifications and then help the supplier to standardise them. Finally, the supplier and the OEM can jointly try to reduce the costs in the entire supply chain. An example of bottleneck components is the software for the HVAC (heating, ventilation and air conditioning) control mechanism at Toyota. This software is not considered a strategic purchase; thus, its development is outsourced. However, the purchase is complex because there are few suppliers able to develop the software. Managers within the auto and truck OEM also classified the HVAC software as a bottleneck component. In spite of this, both the European OEMs did their own in-house development of the software. Their underlying logic was to prevent a situation where they would be at the mercy of their suppliers. But in doing so they spread their resources from their core competencies to non-core items leading to project delays. It appears that the specification issue was misunderstood. In fact, co-development could be done with the software supplier. This would give a basic access and mastery of the technology, minimising the risk of being too dependent on the supplier. At the same time, co-development would prevent divergence of resources from the core design activities of the OEM.

This essentially points out that the supplier does the initial development of a rough specification and thus restricts the design and technology from the start. After involvement of the OEM, the specification becomes collaborative. Relating the above discussion to the supplier typology previously analysed, it becomes clear that the supplier of bottleneck components is not considered a partner supplier as they are not involved in the specification generation at first. They are, in fact, considered experts in a complex technology field which is, however, not strategic for the OEM. Suppliers of bottleneck components are not true mature suppliers because they are themselves responsible for the definition of the rough specifications. This indicates that they are positioned in-between the partner and mature suppliers. The supplier of bottleneck components can be seen as a mature supplier with one difference. They develop components based on their own rough specifications presented to the OEM, as opposed to the mature supplier who develops after getting the rough specifications from the OEM. This leads to an extension in the typologies proposed by Kamath and Liker.

In the case of strategic components, the main aim is to be the first to market. There is a need for close relationships with the suppliers and early or even continuous involvement. Without integrated development, there will be a drop in competitiveness instead of continuous improvement of component performance. At Toyota Motor Corporation, it was observed that suppliers of strategic components were engaged in a collaborative specification setting where both the buyer and the supplier together generated the specifications. In the auto and truck OEM, on the contrary, there were tendencies to over-manage suppliers of strategic components even though the OEMs lacked expertise in the relevant technology. For example, the OEMs provided too detailed specification where state-of-the-art technology mastered by the suppliers was ignored. This led to the suppliers not offering their best. It appears that in a critical area such as that of battery-powered cars or cars that meet a certain corporate average fuel economy, there is a great need for involvement of suppliers and co-generation of specifications or else the innovativeness in the components may be hampered. If there is to be co-generation of the specifications, then the specifications have to be collaborative and thus not restrict the input of the suppliers. Relating the characteristics of the supplier to the typology of Kamath and Liker, it seems that this situation calls for partner suppliers who are expected to be involved from the start of development or even before the development commences.

Supplier relationships and sourcing strategies

The above discussion has allowed us to articulate the different specifications and their relations to the component constituents of the portfolio approach. Following the three-stage approach, it would be appropriate to further relate this study to the other two stages as well (supplier relationships and action plans).

Several of the examples that we have discussed show that problems in terms of strength of relationship between buyers and suppliers can be the main source of difficulties. Moreover, it is necessary to assess the attractiveness of the supplier, i.e. its financial, technological and organisational performance. Step two in the portfolio approach would therefore be entirely relevant. First, the supplier of strategic parts needs to have a strong attractiveness and a strong relationship with the OEM. However, frequent changes in the technologies and the advent of game changing technologies may reduce the supplier attractiveness for certain periods in time. Thus, it would be important to maintain relationships with two parallel suppliers for these critical parts. This would also help in balancing any shortfalls in the attractiveness through mutual co-operation between the suppliers or between the individual suppliers and the OEM. This has been discussed in depth by Richardson (1993), who refutes the misconception that the Japanese and especially Toyota engage in single sourcing, where a part is procured from a single supplier across multiple projects. Richardson states that Toyota engages in parallel sourcing, instead of single or multiple sourcing. This was confirmed from our interviews at Toyota as far as strategic components and bottleneck components are concerned.

Bottleneck components are sourced by the OEMs from a limited number of suppliers. There is a need to have at least moderate to high attractiveness and average to high strength of relationship. There would be a strong emphasis on developing the relationship, i.e. average to high, otherwise, the supplier may not be willing to co-develop with the OEM after generation of the rough specification. The bottleneck suppliers can be from other industries and since their components are not completely adapted to the automotive industry, they may have moderate attractiveness. An effort to better align them to the specific needs of the auto industry would increase their attractiveness. If they adapt their components solely for the automotive industry, their attractiveness may be high. In any event, for any type of work that has to be done together between the buyer and the supplier, there is a requirement of at least a healthy working relationship.

With leverage components, the requirement on the suppliers is to have moderate to high attractiveness as they are expected to add on the 'extra' to the specifications. Low to average strength relationships appear to suffice, as the leverage has to be maintained by the OEM. For the non-critical parts where the OEM generates complete specifications, low attractiveness and low strength relationships might suffice, as the supplier is not expected to contribute to the specification. We observed that Toyota engages in multiple sourcing for non-critical and leverage parts. The above discussion on the relationship required with the supplier for each component category can be summarised as shown in Figure 7.3.

The above discussion can be further related to the third step in the portfolio model, the development of action plans. Olsen and Ellram, and Kraljic propose that suppliers who are low on the attractiveness dimension should be removed, especially if the relationship is weak. However, this may not be correct according to our findings. Suppliers of non-critical components are less attractive by definition as they simply follow the specification. These suppliers also require a low

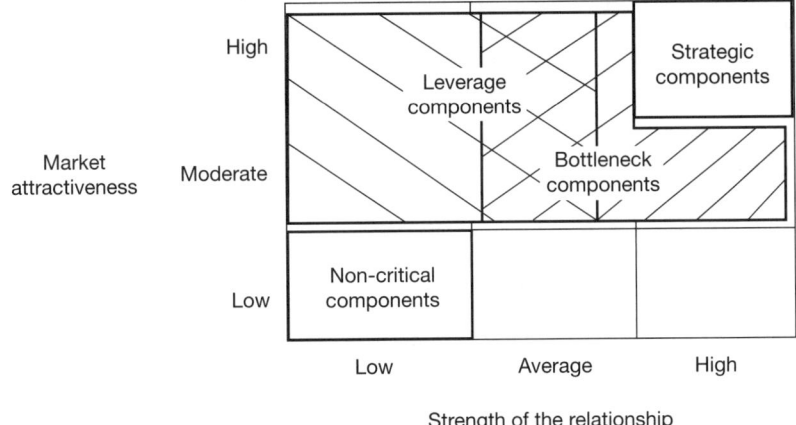

Figure 7.3 Analysis of supplier relationships
Source: Matrix dimensions adopted from Fiocca (1982)

strength relationship since for the most part, the ordering is done on-line and there is no need for any particular relationship. If a supplier of non-critical items has a strong relationship, then the OEM may be diverting its resources from improving relationships with the more important suppliers. One solution would be to develop industry standard specifications. However, even if the relationship is weak, and should be so, we would recommend that it contributes to the development of some particular capabilities such as financial and organisational strength in order to ensure viability of the supplier.

Suppliers of strategic components are required to be highly attractive and have a strong relationship with the OEM. We agree with Olsen and Ellram, Kraljic, and Bensaou that the OEMs may have to invest in maintaining the relationship and the attractiveness by different means, such as through supplier engineers, investing in communication methods, etc. (that the suppliers need to make specific investments is evident). However, in order to keep up with the competition and to prevent slack times, there may be a need to engage in these activities with two suppliers so that efficiencies of scale may be achieved.

With low to average strength relationships and high to moderate attractiveness, there is a need to use more of the leverage power to get the suppliers to increase their attractiveness. Since suppliers of leverage components further develop the initially restrictive specifications, there is a need to have at least an average strength relationship in order to allow a collaborative working atmosphere. There is no need to achieve strong relationships in terms of specification generation as these are only required when dealing with suppliers of strategic components.

We would like to comment on the specific case of bottleneck components, which, according to our findings, require moderate to high attractiveness and average to high strength of relationships. A bottleneck supplier has to have an average relationship with the OEM and can have moderate to high attractiveness with the

OEM. Thus the emphasis in bottleneck components is to get the suppliers to increase their strength of relationship to a strong level with the OEM while having at the same time a moderate attractiveness. Since the bottleneck components are not critical, there is no sense in investing in developing a strong level of relationship.

Conclusion

In conclusion, we would like to elaborate on the missing link between portfolio approaches to procurement and specifications. However, we would like to highlight the criticisms of portfolio approaches, to allow the readers to examine the conclusions in light of the limitations.

Portfolio models can be criticised in general for providing very limited explanations of how to actually manage each category once a classification has been made (Derkinderen and Crum, 1994). This might be due to the fact that companies focus too much on developing very complex dimensions in order to classify components, customers or suppliers, thus falling into the trap of means–end confusion. The classification is not an end in itself, but a means to aid in the development of appropriate action plans. Moreover, the classification in itself is problem-ridden. The initial classification of all the components takes time and there may be confusion. Above all, many parts and many suppliers will not fit exactly into the discrete categories. For example, a systems supplier may be integrating many leverage and bottleneck components together and supplying a strategic part to the OEM. The specification–portfolio link may provide some helpful insights facilitating this process. The strategic supplier may be asked to break down the overall specifications to the different components, for example, a strategic interior supplier may have components such as airbags, seats, foam, leather upholstery, etc. For each of these components the ideal component classification can be found and the specification generator determined. This is also helpful for the strategic seat supplier, as it will contribute to better managing its suppliers, who may be from a different industry.

Another main criticism is that the different dimensions used in the portfolio models are only approximate estimations of the parameters that are supposed to be measured. In the Boston matrix, for example, relative market share is supposed to be a good proxy for competitive position and market share. It has been argued that this is often not true. In order to limit the impact of such problems, we stress that the interrelationship between the category of the supplier and the specification at hand is more important than the initial classification of components. Again, the objective of the portfolio models, i.e. to optimise the use of the capabilities of different suppliers, must be kept in mind.

A final potential risk is that portfolio models have a tendency to result in strategies that are independent or even contradictory. As demonstrated in this chapter, the use of a portfolio approach to classify components, suppliers, and specifications should result in the development of a set of action plans and strategies. Instead of being contradictory, these strategies should be complementary in order to leverage the different situations depicted in the portfolio analysis.

The portfolio approach is a three-step approach to managing supplier relationships. The first step is to classify the components into the different dimensions of the portfolio model. The second step is to classify the suppliers based on their attractiveness to the OEM and the strength of the buyer–supplier relationship. Finally, strategies are drawn up in order to improve the suppliers' strength and/or relationship in order to deliver the component in optimal conditions.

Focused on the use of portfolio models for strategic procurement in the product development process, the present study proposes an expansion of the three stages by incorporating a number of intricate issues. The starting point is essentially the same, with the classification of the components. Then the type of supplier is designated. It is not enough to simply state the characteristics of the suppliers in terms of attractiveness and relationship to deliver a certain component; one must designate the characteristics of the supplier with regard to the specification generator, the relationship required and the type of specification required for a given component in the portfolio dimension. Then strategies can be developed to align the supplier to the required attractiveness and relationship so that the supplier can deliver as required. We have elaborated on the portfolio models, thereby increasing their relevance in manufacturing industries dealing with a very important component volume and outsourcing.

In our in-depth case studies and interviews, we have observed the lack of research in the field of specification management when discussing different types of components and different types of suppliers. We have concluded that specification guidelines may have to be made available to development engineers and suppliers, depending upon the split of components or suppliers according to the portfolio model. It is important to articulate who generates the specification in order to avoid confusion. Specifications are the language of the engineers and even if purchasing organises the purchased materials according to the portfolio approach, the specification–portfolio link will still have to be clarified in order to avoid confusion.

The most important findings from this study are as follow:

- Allow the engineers to be involved in the purchasing process through a close link between the category of purchase and the specification generator classification.
- If it is clear who will generate the specification, then both purchasing and engineering can reap the benefits through reducing costs and late changes in the product development process.
- The specification generation matrix will allow the full talent of the suppliers to be tapped and will avoid over- and under-management of the suppliers.
- Any kind of portfolio model for purchasing can be used in OEMs, but the specification link needs to be considered in the process.
- Even when the suppliers are classified into different categories, there could be different combinations of who does what in the specification and development process.

132 *Outsourcing: portfolio approaches*

The complexity of classifying components and suppliers stressed in the criticism of the portfolio approach remains, of course, totally relevant. We think that the management process described might help managers to deal with these issues in an integrated and proactive manner.

8 Contracts to help validate specifications

The role of contracts in validating specifications has been ignored in research, as they are thought of as commercial documents with little value as far as specification validation is concerned. This chapter demonstrates the role of contracts in validating specifications by proposing the elements of a contract that can aid validation. A strategic contract structure encompassing two categories of elements, namely, the validation criteria for entry and the validation criteria for remaining in the business, is proposed. The strategic contract structure can help managers involved in the specification process to structure development projects with suppliers in order to attain planned goals.

Introduction to commercial contracts

Contracts have no formal definition, according to the law (Thorpe and Bailey, 1996), which seems very surprising. One definition of contracts offered by Thorpe *et al.* is 'an agreement, which the parties intend to be legally binding'. This definition is also shared by Llewellyn (1931), who states that contracts are

> a framework which almost never accurately indicates real working relations, but which affords a rough indication around which such relations vary, an occasional guide in cases of doubt, and a norm of ultimate appeal when the relations cease in fact to work.

Keith (1931) states that contracts are a type of agreement that creates between the parties a legal obligation. The legal obligation that contracts offer is a common theme in all the above definitions. This legal obligation according to Thorpe and Bailey cannot be transferred to anyone who is not a party to the contract. Parallel to the present research, the legal obligation is considered to exist between the buyer and the supplier.

The content of contracts is hard to understand and individuals not used to dealing with contracts will often abandon the attempt, baffled by long, tortuous statements, and numerous cross-references (Thorpe and Bailey, 1996). They further state that commercial contracts will have been drafted by a lawyer. This means that since the lawyers will use words in a legal sense, one will need to recognise these words in order to understand a formal contract. This has also been expressed by Keith (1931), who states that:

> [The] terms of a contract are seldom fully expressed in the actual instrument, and to the express terms legal science adds implied terms, which are assumed to accord with what would have been agreed to by the parties, had the contingencies in question presented themselves to their minds when they were engaged in the making of their agreement.

A contract as described above generally includes all the legal obligations. In the relationship between the buyer and the supplier the latter is expected to satisfy the specifications given by the former. However, the presence of the legal obligations alone does not ensure that the supplier has understood the specifications, never mind the contents of the contract as they are hard to understand.

The contents of the contract can include many implicit terms (Keith, 1931) that could ensure the satisfaction of the specifications but not understood by the supplier. Hence, using validation elements to make the suppliers understand the specifications can be beneficial in satisfying the specifications. This can be made a part of the contract along with the legal obligations. The validation elements can be seen as aiding the understanding of the legal obligations. We will not discuss the legal obligations as it is beyond the remit of this chapter but rather concentrate on the role of contracts as validating mechanisms in order to satisfy the specifications and thus, the legal obligations.

Specification flows between the buyer and supplier may need to be channelled or controlled. OEM firms do not rely on the suppliers to deliver a product, but instead on their ability to take over design, styling, development, component sourcing, cost and weight management, quality, manufacturing, etc. (Ponticel, 1996). This also includes delivery of ready systems and modules to the plants for installation. First-tier suppliers are increasingly under pressure to become integrators, designers and assemblers of the second-tier suppliers, and so on (Lamming, 1993).[1] This would mean creative thinking on the part of the suppliers, being more focused and stronger in their core competencies. All these are new demands on the suppliers and hence there is a need to confirm whether or not these demands can be fulfilled. Cooper (1975) and Beecham (1996) articulate that the contracts can encompass negotiations such as results to be delivered, industry demands, etc. These negotiations can be seen as a way of confirming that the supplier can deliver what has been promised. However, no explicit link is made between the negotiation criteria and the specification, nor is the content of the contract discussed in order to aid the process of specification validation in the literature. There is also no indication as to when these negotiations should be conducted, i.e. at the start of the business or during the business. However, an important point emerges i.e. contracts could be used as a mechanism to assist in the validation of the specification.

The validation aspect becomes all the more important if buyers and suppliers have different perceptions of their relationship (Arkader and Fleury, 1998).

Validation could certainly help narrow the gap between these different perceptions by allowing the articulated demands to be checked. Newer demands require newer ways of working and this would in turn demand a new type of validation mechanism to ensure that demands are being fulfilled. Written contracts could form a guiding or controlling mechanism in product development as they may help verify that the suppliers can meet the specifications. They could help play a major role in incorporating quality into the specifications and, thus, into the final product by ensuring that the suppliers perform as required. There are other types of contracts such as verbal, simple, speciality contracts, etc. (Major and Taylor, 1996). However, these contracts cannot assist in validation to the same extent as written contracts. This is because the written contracts have many validation criteria that are written down and are explicit. In the case of a verbal contract, the validation elements are not explicit and, thus, the OEM or the suppliers may misinterpret or forget the validation parameters. In validating the specifications, it is important to cross-check that specification parameters are being fulfilled by having a contents list. While the content of the contract is important, it cannot be changed all the time as this will only lead to confusion.

Theories that focus on the division of activities between firms often propose two governance modes for transactions: to internalise through vertical integration (hierarchy), or to externalise to suppliers (market) (Williamson, 1975). Vertical integration is preferred when assets are highly specific, when uncertainty surrounds the transaction, and if such transactions occur frequently (ibid.). Externalisation is preferred under the opposite conditions.

Contracts are associated with the market mode, where firms meet to exchange goods with low asset specificity under conditions of low uncertainty (Lieberman, 1991; Teece, 1987). As long as contracts will be able to cover all possible contingencies in the transactions, markets are seen as the optimal governance mode (Lieberman, 1991). Parties reaching an agreement or deemed to have reached an agreement are said to have made a contract (Major and Taylor, 1996). The agreement can be done in writing, verbally or, by inference from the opposite party or parties.

An intermediate situation, a quasi-vertical integration, has been developed as a governance mode in its own right (Håkansson, 1982; Turnbull and Valla, 1986). In this mode, the relationship is the focal point of interest and 'firms gain the advantage of vertical integration without assuming the risks and rigidity of ownership' (Blois, 1971).

A contract is used in a market mode as the major mechanism to ensure that business takes place under conditions of mutual benefit to the buyer and supplier. Contracts are generally not used in a hierarchy mode, as the latter is internal to the OEM (Teece, 1987). However, a central question is whether contracts can be used in the relationship mode. Crocker and Morgan (1998) argue that contracts cannot cover all the contingencies in this mode, due to the intricate interdependencies between all the firms. Instead, they agree with the argument of Cooper (1975) that contracts can be used as a *forum* to create an optimal relationship and ensure that the parties (suppliers and buyers) perform what is necessary when it is necessary. This argument is also supported by Adler (1999), who states that compared to trust, price and authority are relatively ineffective mechanisms when dealing with assets based on knowledge. In other words, the complex products based on knowledge that are interchanged between the buyer and supplier in the automotive industry need trust to serve as a governance mechanism. Adler cautions that this trust is reflective and not blind. The reflective trust ensures that there are rules to ensure stability and equity, and competition to ensure flexibility and opportunity. Trust is important in the relationship mode (Sako, 1992). However, trust is a cognitive–emotive result of experience with someone or something, making it very difficult to set targets and ultimately evaluate whether a task or activity has been realised according to expectations. Contracts could be seen as means of ensuring that tasks and activities are executed as presumed in a buyer–supplier relationship based on trust and support the argument of reflective trust proposed by Adler (1999).

A review of relevant literature

What is a contract?

Major and Taylor (1996) observe contracts to have three fundamental elements, namely, the agreement, the intention, and the consideration:

- Agreement is reached when there is existence of a clear offer and acceptance of that offer.
- Intention is the need to create legal relations to protect the interests of the concerned parties.
- The consideration or understanding is arrived at when the parties have reached an exchange of benefits and losses.

There is extensive literature on the use of contracts as legal documents for commercial purposes in a market situation referring to the transaction cost framework (Major and Taylor, 1996; Teece, 1987). As the present research focuses on the intermediate mode, we turn to literature dealing specifically with the role of contracts in outsourced product development where specifications are developed in collaboration between buyers and suppliers.

Asmus and Griffin (1993) argue that best practice procurement requires optimisation of three major elements of the supply management process, namely, product development/specifications, sourcing, and contract execution:

- Product development/specifications concerns the link between R&D, engineering, and suppliers. Suppliers who will be given development responsibilities need to be selected before product engineering starts so that they become an integral part of the product development team. These suppliers must be capable of leading new technology development. These affirmations are shared by the product development literature (Schilling and Hill, 1998).
- Sourcing concerns the overall determination of the number of suppliers to

work with, supplier auditing and selection, and determination of contractual agreements. Sourcing refers to the core activities of the purchasing department (Dowlatshahi, 1992).
- Contract execution relates to how OEMs will work with their suppliers on a day-to-day basis, for example, Honda has dedicated teams at its suppliers' premises to reduce costs.

Asmus and Griffin discuss specifications and contracts independently of each other and do not explore the link between them. Cooper (1975), on the other hand, argues that the negotiation of contracts is a central part of strategic planning in purchasing. Taking the example of the construction industry, he suggests that contracts can be used as a forum to raise and answer questions that need to be the object of negotiations before suppliers are chosen. The aim of these negotiations is to check that the suppliers are capable of fulfilling the demands that are imposed on them by the specifications.

The notion of validation merits further investigation, as Cooper does not state how validation will be performed during the course of the business. Moreover, there is no consideration of the link between contracts and specifications. Our working assumption is that any establishment and modification of contracts has to refer to the specifications, as the latter are the ultimate references that suppliers are expected to satisfy.

There are also risks related to contracts. Companies signing long-term contracts with suppliers within the framework of outsourcing run the risk of paying the supplier for extra contractual charges and of getting stuck with old technology when the technological environment changes (Harris *et al.*, 1998). If contracts have flexible options, such as early termination, incentive contracts, price flexibility, renegotiation flexibility, and flexibility in terms of duration, these problems could be reduced. A certain flexibility in the contract would be necessary in order to keep up with the evolution of specifications that takes place in integrated product development between buyers and suppliers (Harris *et al.*, 1998).

Although the importance of contracts in outsourcing is emphasised in the literature, there is very little discussion of their role in assisting the validation of technical specifications. If flexible contacts with a clause for early termination are used, the OEM can remove a supplier from business if the supplier does not supply the 'right' technology. However, removing suppliers instead of helping them to improve themselves would mean non-continuous evaluation of the specifications which could lead to late design changes and a risk of modification of related components and systems in a cascade. Thus, flexible contracts do not solve all problems. Rather, contracts might have an important role to play in terms of *continuous* validation of supplier performance compared to the evolution of specifications in order to avoid such drastic action as removing a supplier during the course of a project.

As we have argued, specifications are dynamic. In each stage in the process of specifying there is compilation and adding of information, and the content of the specification is progressively extended (Kaulio, 1996; Smith and Rhodes, 1992).

The validation aspect becomes all the more important if buyers and suppliers have different perceptions of their relationships as in the case of development responsibility (Arkader and Fleury, 1998). Validation might narrow the gap between different perceptions by allowing the articulated demands to be checked for completion. Changing product development demands on suppliers and OEMs in the framework of black box engineering require new ways of working. This would, in turn, demand validation mechanisms to ensure that the demands are being fulfilled. Written contracts can form a guiding or controlling mechanism in integrated product development as they can verify that the other party does what they have promised. Let us now explore whether the literature has explicitly stated what validation parameters can be contained in a contract.

Validation parameters

The literature on the validation parameters is mainly based on purchasing. In outsourced product development the suppliers and buyers do the work in varying degrees of collaboration (Lamming, 1993). Besides focusing on *product* validation, it is important that OEMs ensure that the suppliers have the *capacities* and *capabilities* to remain sustainable partners, particularly if they are to take a major role in the OEM development process (Lamming, 1993). In other words, contracts can contain criteria specific to the product and also criteria specific to the suppliers who are to execute the specifications.

Today, all OEMs conduct extensive capability audits before selecting suppliers, and also regularly audit suppliers in ongoing relationships (Kolay, 1993; Monszka *et al.*, 1995). These audits might concern the contribution to product development, technological capability, innovation capability, contribution to the OEM product advantage, use of total quality management, potential for further improvement, potential for price reduction, suppliers' financial stability, management commitment to excellence, flexibility, cost competitiveness, cycle time concentration and manufacturing skills (Cash, 1996; Harrison, 1990; Hyun, 1994; Kolay, 1993; LaLonde and Masters, 1994; Larson, 1994; Levy *et al.*, 1995; Mohanty and Deshmukh, 1993; Monszka *et al.*, 1995; Turnbull and Valla, 1986). Payment terms were also considered to be important in source audits (Leenders *et al.*, 1994). All parameters considered relevant by the OEM are likely to be contained in the contract. The different performance criteria for suppliers may be considered in advance if an OEM wishes to make a useful contract that can reduce tensions with suppliers and at the same time keep the relationship working. The fulfilment of goals relative to these criteria is expected to improve the relationship, thus leading to partnership.

The above identified validation criteria can be regrouped into levels of importance in order to support the validation of specifications. The study will explore how validation criteria can be integrated and used in contracts as a means of assisting the validation of the specifications.

Kanter (1994), studying partnerships within the framework of alliances (i.e. long- or short-term collaboration between firms and other organisations involving partial or contractual ownership which are developed for strategic reasons (Forrest, 1989)), argues that there should be strategic integration (goals, objectives), tactical integration (to develop plans for projects), operational integration (working procedures), interpersonal integration (meetings, conferences), and cultural integration (learning each other's culture) at all levels in an organisation. This typology provides an interesting benchmark for the anticipated findings of the present study.

Specifications and contracts – reciprocal interdependence

The analysis above prompts us to investigate the reciprocal interdependence between contracts and specifications. Let us explore this further in order to position the research question better. Kaulio (1996) discusses the connection between specifications and contracts. According to him, the specification takes on the role of knowledge gathering during non-contractual situations and the role of market investigation during contractual situations. Hence, according to Kaulio, the role of specification varies with the contractual situation. The contractual situation is engaged with suppliers who possess different capabilities and capacities. When contracts are developed and specifications exchanged, it might, therefore, be very useful to classify suppliers in relation to their capabilities relative to integrated product development. If suppliers possess different capabilities, then they may perform different specification roles irrespective of whether a contract is present or not. For example, when a supplier presents concepts to an OEM, the supplier has already performed the knowledge-gathering role even though the supplier was not under contract. Hence, the contract–specification link, as explained by Kaulio, has to be relevant to the categories of suppliers as certain categories of suppliers may or may not follow the proposals of Kaulio. If the roles of the specifications are variable, then the contract must reflect these variations. If the nature of the specifications turns out to be very different from those in current use, then the contracts will have to be updated in order to reflect these changes. Without contracts, the specifications cannot be satisfied, and without the specifications, the contracts are of no use as their primary purpose is to validate the specifications. In effect, there is reciprocal influence between specifications and contracts.

Exploring contracts in the auto and aircraft OEMs

Four different types of written contracts[2] (A, B, C and D) are used between the auto OEM and its suppliers in development projects. The aircraft OEM, on the other hand, uses only one type of contract (E) when dealing with its suppliers. By examining these different types of contracts we will be able to analyse the different ways in which contracts are promulgated in the specification process between the buyer and the suppliers. The auto OEM contracts are explored at first, followed by the contract at the aircraft OEM. The contracts varied in length between one to fifty pages in the auto OEM and were ten pages long in the aircraft OEM.

Table 8.1 The contract data

	Column A Items mentioned in the contracts	Column B Elements
Transversal items in all the auto OEM contracts	Price, service and quality are the important performance criteria for getting the business	Performance criteria
	Suppliers must adopt Odette	Communication
Type A contract auto OEM	The purpose of the contract was mentioned, which was in fact to use the suppliers' resources to produce drawings according to the product development process.	Purpose
	The people to contact were mentioned both at the suppliers' end and at the OEM's end. Expenses to be calculated on an incurred basis.	Communication
Type B contract auto OEM	The supplier should produce FLPS drawings. The supplier should produce NUFO drawings. Prototype parts to be produced by the supplier. The supplier is responsible for all his sub-suppliers.	Supplier responsibility
	The supplier should have full responsibility for the testing. Types of tests not mentioned in the specification should be agreed and determined by both the supplier and the OEM before the start of the test programme. Test results are to be handed in to the OEM within a week after the tests.	Testing
	The OEM can cancel the contract at any time. If the OEM is responsible for the delay such as by enforcing late changes, the supplier is not liable for any penalties. x% of the final quoted price to be paid in penalty if the supplier does not fulfil the terms in the contract. The OEM will give all information to the supplier regarding specification, description and drawings.	Legal issues
	There should be fortnightly project meetings The supplier should have a full time project manager and the capacity to provide a resident engineer if needed.	OEM responsibility Communication
	The supplier should present to the OEM reports regarding compliance with quality targets. The supplier should inform the OEM about any existing quality problems.	Quality systems

Table 8.1 continued

Type C contract auto OEM	The supplier must submit service literature, parts and accessories, to the OEM at the same price as the original quote.	Supplier responsibility
	No price increases are to be tolerated	Communication.
	Cost, progress of tool and sample development must be followed	
Type D contract auto OEM	The supplier is expected to deliver the drawings, specifications on x dates	Supplier responsibilities
	The supplier must give suggestions to the OEM	Communication
	The personnel at the supplier should be organised so that they can work in-house at the OEM.	Legal issues
	In case the serial production is not awarded to the same supplier, the auto OEM will pay for the complete design work.	
	Column A	Column B
	Items mentioned in the Contracts	Elements
Contract in the Aircraft OEM	Suppliers need ISO9001 certification.	Quality system
	Supplier should help the OEM market the final product	Supplier responsibility
		Legal issues
	Suppliers will be paid in case of termination	
	Supplier liable to pay the OEM in case of delays	
	Changes to be negotiated in good faith.	Changes
	Price, service, delivery performance and quality are the important performance criteria for getting the business	Performance criteria
	The suppliers must adopt Odette	
	The suppliers must acknowledge receipt of messages and elucidate response dates.	Communication

The first part of the data collection consisted of listing the discrete items that the different contracts contained. The result of this analysis is presented in Table 8.1, column A.

In the second step of the data collection, twelve managers[3] – six from the suppliers and six from the auto OEM – were asked to meet in a focus group and to analyse the items contained in column A of Table 8.1 with the aim of identifying the important contract elements hidden in the listed contract items. The result of this step is shown in column B in Table 8.1. A total of nine elements were identified: Purpose, OEM Responsibility, Supplier Responsibility, Performance Criteria, Testing, Legal Issues, Changes, Quality Systems and Communication. Table 8.2 summarises the nine elements and indicates the extent to which they were present in the different contracts. Table 8.2 also provides an added value as it presents the nine elements in a sequence agreed upon by the twelve managers, in order to impose a better order on the contract structure.

The elements are partly reflective of the background of the individuals in the focus group, but the final result emerged as a consensus after three rounds of discussions. It is to be noted that elements like the specification–contract link (Harris *et al.*, 1998) and payments (that are necessary for the suppliers to remain in business by appropriately using their cash flow and managing their commitment to the sub-suppliers; Leenders, 1994) were missing from the content of the examined contracts, and therefore naturally are lacking as main contract elements, while observed to be important in the literature review.

Table 8.2 Contract parameters, sequenced

ID Contract elements	Auto OEM				Aircraft OEM
	Contract A	Contract B	Contract C	Contact D	Contract E
1 Purpose of the contract	Mentioned	Not mentioned	Not mentioned	Not mentioned	Not mentioned
2 OEM responsibility	Not clear	Mentioned	Not clear	Not clear	Not clear
3 Supplier responsibility	Not clear	Clear	Not clear	Not clear	Not clear
4 Performance criteria	Price, service, quality	Price, service, quality	Price, service, quality	Price, service, quality	Price, service, quality, delivery performance
5 Testing	Not mentioned	Mentioned	Not mentioned	Mentioned	Mentioned
6 Legal issues	Not mentioned	Mentioned	Mentioned	Mentioned	Mentioned
7 Changes	Not clear	Not clear	Not clear	Not clear	Negotiated
8 Quality systems	Yes	Yes	Yes	Yes	Yes
9 Communication	Not mentioned	Not mentioned	Not mentioned	Not mentioned	Mentioned

Table 8.3 Regrouping contract parameters

ID No.	Contract elements (Main)	Contract elements (Sub)	Reason for including the sub-contract elements
1	Types[1]		
2	Purpose		
3	Responsibility	OEM responsibility Supplier responsibility Quality systems	Responsibility concerns both the supplier and the OEM; what are the responsibilities of each partner and what are the joint responsibilities? A good contract would need to specify this. The quality system that links the OEMs and the suppliers specifies detailed responsibilities both during development and during running delivery and production. I therefore consider that the quality system pertains to the category responsibility.
4	Performance criteria		
5	Legal issues		
6	Communication	Changes	Integrated product development calls for extensive communication (Clark and Fujimoto, 1991). Söderquist (1997), studying the role of expert suppliers in integrated component development, argues that operational design engineers and technicians invent their own communication modes and channels in an improvised and *ad hoc* manner, and that appropriate support structures and guidelines for communication are lacking. Contracts could help in developing clearer communication paths. How and when design changes are dealt with are, to a large extent, a question of communication (Karlsson, 1994). I therefore consider the contract parameter changes as pertaining to communication.
7	Payments		
8	Specification–contract link	Testing	How testing of prototypes will be carried out is one of the main elements in a specification (Karlsson *et al.*, 1998). The contract can help in validating and checking testing procedures. I therefore consider that testing pertains to the specification–contract link.

Note: 1 Types refer to having one contract or multiple contracts for suppliers.

144 *Contracts to validate specifications*

Further interviews were conducted to gain an in-depth understanding of the nine elements within the firms, and also to explore the specification–contract link. Given the technique of the open coding procedure, it was further decided to reduce the number of contract elements by regrouping. The coding, the categories and sub-categories are as shown in Table 8.3. These categories will be examined in the analysis section.

Types of contracts

As observed, there are many different types of contracts in the auto OEM. The auto OEM contract variants were used at random with the suppliers, so there was no specific rationale behind this difference. Rather, it was due to the fact that each contract contained certain elements that the other contracts might or might not contain. This can lead to confusion, especially when the decision regarding the type of contract to be awarded to suppliers is made. This problem can be illustrated with an example. The seats are positioned on rails in the car. The interior department in the OEM handles the seats, whereas the chassis department handles the rails. When different departments are handling different parts of the same system, the system supplier, who is responsible for the complete seat including the rails, could get different and conflicting messages.

The aircraft OEM contract contained supplier-specific parameters connected to individual supplier requirements. Both these variants have advantages and disadvantages as shown in Table 8.4. The use of a single contract or multiple contracts would depend on the level of detail that the OEM would like to attain in the contracts. A single contract could contain only very generic clauses applicable to all suppliers. On the other hand, there will be little use in having multiple contracts or individualised clauses unless the differences are linked to some rationale, such as different categories of suppliers, as discussed in the literature section. A link to different types of suppliers could help to put clauses in the contract to anticipate problems and prevent them from occurring. Based on research in the insurance business, Crocker and Morgan (1998) suggest that the main role of contracts is to prevent the same mistake from happening again.

Purpose

Even though the definition of a contract, according to Major and Taylor (1996), states that a contract is made after an agreement is reached between parties, it was observed that both the OEMs sign contracts before the intention is reached in many instances. As a result, there are still fights over responsibility, costs, timings, quality, etc., after the contract signature. This demonstrates that the basic purpose of a contract, i.e., to reach an agreement acceptable for the contractual partners, has not been fulfilled. If such basic premises are not met, trust and partnership will fail to emerge.

If the elements contended in the contract are not agreed upon, the contract will not be well defined, and the validation of the specifications may be difficult, as the

Table 8.4 Different contractual possibilities

Many contracts	One contract
There will be no match between the contract and the capabilities of the supplier if the contract is supplied at random. In other words, the contract will not be able to validate the capability of the supplier to deliver as promised.	A match between the contract and the suppliers' capability to deliver will occur only when the supplier specific parameters related to the supplier types are included in the contract. In other words, contracts cannot have both generic parameters and parameters related to individual supplier requirements but rather specific requirements connected to the different types of supplier categories else the problems of randomness associated with the many contract scenario will be visible.
Problems will occur with multiple contracts especially when different departments are involved in the development/sourcing of a particular system/component.	One contract would mean one message as all the departments would have to caucus to see that their individual needs and requirements are stipulated in the contract.
Generic contract parameters can be forgotten in case there are too many variants of the contract	Generic contract parameters are never forgotten and always present in the contract. In fact as problems arise and solutions are generated they are continuously updated as part of the generic parameters if possible.
There are no visible synergies in the different contracts. For example, it is not clear whether solutions to problems arising from one contract will be put into the other contracts as part of continuous improvement.	It is easy to check problems and put clauses back into all the contracts to prevent them from reoccurring, thereby drawing on synergies.

'what' to be validated will not be clear. The very purpose of contracts is to set the scene so that no conflicts will occur or so that the partners know how to deal with conflict (Major and Taylor, 1996).

The present study complements this conclusion by emphasising that everything cannot be made clear from the first instant, and hence validation of the agreements on a regular and ongoing basis may become an additional purpose of the contract. Neither the OEM nor the supplier should expect and specify the impossible. The purpose of a contract could be to oblige a clear discussion of what is expected and what is not, what is acceptable and what is not, and what is possible to anticipate and what is not. This is applicable not only to what the suppliers promise the OEM or to the demands of the OEM, but also to the generators of the specification who need to know the capabilities of different suppliers better.

To aid in this process, successive agreements have to be reached in order to validate common understanding of all sorts of compromises that the final product – the car or the aircraft – is subject to. Supplier attitude to reaching agreement and assuming changing situations, which could be chaotic at times, could be seen as a validation criterion for acceptance as a supplier because, without the right attitude, the suppliers cannot be expected to deliver as promised.

Responsibility

Responsibility does not simply mean stating a list of tasks for the supplier to do. It also means ensuring that the demands are met and validated in a timely fashion. There is a need for the responsibility to be clearly visible and appropriately linked to the job at hand. I will illustrate the above statements better with an example.

A supplier was hired for design only and the contract ended when the supplier submitted the drawings. However, it was very difficult to judge the effectiveness of the drawings at an early stage in the development. Another supplier, who only manufactures and did not have any input in the design, manufactured the parts according to the drawings given by the design supplier and faults were noticed, as defective parts were being produced. But by the time the defects were noticed, the drawing supplier had already completed the contract. Hence the OEM had to assume the changes in the design alone. The manufacturing supplier was of little help due to its lack of experience in solving design-related problems. This meant wasted resources and duplication of work.

This example shows that the quality of the specifications was affected by the misjudgement of the responsibility level of the supplier. Had the supplier been given both development manufacturability and responsibility, then the supplier alone would have been responsible for solving all the design-related problems that became obvious in manufacturing.

A very important part of the contract is to ensure that the OEM gets what it asks for. The supplier responsibility, the OEM responsibility, and joint responsibility must be made clear from the beginning and mentioned in the contracts. This is to avoid over- or under-management of suppliers. In the example above, the design supplier could have been contracted at least until the design had been validated in ramp-up production. The case of air bags to be fitted on to the dashboards further illustrates this point. In case of failure of the air bag under use, will the responsibility lie with the OEM, the dashboard supplier or the air bag supplier, both suppliers, or all three partners? For example, if the OEM clearly indicates that the dashboard supplier is solely responsible for air bag integration, then the sphere of responsibility for all the three players would be clearly visible.

The possibility of making responsibilities clear from the beginning would form the validation criterion for entry, as it would improve visibility should problems arise. It would lead to faster problem-solving time. It might not only mean that the OEM alone articulates what the suppliers' responsibilities are, but that the suppliers do the same based on their capabilities and capacities. The suppliers need to become more proactive and ask relevant questions of the OEM in order to take their part of the responsibility for integrated development. This could avoid missing areas when the OEM alone dictates what the supplier is responsible for. Understanding their responsibilities would allow suppliers to understand the importance of quality, and undertake continuous education and training in order to satisfy the demands of the OEM. Increasing levels of quality, continuous education and training would thus form validation criteria for remaining a supplier.

Performance criteria

The contracts (A,B,C,D) judge suppliers on the dimensions of service, price and quality. The essential role of the contracts is to express these parameters in quantitative terms that, ideally, should be agreed to by both parties. However, none of the following selection factors, identified from the literature as essential for good relationship and product performance, were considered:

- the suppliers' capability in general to contribute to the OEM's product development process;
- technological and innovation capabilities;
- the potential for price reduction;
- suppliers' financial stability;
- environmental standards;
- suppliers' industrial relations;
- strategic, tactical, operational and interpersonal integration.

This indicates that the auto OEM has a narrow vision of performance criteria in its contracts focused on price, quality and service. The concentration of price as a selection criterion is in complete opposition to the argument that price should be the consequence and not the initiator of the discussion (Frey and Schlosser, 1993; Lamming, 1993).

Contract E in the aircraft OEM takes an additional factor into account, namely, delivery performance. They have, in fact, hired a company to monitor the delivery so that they get the information as soon as the goods have left the suppliers. This means that instead of having many people monitoring the delivery, both at the aircraft OEM and at the suppliers, there is only one monitoring unit.

The performance criteria of the suppliers will impact on the quality of the specifications. For example, if suppliers are selected with no connection to the specification at hand, then there is little hope that the specifications will turn out as planned. Relating to the supplier typologies proposed by Kamath and Liker (1994), open specifications cannot be given to contractual suppliers, for example. Also, giving detailed specifications to a partner supplier would be considered an act of over-management. Although there will be generic parameters that are applicable to all these suppliers, there will also be some specific parameters in the contracts that depend on the specific capacities and capabilities of individual suppliers.

There is no doubt that a reasonable initial cost level at the suppliers forms an important criterion during the first discussions between the OEM and the suppliers. However, the attitude to price reductions is very important as the business dealings commence. Unless suppliers are financially stable, they will not be able to invest in productivity improvements and thus will not be able to reduce the prices for the OEMs without reducing profit margins. The question of cost reductions, as well as parameters such as continuous improvement and innovation capabilities, are very much related to the culture, mission and strategy of a supplier. The opportunities to develop integrated buyer–supplier visions, and a fit of the mission, strategy and culture between and within the buyer and the suppliers can be seen as validation criteria for entry as they form the foundation on which business can be conducted.

Concern for sensitive issues like emissions and recycling matters must also be reflected in the initial discussions between OEMs and suppliers. This is to ensure that the suppliers can deliver within the constraints faced by the OEMs. Concern for environmental issues can be seen as an important criterion for entry as it determines the constituents of the product and the processes that the suppliers use. Questions on compatibility can be addressed at the beginning so as to reduce the problems that may occur during the development process.

Closer integration between the buyer and the suppliers at the strategic, operational, interpersonal and tactical level will lead to better understanding and improvement in productivity during the development process. However, these cannot be achieved at the start of the relationship and hence it is necessary that they be achieved during the course of the relationship and can be seen as validation criteria for remaining in the business.

Another important performance criterion for suppliers was observed to be a fit between the suppliers' existing portfolio of projects and the new projects accepted. Suppliers cannot be expected to have individual projects for every OEM without any synergies between them. It is essential to have synergies between the projects and this will be possible when the suppliers work with the same units of OEMs. A clear explanation of the portfolio of projects by the suppliers to the OEMs may be seen as a validation criterion for entry as it makes the assumptions clear from the beginning.

Legal issues

Although there are provisions for legal fines in the contracts, essentially for suppliers not delivering on time, they are not strictly enforced, as it is hard to determine where the fault lies. Also, the fact remains that if there is a high penalty imposed, the supplier will be unwilling to sign any contract. On the other hand, there can be legal fines based on the specific demands placed on the supplier that are explicitly mentioned in the contracts. For example, if suppliers are asked to fulfil a certain durability demand and they do not do so, then they could be asked to reimburse the cost for that part. Let us assume that the cost for a product such as an equipment option sold to the OEM is $150 (the actual cost to the supplier is $100) and the OEM sells it to the importer at $200. In case of rejection by the customer, the supplier has to pay the OEM $200 plus interest charges and not just $150. This is because the demand was to satisfy the durability requirements for the final customer and not for the importer or for the OEM. The example demonstrates that fines should be directly linked to the responsibility assigned to the suppliers.

Let us take another example. The OEM had passed a component, which was 95 per cent complete compared to the specifications, into customer cars. This was because the OEM judged that the 5 per cent incomplete specifications concerned minor issues that would not be noticed by the customer. If the customer notices the defects, then the OEM will be blamed, as they passed the product and are responsible for the overall quality of the car. While the suppliers can be penalised for not satisfying specifications given to them or agreed upon with them and thus bear the warranty costs, the OEMs would be required to accept and reimburse losses in cases of incomplete specifications, wrong specifications, design miscalculations, interfacing problems between the components from different suppliers, etc., i.e. if the source of problems originated due to the OEM. This example shows that the problems were due to the poor usage of the contract as a mechanism for validating the requirements. If the contracts make the responsibilities clear from the beginning such as that of the OEM and the suppliers, then the contract functions as a validating mechanism.

In a related example, Sorabjee (1997) comments that a steel supplier and steering gear supplier are jointly footing the bill for having supplied defective steering gears to a particular automotive OEM, thus paying for the recall exercise (where a number of cars were recalled) by the OEM. This confirms the fact that when the steel was accepted for use in the steering gears, the steering gear supplier accepted full responsibility for its quality. However, since the quality of the steel was bad, he footed the bill together with the steel supplier as it was the steel supplier's mistake to supply defects and the steering gear supplier's mistake to accept defects.

The ability to understand the legal demands and liabilities on a continuous basis would form a validation criterion for remaining in the business. This can also be seen as continuous environmental scan by the suppliers in order to aid the OEM and also to make the products with the right ingredients[4] so that the final customers will accept them.

Communication

Communication between the buyer and the supplier is all the more necessary given the fact that their work is interrelated. The success of the specifications depends on the in-depth discussions and joint problem-solving carried out by both the buyer and the supplier. Contracts could also state when design reviews should take place and what information should be made accessible on such occasions. Contracts can assist communication by making sure that both the buyer and the supplier have compatible modes of communication and know-how, for example, for EDI. The suppliers are increasingly under pressure to adopt Odette[5] as a means of communication. As most of the suppliers to the auto OEM supply to multiple customers, investment in Odette would be considered to be specialised unless the suppliers use Odette in dealing with other customers as well. Common communication standards can be a vehicle for cross-organisational learning (Söderquist and Nellore, 2000). Either the auto OEM can encourage all other automotive companies around the world to adopt Odette or itself adopt a common industry standard. If there are common standards, the suppliers do not have to invest in specialised transmission modes for each customer, and information will not be distorted if cross-organisational learning is desired.

Contract E uses communication as both an entry criterion and a criterion to remain in the business. For example, if the OEM sends a message to the supplier, the supplier may have to respond immediately, and if possible with a decisive answer or at least with a message indicating when this answer will be ready. In the aircraft OEM, a small technical problem can cause the whole aircraft to shut down. Hence, the buyer and supplier are required to work very closely together at all times to be able to solve the problems immediately they occur. Lacking a common information system might lead to problems in understanding and working with the specification.

Good communication means timely information about different parameters that require attention in specifications. In outsourced product development there are constant changes to the acceptable level of quality, cost, and service by the OEMs even after the contracts have been signed. While changes are a necessity, the amount of change is not mentioned in contracts. For example, it was not mentioned that there would be x loops of changes, or how many hours the changes would require. This meant that the OEM could easily be cheated into losing money. The contracts can state the number of hours, cost per hour and the maximum loops of changes. In the aircraft OEM, all changes are negotiated. Price increases are tolerated for materials and labour according to an escalation clause which works with a predetermined formula. In order to keep the competitiveness of the suppliers, the aircraft OEM reduces a small percentage of the escalation price. The aircraft OEM is prepared to pay any cost, as safety is of utmost consideration. Early decisions on changes ensure that the specifications are satisfied within agreed costs. These also ensure that both the buyer and the supplier understand all the possible changes so that there are no surprises when the specifications are to be validated.

The existence or strong potential for development of a common information system between the OEM and the supplier would form the validation criterion for entry. Without common information systems, there could be distortion of information, delays in reception, etc. The ability to estimate changes and avoid movements outside the set of solutions, costs and delivery conditions would allow the supplier to be validated for entry. Ability to work with a set of solutions is a critical success factor for Toyota according to Ward *et al.* (1995). The commitment to work within a set that includes cost, number of solutions and changes, extends the conclusions of Ward *et al.* It is not only sets of solutions that are important, but also the ability to work within a set of changes and costs that is equally important. This appears to be an important validation criterion for remaining in the business as the existence of a continued profitable relationship depends on reducing costs and bringing to the market the best solution when required.

Payments

A lot has been written about the successful Japanese practices of early supplier involvement. However, the case study companies rarely want to reveal information regarding their cost structure and production planning, something that might indicate a lack of trust in the suppliers (Helper, 1991). This leads to the conclusion that while the Japanese may be right in not relying on contracts but on long-term partnerships based on trust, Western OEMs may be committing a big mistake if they think that this can be replicated overnight. The Japanese have taken years of working together with the suppliers to attain their current levels of partnership (Lecler, 1993). For example, other suppliers pitched in when Aisin, a Toyota supplier, caught fire and Toyota helped in reimbursing all the suppliers for their assistance (Nishiguchi and Beaudet, 1998).

Monetary resources are important for the continuation of businesses. The suppliers need information about payment schedules in order to plan their activities. They often think that if they deliver early, they might receive early payment. This is, however, very rarely the case. By clearly defining pay schedules in the contract, mistrust due to misunderstandings between the partners can be avoided. For example, in the aircraft OEM, the cost of each prototype is quite considerable. Hence the suppliers are told from the beginning that their products will be paid for after delivery to the final customer. That is because the OEM also gets the payment after delivery. If long-term relationships are desired, then both the parties can share the risks.

In order to develop a healthy relationship, a number of activities can be undertaken at the start of the business and others could be undertaken as the business progresses. For example, the issue of payment can be made clear from the start so that activities can be planned accordingly and can be seen as a validation criterion for entry. Timely dispatch of information, such as budget release dates, would help develop trust during the course of the business and hence can be seen as a validation criterion for remaining in the business. Validation criteria do not have to pertain to the suppliers alone. They could also pertain to the OEMs. Both parties can contribute their best in order to see that the final product is validated.

Specification–contract link

Contracts should help in assuring that the necessary steps to achieve the specifications will be taken by the suppliers and the OEMs. The specifications are an essential base before the contracts are to be signed because without the specifications, it would be hard, even impossible, to understand the expectations in terms of cost, quality, lead time, functional performance, and so on.

Specifications are subject to changes as the development projects proceed. However, the basic component or system concept needs to be explained to the supplier at the design outset, and the contract process can be helpful in doing that. Changes mean risks to both the buyer and the supplier.[6] If the suppliers are to enter into long-term relationships and become an integral part of the development team, then the risks should be shared (Asmus and Griffin, 1993). Contracts can confirm that suppliers estimate the number of change loops in the specifications, and quote a price accordingly. If there is a saving or increase in price, then it can be shared between the partners. However, with this technique the project estimates will go up initially.

The notion of autonomous or systematic technology[7] is important in the specification process. The current contracts in the auto and aircraft OEMs do not analyse this, however. If suppliers understand the technology that they are working with, then they will quote for jobs that can be carried out within their existing infrastructure of process technology and competence. This will lead to satisfaction within the suppliers, as they do not accept jobs that are beyond their capability.

The specifications normally outline several critical parameters such as materials, dimensions, product and process technology, testing procedures, and number of possible changes. Contracts could play an important role in checking that the suppliers understand these criteria. For example, a certain supplier knew that testing had to take place, but did not understand the importance of testing during the designated time period, which was winter. The supplier carried out tests during the autumn and was happy to be ahead of schedule. The result was that the components had to be re-tested in the right conditions, and this test revealed problems, leading to redesign and delay. Another example concerns the aircraft OEM, where only two prototypes can be built due to cost considerations. One prototype is used for destructive testing while the other is used for functional testing. The nature of the tests can be important and clarifying this to the suppliers as early as possible will allow the suppliers to build the prototypes with the right constituents[8] for the different tests.

Specification generation is interdependent between the buyer and supplier. There is a need for co-ordination and development of a common cognitive ground between the people involved (Karlson, 1994). This means that specifications cannot be simply handed down from the buyer to the supplier. Instead, a seminar could be arranged in order to discuss the issues in the specifications so that the concerned people can get together and discuss the alternatives and options. Contracts can state the conditions for these seminars and help in ensuring that both the buyer and the suppliers have understood the importance of having them. The seminars could be useful in articulating events that require the suppliers' physical presence.[9]

It was observed during the course of the interviews that benchmarking was an important requirement if the specifications were to take account of changing situations such as changes in the competitor offerings. Contracts can emphasise the importance of benchmarking both for the buyer and supplier. Furthermore, they could state how suppliers would deal with supply to several competing OEMs.

There are a number of messages from the above analysis. Getting feedback from each other (buyer–supplier) seems to be both a validation criterion for entry and a validation criterion for remaining in the business. If there is feedback from the early stages of the relationship, then development of trust can be facilitated. Understanding the tests, their nature, validity, and the right period to execute them appears to be an important criterion for remaining in the business. If there is poor understanding of the product at hand, then there are bound to be problems. This understanding could be extended to suppliers' physical presence on project platforms. In certain cases, the physical presence of the suppliers is required and the suppliers may have to promote this understanding at the early stages of the relationship. Having a separate project team for each of the OEMs with synergy effects[10] between them can be seen as an important criterion for entry into the business. This is because the suppliers will be able to devote adequate attention to the needs of the individual OEMs, which may be different. Benchmarking throughout the development process, and providing evidence of it at the outset and throughout the duration of the project will be necessary. Finally, the use of seminars to reflect on the specifications will be seen as a validation criterion for remaining in the business. This is because the development staff will be more willing to accept the specification as a working document rather than a document that is to be written just for the sake of writing it (Smith and Reinartsen, 1991).

Conclusions – the elements of a contract to validate the specifications

The above section has analysed the different types of contracts. The analysis indicated that the different contract categories can be split into validation criteria for entry – to be used before the supplier starts the project – and validation criteria for remaining in the business – to be used after the supplier starts working with the OEM (Table 8.5). The understanding of the two different types of criteria and the classification of the different contract categories into these different criteria appear to be important in order to validate the specifications. The criteria developed in Table 8.5 are the outcome of the analysis, the observation of the different contracts, and the interviews.

The two types of validation criteria must be separated, as suppliers can remain in the business and yet not deliver what they are asked for. The OEMs seemed to either ignore the difference between the validation criteria or did not pursue the two types of criteria with full vigour.

The checklist proposed in Table 8.5 is a set of issues that can be included in the contract to assist validation, thereby adding to the list of partnering activities, leading to satisfying results. The supplier can either be asked these questions during auditing, or they can be articulated by the supplier on his own. For example, both the OEM and the supplier can check whether suppliers' visions are present. Understanding the tests would mean deciding who should do what in the tests. This means that each validation parameter is discussed by the parties in the broadest sense.

Let us take an example to demonstrate this. The auto OEM engaged a telephone supplier to develop an integrated telephone for a new model. However,

Table 8.5 Validation criteria for entry and remaining in the business

ID	Parameter	Validation criteria for entry	Validation criteria for remaining in the business
1	Types	• Clear linkage between the contract and the types of suppliers	• Continuous input of clauses to prevent mistakes from reoccurring
2	Purpose	• Ability to reach agreements and feel comfortable with uncertain situations	• Increasing levels of quality • Increasing education and training
3	Responsibility	• Ability to make responsibilities clear from the beginning • Number of value-added questions asked • Demonstrating both internal and external commitment to the project/s	
4	Selection criteria	• Development of supplier visions • Understanding of the mission, culture and strategy (both OEM and the supplier) • Concern for environmental issues • Match between the project and the portfolio of projects	• Show strategic, tactical, interpersonal and operational integration as time passes
5	Legal issues		• Ability to understand and estimate legal, liability issues, etc. • Ability to work within a set that encompasses solutions, cost and changes
6	Communication	• Common information systems	• Timely dispatch of information such as budget release dates
7	Payments	• Clear proposal of when, how and the parameters on which the payment will be made • Getting feedback	• Getting regular feedback
8	Specifications	• Having separate project teams for the individual OEMs • Early benchmark report before the start of the project	• Understanding the tests, nature of the tests, etc. • Use of seminars to discuss the specifications • Benchmarking throughout the project

the protocols in the telephone change once every six months and the OEM was not aware of this. Since the auto OEM project was delayed, the protocols changed and thus the OEM had to remove the option of installing the integrated telephone. Using the strategic validation contract could have helped avoid this. For example, getting feedback as a validation criterion for entry, at the start of the business, would have meant clear articulation between the parties about the protocol life cycle and this could have helped the auto OEM to understand the relation between the change in the protocols and the length of delay of the models.

Let us now summarise the most significant learnings from the study:

1 Written contracts can be used to reach agreements on an ongoing basis in the specifications. Since a final product always is a compromise, agreements will have to be reached continuously and hence the contract can be seen as a vehicle that helps to reach these agreements, thus leading to good specifications.
2 If frequent or important gaps in the suppliers' performance occur, during the course of a project then the OEM may have to validate the supplier all over from the beginning, i.e., use the validation criteria for entry. This extends the limitations in the proposals by Cooper (1975), i.e. by developing clear validation criteria for specifications and also arguing for the suppliers who have a gap in their business dealings with an OEM. Entering and staying in a business are two separate issues.
3 The warranty issues can be traced and solved at the source. The issue of warranty payments to the customer may be decided from the beginning in the contract. In other words, matters that could be the cause of problems can be discussed and settled early enough. The warranty issues allow both the buyer and the supplier to check that the final customer is not dissatisfied in any way. The contract allows the validation in the sense that it decides the settlement of the claims if the specifications (the needs of the customer) are not satisfied. In effect, it can be concluded that the earlier the contract validates the understanding of the warranty issues, the better the chances are of customer satisfaction as the action to solve customer complaints is immediate.
4 Contracts provide an ideal setting for discussions on the specification. Different issues may be raised and discussed at this point. This allows both the buyer and supplier to understand the specifications, each other's capabilities and the resources needed to do the job. Every point needs to be checked. For example, if a supplier makes suggestions to the OEM about delivering a new seat, then the OEM will have to draw up a framework to check that the supplier performs as promised. It is not only validation of the product by the specifications, but also validation of the specifications that is important in outsourced product development. The earlier in the process the contract is used, the better the chances are that the specifications will be satisfied and the product will turn out as planned.

Notes

1 Evidence of this is slowly emerging from the automotive industry. See Buchholz (1997).
2 There is no rationale as to why there are different types of contracts and also the type of contract to be given to a particular supplier.
3 The managers from the auto OEM belonged to the purchasing, engineering, projects, R&D, legal and marketing departments. The managers from the supplier firms belonged to marketing, purchasing, engineering, R&D, projects departments, including the CEO of the firm.
4 This means in order to meet the rules and regulations of the different countries.
5 Odette is a communication system that identifies the protocols that have to be used between the buyer and the supplier, for example, the composition of a delivery schedule, invoices, etc.
6 The risks could be that more money is spent than initially estimated, the concept turns out to be very different at the later stages in the development and hence has to be started all over again, the project is scrapped, etc.
7 Autonomous technology does not require complementary investments in manufacturing or managerial processes, whereas systematic technology requires complementary investments.
8 Different prototype tests require a different level of ingredients or level of perfection. The early prototype tests do not require a high level of perfection as compared to the prototype tests conducted later in the process.
9 When the suppliers quote for the contract, they often do not do any intellectual work, i.e., asking questions of why, what, etc., about the parameters in the specification. For example, when a supplier quoted for door trims, he did not realise the temperature implications. This was because of their desire to get the contract at any cost. When the car was tested in a strategic Middle East country, where temperatures are extremely high, the door trims melted. This was because the supplier did not consider the impact of temperature. The supplier had to change the door trims, which implied a price increase for the auto OEM. The suppliers can easily misunderstand and underestimate the critical nature of activities unless they question the importance of each project with respect to the portfolio of projects that they are engaged in.
10 The project teams need to be dedicated to the individual OEMs but experiences, etc., can be shared.

9 Managing systems suppliers
An uphill task

Alliances and partnerships are commonly thought of as collaborative arrangements an organisation may have with its suppliers, but a systems supplier is another example of a collaborative arrangement that many supply managers may not be aware of but that is useful in their industry. Many firms, especially those in the automotive industry, state that they want all their suppliers to become systems suppliers without emphasising the requirements. The only explanation given to the suppliers is the need for strong technological contribution. The term 'systems suppliers' is synonymous with partner suppliers, a term widely used in the automotive industry. A wide range of suppliers from those delivering complex parts to those delivering simple components, call themselves 'systems suppliers', leading to confusion. In order to enable firms to distinguish and use the so-called 'systems suppliers', this chapter will attempt to map out why suppliers label themselves as systems suppliers and the requirements that could allow suppliers to function as systems suppliers. In doing this, we will propose the structural changes necessary in order to accommodate such systems suppliers. The conclusion highlights that systems suppliers supply one function as opposed to the supply of simple components or parts. We also identify mega-systems suppliers who produce more than one function. Identification of systems and mega-systems suppliers also reveals the need to classify the remaining suppliers that an OEM might engage with. This will also help in managing the supply base and tapping their capabilities to the fullest extent. Management of the different categories of suppliers was found to depend on the knowledge and importance of individual projects to suppliers.

Introduction

In spite of extensive research on the benefits of early supplier involvement in product development, little has been said about the use of the different categories of systems suppliers. This appears to be a disadvantage to many firms as they clamour for these systems suppliers. However, neither the suppliers nor the OEMs understand what the term actually means and the internal changes that are necessary in order to accommodate such suppliers.

158 *Managing systems suppliers*

Consider a global automotive OEM operating in the luxury segment in the process of building a new generation platform. The OEM has decided to engage a 'systems supplier' to develop and manufacture the key (mechanical and remote part) and has requested purchasing to solicit bids accordingly. Purchasing has requested suppliers to inform them if they were 'systems suppliers' along with the quotes to be submitted. Nearly all the suppliers indicated that they were systems suppliers and purchasing selected a particular supplier whose quote was the lowest. However, the supplier was a leader in the area of keys. After the selection process, the supplier was expected to develop and produce the key with help from the initial specifications given by engineering. Three months before the project completion date, road tests in the United States revealed that the key was faulty. It did not have the desired range to open the car remotely. Most importantly, the key could be accidentally put into the off position, which meant that the car could lose control. This surprised the OEM as they had expected the 'systems supplier' to deliver a key that would be functional since the supplier was the world's leading supplier of keys. Most importantly, other OEMs who were developing their keys through the same supplier had no problems. This led to several questions for the management: Why was the supplier called a systems supplier? What are the requirements on a systems supplier? Why were there problems especially when the supplier was a leading supplier?

The above questions require that the characteristics of the systems supplier be clearly articulated within a company in order to use the capabilities/capacities of the supplier to the fullest extent. The entire organisation will need to have the same view of the involvement of the supplier if the supplier contribution is to be realised, i.e., the organisation, as a whole, has to be ready to accept systems suppliers. Furthermore, the OEM needs to map the identified systems suppliers in the context of the total work that they engage in. We would like to explore characteristics of systems suppliers, draw a model of their involvement, and explore whey these leading edge systems suppliers create problems for OEMs.

Systems suppliers – constituents

Why do suppliers call themselves systems suppliers? The answers are displayed in Table 9.1. The reasons why suppliers considers themselves to be systems suppliers can be grouped into three categories: product range, product development responsibility and experience using the open coding technique (Table 9.2).

In the OEM, the complete system of the automobile has been split up into six sub-systems: electronics, electrical, chassis, body, engine and climate. The sub-systems have to work together if the car is to function. The sub-systems are made up of objects, which in turn are made up of components. The line of difference between an object and a component is very thin and depends on the individual firms. An object in a particular company may be considered a component in another firm. An object can be defined as a collection of components which are integrated together by a group of dedicated cross-functional people from marketing, purchasing, finance, production, after-sales, etc. For example, the sub-

Table 9.1 Why are you a systems supplier?

ID	Why are you a systems supplier?	% of suppliers answering
1	We design and supply ready systems	11
2	Complete transmission	2
3	We offer a full range of products	12
4	We develop and supply complete door sealing systems	1
5	Not enough capacity	16
6	Too small and cheap products	22
7	Today's business is systems driven	45
8	Responsible for the design, development and manufacture of a complete assembly system	1
9	Core products are of a control nature, integral to an automotive system	6
10	We supply chemicals for surface treatment	2
11	We are doing antennas and a system would mean the whole audio chain	6
12	We develop and produce in house	2
13	We develop steering gears with the understanding of the whole system and its application to the vehicle	5
14	We produce parts which are vital to systems but require very detailed work to manufacture	4
15	We supply complete systems and modules consisting of up to 70 single components and take over responsibility of the product as a whole regarding functionality	10
16	We are able to develop, produce and assemble complete systems due to long experience	4

Table 9.2 Categorisation of reasons

Category	Reasons
Product range	1, 3, 4, 5, 6, 11, 12
Product development responsibility	2, 5, 7, 8, 11, 12, 13, 15, 16
Experience	7, 12, 13, 16

system electronics contains the following objects: audio or entertainment system, telephone, main instrument panel, side instrument panel, etc. The object audio system will contain the radio, amplifiers, loudspeakers, antennas, CD changer, etc. The total number of objects will be decided by the resources, time, etc. that a company can afford.

The OEM also uses the term *expert supplier*. An expert supplier could be a RDS (radio data system) software supplier. The RDS is used in the radio and manages the radio stations and takes care of traffic information. The RDS supplier can get the entire radio object or the electronics sub system, feed the RDS to the computer, test it and then dispatch it to the OEM. However, there are other possibilities, as we will observe later.

The reason why many different suppliers call themselves systems suppliers is because they have been told to do so by auto OEM. The explanation provided by some suppliers justifies this as they were told that the auto business is systems driven. There is a lot of confusion within both the OEM and the suppliers as to what a system, component, object, etc., actually mean. This is obvious from the questionnaire study and the interviews in the OEM firm. In order to develop ideas and identify factors in the so-called 'systems supplier', the following discussions will assume that systems is a function that needs to be satisfied which also corroborates Lamming's (1993) discussion. Let us examine the various parameters.

Range of products

The system supplier may be required to supply a full line of products ranging from simple amplifiers, on one hand, to complex amplifiers, on the other. This means that the systems supplier needs to be financially stable. This in turn will affect their ability to test/define/experiment with a number of different solutions. The systems suppliers should be able to develop and deliver concepts suited to the budget and the technological expectations of the OEM. The supplier could deliver ready functions. Simple components do not qualify to be considered as the domain of systems suppliers. They do not have to produce all the objects for the system but need to carry out assembly and testing under their supervision. A system supplier can have a value chain approach for the system that is being delivered to the OEM and also focus on core products. Cheap and small products do not qualify to be a system.

The approach of the systems supplier suggests the need for a number of minor gate checks instead of a few major gates in the development process. Hence, the product throughput is monitored on a continuous basis. A modularised architecture combined with parallel sourcing can be utilised so that the dependency on the suppliers is reduced to some extent and the customers' wishes are always satisfied. The interfaces between the different systems suppliers need to be made clear. For example, if there are problems between the different systems suppliers, one of them will have to take the responsibility for solving the problems. Some parts of the car may be core to the OEM and cannot be given to the systems suppliers, for example, the interface to the driver. Hence, these items may be retained in-house and outsourced after the design has been finalised. It is important to understand the life of the different items that are being delivered by the systems supplier, as shown in Table 9.3.

A modularised architecture can be applied to the long and medium life span items while short life span items cannot benefit from it. The systems suppliers will have to identify the object life cycles, identify static and dynamic technologies and work accordingly. When discussing the range of products it must be understood that the OEM firm can exercise different degrees of control over the systems supplier, which will depend on the following:

Table 9.3 Life span of items in the car

Duration	Life span		
	Long life span	Medium life span	Short life span
6–8 years	Chassis, interior		
2–3 years		On board computer, microprocessor	
2–8 months			Telephones, specialised software

- the technical functionality of the system/object;
- the material properties of the system/object;
- the interfacing qualities of the system/object.

The first point concerns the product technology in terms of the function of the system. If a system/object represents the core technology in a system, i.e. its performance is directly visible to the final user, the automobile manufacturer will explicitly maintain a direct relationship.

The second point deals with product technology in terms of the material. The use of new materials often leads to a complete reconfiguration of a product's functional performance and the production process. This, in turn, affects the product and process technologies of related system/objects. Moreover, the potential for innovation is often important when new materials are used. These factors taken together lead the OEM to preserve direct design relationships with suppliers responsible for components where material and/or process technology often changes. A typical example is technical plastic components.

The third case is where the OEM would like to preserve a direct influence over the design. This includes systems/objects that have important interface elements between several parts of a system. Without direct contact and integrated development with suppliers of interface elements, there is a risk of increased co-ordination cost in product development.

Product development responsibility

The systems supplier would be required to carry out the design, development and manufacture of entire systems. In addition, the supplier may have to take over all the responsibilities associated with the system such as ensuring that the functionality is fulfilled, testing is complete, etc. There are three different ways in which the systems supplier can work with the OEM and should be prepared to manage any of these three situations. Hence, parallel to a typology based on different kind of suppliers (e.g. Lamming, 1993), it is relevant to define a typology relative to different customer relationships with one and the same supplier.

In the first case, the systems supplier (Sys) is a first-tier supplier without interchange of intelligence. In this case the auto OEM keeps the design of system X vertically integrated, and buys a function Y 'off-the-shelf' from supplier Sys. The best example of a direct arm's length situation could be when an evaporator unit (an object within the climate system) is purchased. It can be used by the OEM and does not require any transfer of knowledge or intelligence. However, in cases where intelligence is not transferred, the OEM may become overly dependent on the supplier and be forced to run to the supplier every time a problem occurs.

In the second case, the systems supplier (Sys) is a direct supplier in terms of development intelligence, as the system X is designed via close collaboration between the auto OEM, the expert supplier and Sys. This practice, which was found to be very common in reality, but is not often discussed in theory, can be called *triangulation*. It is mentioned by Lamming (1993) who illustrates it with a door lock supplier who designs and develops the components in close cooperation with the assembler but delivers to a first-tier door supplier. This direct contact is crucial for any supplier that wants to remain a systems supplier. The best example of this category would be the electronics unit. The entire unit can be given to the RDS supplier who can then test the RDS technology and prove that the entire system works in cohesion.

In the final case the systems supplier is a first-tier supplier in terms of both physical supply and development intelligence for parts of a system X, that is not yet integrated by system suppliers. In opposition to triangulation, this situation might comprise substantial competition between *complementary systems suppliers* in terms of tier position. These are two or more suppliers who directly provide the automobile manufacturer with functions that are technically interdependent, but where this interdependency is managed by the car maker. The best example of this type could be in competitive areas of the car, i.e. areas the OEM wants to retain in-house, for example, the interior can be outsourced while the OEM can provide the comfort validation for the seat in-house.

Experience

The supplier must have had a long experience in the industry. This experience will be necessary to ask questions about the whole system and its interfaces with the other systems. A systems supplier cannot exist without several years experience in the industry. Longevity in experience will lead to sufficient capacity planning to ensure that there is sufficient capacity to build systems. Lack of capacity may hinder a supplier from becoming a systems supplier.

The OEM cannot afford to have too many people working for the outsourced system when it has a system supplier. This could lead to over-managing the suppliers. The people in the OEM should concentrate on functionality and interfaces and not details, which should be the systems supplier's domain of responsibility. If there are many people working at the OEM for a system that is outsourced, then most of these people need to be transferred to the supplier so that they can work there. The system supplier also needs to take this into account before bidding for a systems contract. A systems supplier can use multiple sub-systems suppliers, thus making a systems supplier network.

Experience is an important concern in product development projects. Often, in large supplier companies, experience is vested in one or two persons and if these people leave, then things go haywire. The systems supplier must ensure that the necessary experience is retained either through exciting intrinsic and extrinsic rewards or good information systems.

Systems supplier – the requirements

The term 'systems supplier' needs to be applied with caution. Not every supplier can qualify as a systems supplier. Systems suppliers are knowledge suppliers with the ability, capacity and capability to satisfy the needs of the OEM firms (Figure 9.1).

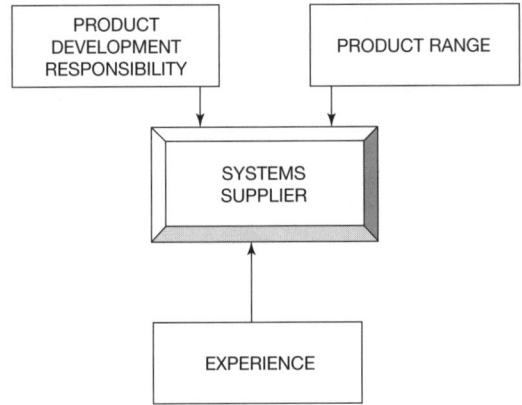

Figure 9.1 The systems supplier framework

A systems supplier does not necessarily have to supply systems but can also supply different objects within a system in OEM-classified competitive areas. A system supplier to a particular OEM does not automatically classify the supplier as a systems supplier to other OEMs.

All the systems suppliers can be further categorised into systems suppliers for development and systems suppliers for production. While systems suppliers for development do the actual systems development with a number of components, the systems suppliers for production actually integrate different systems/components for production. For example, a parking sensor can be developed by a systems developer or be integrated into the bumper of a car by a systems supplier for production. A systems supplier who qualifies as a developer and a systems production supplier would be a true systems supplier.

The mega-systems supplier integrates several different functions together. The systems supplier may also provide integration ideas for assembly to the mega-systems supplier who is then responsible for not only product engineering, but also process engineering.

164 *Managing systems suppliers*

Table 9.4 Different types of supplier

Supplier	Example
Mega-systems supplier	Provides an integration of more than one function and is involved in process engineering as well. For example, the entire electronics function, HVAC function etc. Works on more than five concepts at any given point in time.
Systems/ partner supplier	Works on more than five concepts simultaneously in order to satisfy a function and allows OEMs to choose from them and provides mass customisation to the firms along with process engineering for that function.
Late start/ mature supplier	The supplier starts late and thus waits for critical specifications from the OEM before commencing work. May have to provide mass customisation for all subsequent carry-overs, model year changes, future models, etc.
Labourer/ child supplier	Works on detailed specifications. Cannot contribute to the improvement of specifications. No transfer of knowledge.
Contractual supplier	Supplies parts from a catalogue. There is no customisation and parts are standard. One can purchase only from the catalogue. For example screwdrivers etc.
Indirect suppliers	These suppliers deliver items that are not directly associated with the end product or service such as advertising, overheads, human resources, and technology expenses.
Process system supplier	Supplies integrative systems to the OEM as far as process equipment is concerned. For example the assembly to fix and bolt the tyres on the car in assembly.
Process contractual supplier	Supplies all process-standardised equipment, i.e. equipment that can be used in any auto OEM.

Eight layers of suppliers that an OEM could deal with were identified. It appears that OEMs have to reduce the supplier base, using more of the capabilities of the supplier and concentrating on overall integration and core areas in the car (depends on individual OEM firms). Table 9.4 helps us to differentiate between the different layers of suppliers and their responsibilities in the product development process.

Model of systems supplier and lessons

Figure 9.2 is an understanding of the way the identified suppliers can be employed. The OEM firm deals with mega-systems suppliers who are responsible for the integration of more than one function in areas such as power train, chassis, etc. The interface with the mega-systems suppliers can be cushioned by the packaging people and the total integration area people in the OEM firm. The risk with such a system is that if one supplier fails, the whole system may collapse. So there will be emphasis on joint responsibility. The expert suppliers in this example are the wire harness supplier, the ABS supplier and the engine management supplier.

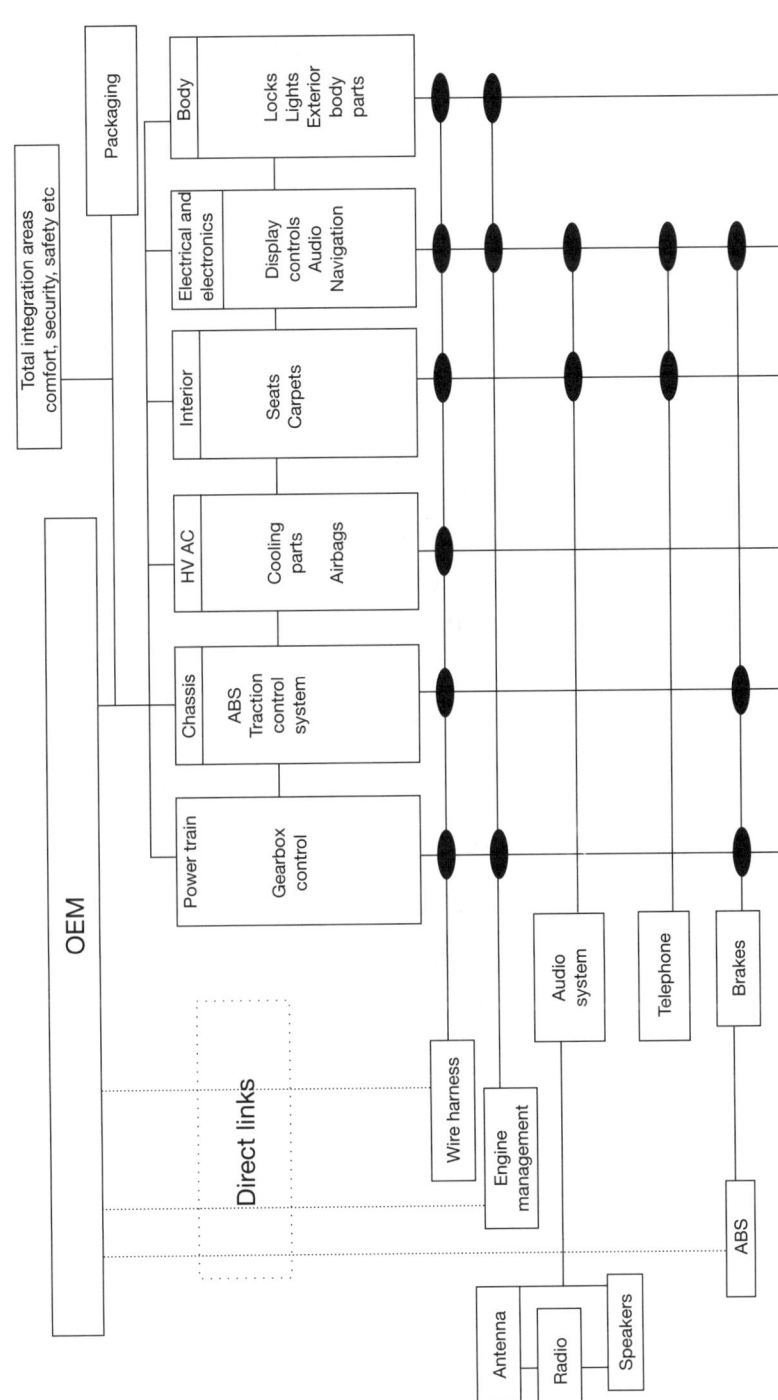

Figure 9.2 The mega-systems approach

The OEM has direct links with these suppliers in order to develop their competencies and to keep in touch with the technologies that the product will be using.

The system suppliers in Figure 9.2 are the telephone and the audio system supplier as they satisfy a function. The audio function system supplier deals with the radio supplier, antenna supplier and the speaker supplier. This function is satisfied by interfacing with the mega-systems suppliers of electrical/electronics, and the interior supplier. There are many checkpoints in this shared destiny relationship. The systems supplier will have to check the function. Next, the mega-systems supplier will check all the functions in his/her domain. Also, there will be a check between all the mega-systems suppliers for overall functionality. Finally, the OEM will check the overall integration along with the mega-systems suppliers and the packaging/total integration departments. It is recognised that there are certain areas that will cut across all the different mega-system units and these will then be dealt at the overall integration level.

Invariably, the system moves from a push (where the OEM creates all the specifications and gives it to the suppliers) to a pull system (where the suppliers generate the specifications as and when required). This model will actually mean a reduction in the number of suppliers. Clear visibility means easier control. Depending upon the option of product development responsibility, the OEM may have direct links, for example, with suppliers other than the systems supplier such as the wire harnesses supplier. In summary, it is to be noted that the system supplier delivers a product range when required by the OEM and that can involve a collection of objects and not components. In spite of all the required characteristics of systems suppliers, many of them have created numerous problems for the case study company. This led us to believe that the requirements placed on the systems suppliers were not sufficient. Further investigation revealed that the systems suppliers were acting as systems suppliers to several other OEMs as well than the case study OEM.

Systems suppliers – are they self-sufficient?

The suppliers can be treated according to the importance of the project to them in terms of turnover, innovation, etc., on one hand, and the amount of knowledge that they possess, on the other. This is summarised in Figure 9.3.

If the knowledge and the importance of the project to the supplier are high, then there can be an atmosphere of trust and regular checks made at major gates in the product development process. Mega-systems suppliers and systems suppliers come under this category. The supplier can be trusted to do the job as the project is important. If the knowledge is low and the importance is high, then detailed specifications could be provided to the suppliers. If the knowledge and the importance of the project to the supplier are low, then the supplier may be allowed to deal only with contractual products. Finally, if the knowledge is high and the importance is low, there may be excessive control with major checks at a number of minor gates. In other words, policeman techniques may be used.

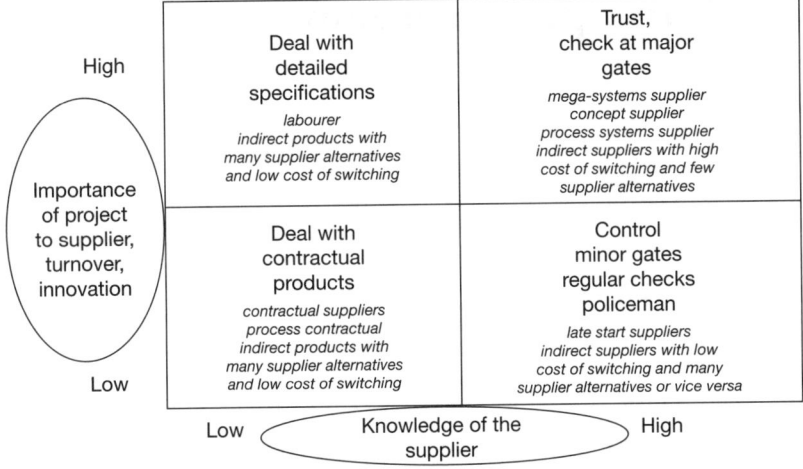

Figure 9.3 The supplier–knowledge importance link

The concept of systems suppliers is not limited to manufacturing industries alone. It can be applied to non-manufacturing industries such as banks or hospitals. A bank could have one mega-systems supplier to handle all their incoming and outgoing mail. The mega-systems supplier can then have a number of systems suppliers. One systems supplier may look after courier mail, registered mail, and express mail in the outgoing mail section, while another systems supplier might look after the delivery by departmental function in the incoming mail section. These systems suppliers can be interfaced with a number of specialised suppliers such as those handling franking, special stamps, duty stamps, etc. Overall, the concept of systems suppliers has value both in the manufacturing and non-manufacturing sectors.

There are certain important lessons from this study, which was described as a part of the learning process when implementing this approach in the case study firm:

- Use the term 'systems suppliers' with caution.
- The term 'systems supplier' encompasses not only design but also production.
- Systems suppliers can be developed for each and every business/OEM, etc., through a period of gestation.
- A systems supplier may supply many objects within a system but that does not qualify them to be called a component supplier.
- Make responsibility levels between the systems suppliers as clear as possible.
- Allow expert suppliers to have direct contact with OEM firms so that the experts can test the product before dispatch to the OEM.
- The mega-systems, systems and concept supplier could belong to the same industry for easy understanding of each other's requirements.

10 Digital procurement

Digital procurement or e-buying is the current trend in buyer–supplier relations. In other words, a number of commodities and/or complex components can be bought online rather than through face-to-face negotiations. All negotiations are carried out through digital means. Consider the following: a leading software producer in Europe is sourcing A4 paper from a variety of sources. These sources are country-specific as this software producer has offices in many different countries within Europe. They are approached by a firm to conduct an online auction (ask suppliers to bid online) for A4 paper. The online auction meant that the software firm had to consolidate all its A4 requirements on a Europe-wide level. They observed that they were buying many grades and some were only for 1000 sheets. They immediately discontinued the grades, which were of small quantity and conducted the auction for the larger grades. They obtained large reductions in the price on the A4 paper requirements as suppliers were quoting for larger orders and furthermore smaller suppliers who would normally not have quoted to such large corporations were quoting as well. The A4 paper is an example of an indirect material but that does not mean that only indirect materials can be procured online. Direct materials such as steel can be procured online through auction houses such as e-steel (the auctions are not conducted in real time like the A4 paper). Irrespective of whether direct or indirect materials are procured there is a need to link it with the internal systems such as (MRP). In this way, the information will be consolidated so that the information to and from the suppliers through the digital process will be visible. Online auction and the linking of the online auction to the internal systems like MRP form the constituents of the digital procurement process. Companies can either decide to outsource one or the other components or do it completely on their own. Based on practice, existing surveys and interviews we will attempt to give the reader a total picture of digital procurement with special reference to the automotive industry in this chapter. Finally, we will describe a case study on digitalisation.

Types of digital procurement

E-business is currently considered one of the most promising drivers for change in the automotive industry, and in particular in its value added chain from R&D and design to the final customer. According to the most enthusiastic observers, it will completely revolutionise the system. Schlott (2000) compares the Internet revolution to the fashion for just-in-time and lean philosophies in the early 1990s. For the most cautious, it will simply be one more supply and sales channel in addition to the already existing and more traditional ones (Licoppe, 2000). According to Lamm (2000), the Internet is not creating a frontal competition with the 'old' system, but is adding a new tool, which is challenging it and requiring its complete reshaping. From an academic point of view, in-depth research is still to be conducted in order to establish some more stable models before any robust managerial recommendations can be formulated.

E-business is concerned with three different channels:

- business-to-business (B2B) between OEMs and their suppliers and between first-tier and second-tier suppliers;
- business-to-business between OEMs and their dealers and other distributors;
- business to customers (B2C) between OEMs and distribution networks and their final customers.

This chapter deals only with the first category, i.e. e-supply. However, companies can only benefit if they are able to link all three different channels together.

The digital scenario

E-commerce is still emerging and at an unexpected speed.[1] Market research shows that e-B2B is growing much faster than e-B2C. Forrester Research reports that 75 per cent of spending through the Internet results from the business-to-business segment and predicts that it will represent total purchases of US$183bn by 2001 (Mann, 1999). The total B2B e-commerce in the USA is estimated at US$2,700bn by 2004, of which 53 per cent will flow through e-marketplaces (Forrester website – Table 10.1).[2]

Wolffe *et al.* (2000) estimate that 900 online exchange systems will be established in the very near future. Deloitte Consulting (Sengès, 2000) predicted that by the end of 2000, 91 per cent of North American corporations would have bought through the Internet against 31 per cent in May 2000, however, Kleinbard (2000) demonstrates that out of 620 B2B websites, only 10 per cent were active, i.e., processing real transactions, in May 2000.

Huge online B2B marketplaces are on their way. Within the automotive industry, there are Covisint, under the leadership of the major OEMs (Ford, GM, DaimlerChrysler, Renault, Nissan and Toyota), and Rubbernetwork in the tyre industry. Electricity power suppliers and steel companies (MetalSite) are also struggling to organise themselves into integrated online exchange systems (Wolffe, *et al.* 2000). The rapid interest in B2B has been prompted by the wide variety of tasks that can be performed online.

170 *Digital procurement*

Table 10.1 Websites for information on digital trade

B2B information sites

Research organisations
Gartner Group: http://www.gartner.com
Taylor Nelson Sofres Intersearch Corporation: http://www.intersearchcorp.com
Forrester Research: http://www.forrester.com
Keenan Vision: http://www.keenanvision.com
Roland Berger & Partners: http://www.rolandberger.com/
Roland Berger Research: http://www.rb-research.de
Forit Internet Business Research: http://www.forit.de

B2B companies
Alliance e-marketplace: http:// www.ibm-i2-ariba.com
Ariba: http://www.ariba.com
i2 Technologies: http://www.i2.com
Trade-match: http://www.trade-match.com
Oracle: http://www.oracle.com and oracleexchange.com
FreeMarkets: http://www.freemarkets.com and www.imark.com and www.b2bexplorer.com
IBM: http://www.ibm.com
Commerce One: http://www.commerceone.com
Covisint: http://www.covisint.com
Vertical Net: http://www.verticalnet.com
Thru-put: http://www.thru-put.com
SAP: http://www.sap.com
Business Objects://www.businessobjects.com
Siebel: http://www.siebel.com
Informix: http://www.informix.com
Vignette: http://www.vigentte.com

Product-specific sites
Steel: http://www.esteel.com and http://metalsite.com
Power, Electricity and Gaz: http://pantellos.com
Chemicals, plastics: http://Chemconnect.com

Support services
Big Step: http://bigstep.com
Smart Age: http://smartage.com

Potential purchasing tasks online

Many different tasks could be performed through the Internet but only a few systems, such as IBM *Websphere* and Oracle *E-Business Suite* offer a wide choice of operations. The potential purchasing-related tasks to be performed online are:

- Auction/bidding
- Online price quoting
- Production specification/information
- Order management and tracking follow-up
- Invoicing and accounting
- Inventory and surplus management

- Project management and meeting planning
- Real-time purchasing accounting
- On-line early warning of quality and logistics problems
- Budgeting, planning and scheduling
- Marketing and business intelligence
- Human resources management and payroll
- Training
- Data interchange

One of the key advantages of e-commerce is indeed to manage all services related to purchasing such as quality, warranty, inventory, deliveries, invoicing, etc. Therefore, the development of e-B2B is likely to lead to a decrease in the usage of Electronic Data Interchange (EDI), if not simply to a complete replacement of EDI by the Internet.

The potential market for e-B2B in the automotive value chain is associated with the nature of the purchased goods such as commodities, services, sub-systems and modules ready to be assembled on the vehicle, etc. It is very likely that the more generic the good and its costing structure, the more it could be traded by digital means. This is because the face-to-face contact and the chances for discussion of the product are minimised. Additionally, the more specific the product, the less the chances of it being digitally traded. Thus far, some companies are already using the Internet to auction raw materials, temporary jobs, maintenance and security jobs, computers, software, electrical equipment for building, energy, etc.

Some recent anecdotes regarding the use of digital procurement are illuminating:

- On 11 February 2000, Commerce One, a leading actor in global e-commerce solutions for business, successfully conducted with GM and Isuzu an Internet-based bid-quote purchasing decision (or reverse auction – where prices can only drop) for direct material supplies on GM TradeXchange website. The transaction was the auto industry's largest ever to be conducted entirely over the Internet. The purchasing decision enabled GM and its partner Isuzu, to buy a large volume of rubber sealing packages for vehicle production in both Europe and North America at a cost of US$147 million. The final price represented significant savings over traditional procurement processes. Eighteen qualified suppliers participated in the bid-quote process, and four suppliers were selected in the final analysis, each receiving a portion of the order. Suppliers were qualified and selected based on four criteria: quality, service, technology and price.
- On 17 May 2000, Ford and e-STEEL, the leading negotiation-based e-commerce exchange for the global steel industry, signed an agreement to 'e-enable' complex procurement programmes with the OEM's global first-tier suppliers. Approximately 4.5 million tons of steel and steel-related products will be purchased via e-STEEL for metal stamping suppliers over

the course of this contract. The scope of the alliance covers the OEM's steel order fulfilment processing, claims, financial controls, and audit reporting throughout its global manufacturing and assembly operations.
- In March 2000, Lear Corporation globally organised a reverse auction for fasteners with twelve pre-selected potential suppliers. All suppliers gradually decreased their price with some stopping when they had reached their limits. The maximum discount was about 30 per cent of the initial pricing. According to one of the suppliers, the cheapest offer was far below the cost of materials. But Lear did not grant the order online to the best bidder. Its buyers came back to their traditional French supplier who had offered online a discount of 10 per cent re-introducing quality, service and technology in the selection criteria. This raises questions as to whether the reverse auction was organised for business intelligence purposes or in order to force the traditional suppliers to decrease their price more than was contractually decided (3 per cent minimum per year)?

B2B implementation strategies

There are four strategies that can be taken by manufacturers as follows:

1   *An aggressive position by forming a joint venture with several OEMs and suppliers*: GM, Ford and DaimlerChrysler have set up *Covisint*, a single giant trade exchange platform, and Renault and Toyota revealed that they will or might follow suit. Such an Internet-based portal will allow suppliers to bid for contracts and OEMs to select suppliers online. The system will streamline the whole supply chain process, including procurement, planning and scheduling, manufacturing and logistics for both sides of the transaction. Initially, the three founders were expecting that the system would handle US$50bn by the end of 2000. But the development has been longer than expected, causing serious delay. The first categories to be transferred would be components bought by auctions and catalogue purchases. Delphi Automotive, Magna International Bethlehem Steel and Compaq Computer were the very first to agree to sell and buy over the exchange system. The total potential turnover is evaluated at more than US$500bn.

    Through mergers and acquisitions, the system might be joined by Mazda, Volvo, Jaguar, Land Rover and perhaps Daewoo (through Ford), Fiat, Suzuki, Isuzu and Subaru (through GM), Nissan (through Renault), Mitsubishi and perhaps Hyundai and Kia (through DaimlerChrysler). Such a move is seen as a major shift in mergers and acquisitions strategies by Silverman (2000). Instead of full-blown mergers and acquisitions, corporations are integrating operations through '*co-opetition*', i.e. starting shared Internet marketplaces for e-B2B while stopping short of other corporate links.

    Some partners are also simultaneously playing different strategies: for instance, DaimlerChrysler has opened a web-based purchasing site for all of its 4500 dealers (Chrysler, Jeep, Dodge) and expects to save US$500 per vehicle sold. It has set up a holding for all Internet-related activities: DCX NET with Euro550m. It has a significant share in PowerWay Inc. for B2B and Cobalt Group for B2C.

2 *A defensive strategy by implementing a specific platform open to additional partners (OEMs and suppliers)*: This is the choice made by BMW. Wilhelm Becker, senior Vice President of purchasing at BMW, states that BMW has not joined *Covisint* because it is perceived as a US-controlled network that could jeopardise industrial secrets of its members. Bosch and Siemens are currently said to be reviewing the offer.
3 *A mixed orientation by setting up a stand-alone solution*: Volkswagen Group decided to set up its own online component sourcing network on the basis of its unwillingness to share its secrets with its competitors (Bursa, 2000) and using its already existing electronic network integrating one-third of its suppliers (Roland Berger and Partners, 2000).
4 *A wait-and-see position*: Some OEMs like Toyota, PSA and Honda are still hesitating and reviewing their positions. One of their main arguments is that e-B2B is quite incompatible with long-term partnership and the need for personal and face-to-face negotiation within the purchasing relationship.[3]

On the other hand, some marginal OEMs like Tata and Autovaz are not in a position to invest significantly in e-business due to their current financial situation. They are likely to join one of the existing platforms or to be taken over by a bigger competitor and then forced to follow its example.

Digital infrastructure providers

FreeMarkets' B2B eMarketplace is one of the leading B2B auction sites with 500 employees and US$2.7bn of purchase orders in 1999, which saved buyers an estimated 2 to 25 per cent.[4] The auction orders for the automotive industry were estimated at US$210m in 1999: springs, fuel system valves, master cylinders, steel blanked gauges, rubber moulded components, printed circuit boards, decorative plastics, cold-headed components, actuators and sensors, die castings, plastic components, filtration mesh, ferrous metal stamped components, copper and brass coils, electric power and temporary labour. By mid-2000, FreeMarkets was claiming 4,000 registered suppliers and within the automotive industry its current customers are Visteon, Delphi, Eaton and Navistar. FreeMarkets includes online auctions, asset recovery services, online surplus asset trade, global database of suppliers, supplier research and call centre support in thirty languages.

Imark, a subsidiary of FreeMarkets, is proposing fifteen families of products: interior and exterior accessories and body parts; brake systems; chassis and frame; drive-train; electrical devices; emission components; engine parts; exhaust; fuel system; glass; tyres and wheels; transmission. But only three such as battery cables have available inventories and only for the replacement market.

By its nature, this segment of the new value chain is very unstable. Dozens of new B2B start-ups are created every month all over the world. Gartner Group estimates that 10,000 electronic trading exchanges using the Internet will deal with US$438bn annual transactions by 2002.

These small start-ups of the so-called new economy are still insignificant and most of the time in deficit despite some remarkable performances on the NASDAQ. Big players such as IBM with its *websphere* technology, Oracle involved in AutoXchange and Microsoft with *Biztalk* are also looking carefully into e-commerce.[5] Consolidation is also already on its way in the e-supply business: FreeMarkets acquired iMark; i2 Technologies merged with Aspect Development for US$9.3bn in March 2000. As far as industrial organisation is concerned, this will give a considerably modified shape to the automotive industry.

In practice, it is quite difficult to identify a 'dominant design' in the emerging organisation of automotive-related e-B2B. Some OEMs and leading global suppliers are simultaneously involved in different groupings (Table 10.2). Given that there is no 'dominant design' in the emerging digital organisation, there are four alternative strategies that firms can pursue when thinking about the digital infrastructure.

Alternative strategies

Research and in-depth observations show that there are four different strategies for the OEMs and the suppliers within the automotive supply chain in dealing with e-B2B:

1   In-house e-B2B solutions with the support of software companies, for example, Oracle.
2   Partial outsourcing of digital procurement through Application Service Providers (ASPs) such as SAP or Oracle.
3   E-commerce solution integrators, such as the alliance IBM-I2-Ariba. In this case there is total outsourcing of the digital procurement function.
4   Out-of-the-Box Vertical Market Solutions, or vertical portals.[6] E-steel is an example of a vertical portal as they link only steel mills and steel users together.

A complex rationale

Most academic literature about e-B2B is based on transaction costs economic theory. Saving such costs related to the organisation and fulfilment of value chain transactions would be considered the main rationale. In organisational behaviour theory, the main concept is '*disintermediation*', meaning that one of the key aims is to reduce the number of intermediary bodies, in other words, to simplify the supply chain.

From in-depth observations, it appears that the important reasons for engaging in e-B2B are reducing operating costs, satisfying OEMs' requirements and improving competitive advantages. But according to the Arthur Andersen survey (Miller, 1999), only 16 per cent of suppliers identified revenue growth. Nearly 50

Table 10.2 Existing e-B2B organisations

e-B2B suppliers	Customers in the automotive industry	Potential turnover
Covisint	GM, FORD, DAIMLERCHRYSLER	US$250bn
Oracle and Commerce One	RENAULT, NISSAN, TOYOTA	Renault: FFR110bn
	MERITOR, JOHNSON CONTROLS, FEDERAL MOGUL, DELPHI, MAGNA, BOSCH, YASAKI, LEAR CORPORATION, BETHLEHEM STEEL, AUTOLIV	
Fast Buyer-AT Kearney-	40 Tier 1,2 or 3 Selected Suppliers for Profit Sharing	
Ernst & Young-Oracle-ITS (Fiat)	Total Expected Turnover	US$750bn
	FIAT	
AutoXchange-Oracle FORD	FORD, HANKOOK TIRE, HALLA CLIMATE CONTROL, PYUNG HWA	US$300bn
TradeXchange-Commerce One	GENERAL MOTORS	US$87bn
GENERAL MOTORS		
FreeMarkets	DELPHI, VISTEON, EATON, NAVISTAR	
Trade-Match	VALEO	
Yet to be named	VALEO, DELPHI, EATON, TRW, MOTOROLA, DANA	
Yet to be named SAP	BOSCH, CONTINENTAL, ZF, INA WÄLZLAGER SCHAEFFLER	
Ariba, IBM	VOLKSWAGEN, DANA, BMW, HONDA OF AMERICA, VOLVO TRUCKS, CUMMINS, VISTEON, DUPONT	VW: US$49bn
i2 Technologies – iStarXchange	TOYOTA	
RubberNetwork.com	MICHELIN, GOODYEAR, CONTINENTAL, PIRELLI, COOPER, SUMITOMO RUBBER[1]	Spare parts in the US > US$60bn
Commerce One	JOHNSON CONTROLS, SIEMENS, MITSUBISHI CORPORATION SUPPLIERS	
EuroAutoSupplier AT Kearney		
Steel24-7 (sales) BuyFor	USINOR, ARBED, CORUS, THYSSENKRUPP	
Metals (purchasing)		
Siebel Systems	DAIMLERCHRYSLER, FORD, ROCKWELL, MOTOROLA	
FreeMarkets	EATON, DELPHI, VISTEON, NAVISTAR	
Vignette	DAIMLERCHRYSLER	
Manugistics Group	DANA, GOODYEAR, MITSUBISHI MOTORS, PACCAR, TENNECO	

Sources: Websites; press cuttings.

Note: Bridgestone left the consortium on 28 August 2000.

Table 10.3 Risks and benefits of e-B2B

Benefits	Risks
Savings in procurement costs such as administration of transactions and operations	Downward pressure on prices
Direct revenues from the exchange system through commissions, transaction fees and service fees	Increasing cost of IT
Savings in design costs through standardisation	Standardisation as opposed to customisation and variety
Savings through a reduced number of tiers in the supply chain	Breaking the anti-trust regulations
Promoting and leveraging supplier efficiency	Expanding the supply base
Optimising purchasing processes	Missing the world-class supplier
Transparency over supplier base	Increasing risk of lost corporate secrets
Satisfying the OEMs request	

per cent indicated that they did not know the expected payback of their e-business investments; 25 per cent were hoping to get a one-year payback period and 25 per cent a one-to-four year time frame.

The costs and benefits of e-purchasing are shown in Table 10.3. It could be noted that information security is the major concern of most of the players using the portals. For example, if it becomes public knowledge that a particular OEM gets A4 paper at a certain price, then the other OEMs will want to get A4 paper at the same price thereby, minimising the competitive advantage that could have been gained by the OEM benefiting from the original price reduction. Further, OEMs may ask that the portals do specialised work just for them but this will be at a price premium which many OEMs will not be willing to or cannot afford.

The available data on the benefits (Table 10.3) of e-procurement vary from one source to another source. Commerce One believes that it could save 5 to 10 per cent in material cost. AT Kearney set a target of realising US$10bn in savings by applying e-commerce initiatives to the European supplier sector (Table 10.4).

According to Tait (2000), most analysts emphasise that benefits are more in process than in direct procurement costs:

- faster cycle: according to Aberdeen Group (1999, 2000), huge benefits are in reducing the purchase and fulfilment cycles from 7.3 to 2 days;
- reduced inventory: Aberdeen Group estimates from 25 up to 50 per cent;
- standardised communication between participants within the supply chain;
- reduced working capital;
- faster overall production cycle.

However, as quoted by Tait (2000), Doughty from Cap Gemini admitted that those benefits will take several years to be fully realised. Above all, it seems that sharing information with existing and potential partners and improving customer service are likely to be the most immediate advantages. According to a survey by

Table 10.4 Released savings thanks to e-business

Company	Savings on materials	Savings on administration costs	Total savings	Source
Deutsche Bank	n.d	n.d	US$ 1,188 per car	FT, 20/06/2000
Commerce One	5–10% up to 20%	80%		Website, May 2000
Covisint	n.d	n.d	15% on a US$ 20,000 car	Geneva Motor Show, March 2000
Oracle	n.d	n.d	20% or more	Oracle (1999)
GlobalNet Xchange	n.d		20–40%	Nairn (2000)
Taylor Nelson Sofres Intersearch	n.d	45%		Baum (1999)
Aberdeen Group	5–10%	n.d	Up to 30%	Aberdeen Group (1999a), (2000)
Fast Buyer (Fiat)	n.d	n.d	Up to 50%	n.d

Sources: Web Sites; company's documentation.

Ernst & Young reported by *Industry Week*,[7] such benefits have been considered as 'major' by more than 40 per cent of questioned enterprises.[8]

Hypotheses about major trends

Five major trends can be hypothesised regarding the involvement/commitment to develop and control e-B2B as strongly positively correlated with the following:

- *Its level of globalisation for direct operations, i.e. mainly design, manufacturing and purchasing*
  The more globalised are design, manufacturing and purchasing, the more likely there will be a strong interest in e-business. When thousands of employees and thousands of suppliers are concerned in a global organisation, there is a need for a highly centralised co-ordination, which is clearly reinforcing the attractiveness of web-based technologies.
- *Its level of consolidation, i.e. the number of business units and brands*
  The more consolidated and centrally co-ordinated an organisation is, the more it has the opportunity to develop electronic transactions internally and externally.

- *Its emphasis on co-makership and modularisation, which include a full transfer of responsibilities onto the suppliers' shoulders*
  The more an OEM is committed to developing modular design and assembly, the more it is interested in diversifying its module suppliers.
- *The level of standardisation or 'commonalisation' of the purchased good or service*[9]
  The more a component, sub-system, system or module is generic, the more it could be purchased through reverse auction on the Internet. The more it is specific to a particular vehicle or a brand, the less likely it would be purchased over the Internet.

A fifth trend is still emerging:

- *Is the level of vertical integration or specific relationships with key first-tier suppliers positively or negatively related to e-B2B declared interest?*
  Some OEMs with specific relationships with affiliated or 'historical' partners, such as GM with Delphi, Ford with Visteon, Fiat with Teksid and Magneti Marelli, are very much involved in e-B2B. Some others, such as Peugeot with Faurecia and Toyota as well as Nissan with their *kereitsu* partners, are still reluctant to impose an all-Internet purchasing strategy.

Disadvantages of utilising digital portals

The following problems have been observed by OEMs using the services of digital infrastructure providers:

- *Contradiction with the so-called co-makership (or full partnership) deal along the whole supply chain*
  The extra cost generated by Internet supply is one of the key issues which will indeed have serious impacts on the relationship between the OEMs and their suppliers and along the whole value chain. According to Bursa (2000), Covisint was considering charging 0.25 per cent to 0.5 per cent on each transaction conducted through its website. Quoting Alan Turfe, then head of GM e-activities, Bursa evaluated an income generation of 3.5 US$bn over the next five years.

- *Threat to competition and potential collusion practices breaking the existing anti-trust laws*
  Suppliers belong to different industries and some like steel makers belong to the capital-intensive category where the machines need to be run at full capacity. Even among steel mills there are global players and smaller regional players. If the giant portals club their orders together, then they will be able to dictate huge price reductions as the suppliers will not be able to bargain given the magnitude of the order. Smaller suppliers will be virtually out of the marketplace, as they cannot offer price reductions of such magnitude or quote against such giant orders. In order to protect these smaller suppliers anti-trust officials have banned clubbing of multi-OEM orders together

(Wolffe et al., 2000), calling it unfair practice. Anti-trust analysts and officials in the USA believe that the century-old anti-trust laws should be applied to the new economy to prevent anti-competitive practices such as collusion and monopoly power. The European Commission published its guidelines for vertical portals in May 2000. In August, a green light was given to horizontal portals through the case of myaircraft.com (aerospace components). For the Commission, the anti-trust regulation does not apply to B2B marketplaces since other trade channels still exist (Fabre and Manteau, 2000). It is said that the prices would drop further if the steel mills in the above example were run at full capacity; however, this would be unfair competition as the smaller suppliers would not be able to compete.

- *Change in the relationships along the value chain*
  Nellore et al. (2000) points out that global sourcing is a way for OEMs to separate the sourcing of development and production to different suppliers in many cases so as to retain their bargaining edge. Digital procurement has built on this principle, calling it dual invoicing. In other words, suppliers may or may not get the dual invoice for development and production of goods. Digital procurement could be seen as a way of regaining the bargaining power lost through outsourcing to global suppliers and the transfer of responsibilities by threatening them with potentially cheaper competitors.

- *Major threat to confidentiality and innovation*
  Olin et al. (1999) state that B2B can be a double-edged sword. It enables design and R&D teams from both OEMs and global suppliers to operate in a virtual design environment, thereby posing security concerns over protection of proprietary information, and in particular innovative ideas and suggestions.

Case study

The phrase 'digital procurement' has struck many industries like lightning. Many companies already procure or are trying to procure online various parts and components both in the sphere of direct and indirect materials. However, not many companies succeed in digital procurement and invariably end up destroying their existing supplier relations, which have been built up over the years. We will investigate a company in the white goods industry that has successfully built up its digital procurement strategy. The firm is one of the top three firms in the white goods industry and is a global player. This case study will describe the firm's implementation of its digital procurement strategy for the sourcing of paper. The term 'paper' does not generally mean a commodity where savings can be achieved but the case study firm through a combination of digital and regular procurement methods achieved 14 per cent net savings on prices that were currently being paid. The savings, though significant, are not the only item of interest as the method and the implementation problems faced by the firm in its digitalisation strategy are also of vital importance.

Best practice

We will now describe the best practice implemented in the case study firm. Digital procurement is procurement online and can occur either in real time (dynamic) or not in real time (static). Since supplier firms participating in the digital procurement bid for a contract for a fixed quantity online they enter what is called an auction. The word auction is generally used to represent the occasion where a group of two or more people/firms have gathered to bid on one or more items with the items going to the highest bidder. However, these auctions are generally done for items that are non-industrial in nature and of very high value such as the paintings by Rembrandt or the dresses worn by the late Princess Diana. These auctions were conducted for many years until industrial houses decided to use the same principles followed in these auctions but with the auctioned items going to the lowest bidder. Since the bidder with the lowest prices gets the contract, this process is called a reverse auction. It was this reverse auction phenomenon that instigated the digitalisation strategy of the case study firm.

Digitalisation

In order to conduct a reverse auction suppliers must be brought together through digital means such as the Internet. In other words, since the suppliers will be bidding for a contract and, thereby a fixed quantity of material, there must be a software mechanism that allows the different bids to be compared in real time and allows feedback to be given to the suppliers almost instantaneously. Companies possessing such software and the ability to bring suppliers together at a fixed time for a reverse auction are called a reverse auction houses. One such auction house was selected by the case study company as they offered to conduct five auctions for a fixed fee without any variable costs. The aim was that the auction house could get subsequent contracts subject to the success of the five pilots. The auction house normally charges clients a fixed and variable fee. The fixed fees are constant irrespective of the savings and are put towards the arrangements necessary in order to get the suppliers together such as telephone calls, renting servers, etc. The variable fees are usually a certain percentage of the net savings, varying between 5 and 20 per cent. Once the auction house was selected, it was decided that paper (A4 and A3 types) would be sourced through an online auction. But in order to do this the first step was to consolidate the requirements. The significant consumption of paper was reported from six European countries (1, 2, 3, 4, 5, 6). It was decided that the requirements could not be clubbed together as there were only about three suppliers that were pan-European and could supply the requirements in all the countries. The auction was therefore, organised such that the suppliers could only quote one country at a time and could of course quote for more than one country as feasible. However, it was mentioned in the auction that the suppliers could not quote above a certain maximum price that was 10 per cent lower than the current prices. The figure of 10 per cent was selected as the paper market was extremely tough showing an upward price trend. Evidence of this was visible through the paper pulp index (ppi) that had been moving upwards for the last two years. This also meant that the starting price would be 10 per cent lower than the maximum price and subsequent bids would be even lower than this. Further, the suppliers had to quote below the lowest price that was visible on the screen. The auction rules also stated that there was no obligation on the part of the case company to choose the supplier with the lowest bid as other factors such as quality and delivery service among a host of other factors would need to be considered. However, the suppliers quoting the lowest price (all in ascending order of bid prices) would be invited for the final negotiations which would not encompass any discussions on price. This was done in order to save time and weed out suppliers that did not have the capability to meet strict pricing requirements.

It was also observed that some of the countries had many different variants of paper, albeit for the same applications such as laser printers, photocopiers, inkjet printers, fax machines and double-sided photocopying. These variants had a price range of almost 40 per cent between them, varied in quality according to the grade, and were sizes A+++, A++, B, A–B+, or recycled both in the A4 and A3 sizes. What was obvious from a visit to the paper market by the case company officials was that there was a price difference and different types of paper within a certain type. Invariably during traditional negotiations when suppliers offer a price reduction they just offer a paper within the same type that is of a lower price. It was decided that the understanding of paper was limited in the case study company and not a core competence. The only knowledge or competence was on the applications of paper. Therefore, it was decided that the auction list would not contain the grades currently in use but only the applications and the quantities of paper. The suppliers would simply quote against the applications and their quotations were legally binding in the sense that they needed to fulfil the applications, failing which they would be responsible to compensate the case study firm for down time losses.

Then, on a parallel basis, negotiations were undertaken with the three pan-European suppliers of paper. These suppliers were invited to the auction by the auction house but were called separately from the auction for a negotiation with the case study company. They were well aware of the fact that the case study company was conducting an auction and they were there to negotiate on all issues, albeit on a pan-European basis. These suppliers were to negotiate one price for the entire six countries. While two of the suppliers quoted more than what the case study company was currently paying, only one supplier agreed to a price that was lower than what was currently being paid. An agreement of intent was signed subject to the fact that no lower bid was obtained at the auction. However, in case the bids were lower at the auction, the selected pan-European supplier had to match it and lower their prices. This was in accordance with the rules of the auction that the lowest bidder takes the bid. One of the suppliers offered a particular type of recycled paper that would be suitable for all applications but the overall cost in five of the six countries turned out to be more than what was being currently paid. Therefore, this grade of paper was not selected. The quotes of the selected pan-European supplier were lower than the 10 per cent maximum

182 Digital procurement

price requirement at the auction. The selected supplier requested permission not to participate in the auction, as they were confident that their prices were the best and could not be matched.

At the auction more than eight suppliers attended per country and some of the suppliers were the same in multiple countries. These eight suppliers were from among a pool of sixteen suppliers that were initially invited to the auction. Eight other suppliers refused to join the auction as the maximum price was below their expectations. This did succeed in weeding out some of the suppliers and acted as an entry gate.

Results

From the auction it was observed that significant savings were not obtained in all countries. The highest savings came from a mixture of the digital procurement and traditional procurement. The results of where the savings were the most significant are indicated in Table 10.5 where 'Pan' indicates the pan-European supplier that was selected. The blanks against certain paper grades in certain countries indicate that these papers were not sourced in those countries. The special papers (spec) indicate their use in special machines.

The net savings per country in units of money are shown in Table 10.6. This resulted in net savings of 14 per cent above current prices. This was achieved by a mixture of both traditional and digital procurement methods. The pan-European supplier was given the results of the auction as soon as it was available. The pan-European supplier could match some of the lowest bids in certain countries and not in all. In cases where they could not better the prices of the auction, they were given to the suppliers participating in the auction. This whole experience of sourcing paper through digital and traditional procurement means is an example of a partnership, which is governed by strict goals, and guidelines of expectations. The savings and, thus, the supplier prices are tied to the paper pulp index. The paper pulp index is reviewed every three months and prices are adjusted. The pan-European supplier agreed to give the company 75 per cent of the increase and absorb 25 per cent of the increases. It also agreed to pass on 100 per cent of the decrease should the ppi index fall. In order to guarantee that the prices were the most competitive and did not become lethargic, the contract contained a

Table 10.5 Distribution of paper

Type of paper	Country 1	Country 2	Country 3	Country 4	Country 5	Country 6
A4	Pan	Auction	Auction	Auction		Pan
A4 punched					Pan	
A4 colour				Pan		
A3	Pan		Auction	Pan	Auction	Pan
A4 spec					Auction	
A4 spec					Auction	

Table 10.6 Net savings

Type of paper	Country 1	Country 2	Country 3	Country 4	Country 5	Country 6
A4	30500	2000	8000	150		5000
A4 punched					200	
A4 colour					100	
A3		2000	200	20000	100	3000
A4 spec					400	
A4 spec					600	

clause that if 50 per cent of the savings were lost due to price increases, then the country lot would be outsourced again. However, the pan-European supplier would be given the first option to quote against the country orders again. The results of the auction are phenomenal and they have been duplicated in the sourcing of direct materials like plastics, steel, leasing of cars, etc. This has led to almost 25 per cent savings in certain cases. Finally, the paper sourced against the applications proved to be of better quality than the paper that was currently being used, proving that digital procurement alone cannot succeed in isolation as it has to be done in consonance with traditional means of procurement.

Outcome

The results can be summarised as shown in Figure 10.1.

Procurement can be carried out through three different methods. The first is through traditional methods such as using buyers and face-to-face negotiations with suppliers. The second method is by using digital suppliers who provide the infrastructure to conduct reverse auctions such as free markets. The final method is by relying on internal digital suppliers, i.e. when the infrastructure to conduct digital procurement is in-house such as over the phone. In the case described above, a combination of traditional and external digital suppliers was used. In general, the traditional methods are used for core activities and digital methods are used for non-core activities. Even in the case of a core activity, part of the activity may be outsourced through digital means. Once the supplier is selected, care should be exercised so that the price increases offsetting more than 50 per cent of the initial savings for items are resourced. In order to obtain effective procurement, clear control needs to be maintained over life cost analysis, supply base certification, quality certification, logistics and demand flow certification and price management. For example, if the case officials had not investigated the market and understood the pricing structure of paper, they would not have been able to set the maximum price. In order to ensure that problems do not arise after the supplier has been selected, the supplier needs to be audited for quality and the logistics infrastructure. The supply base needs to be constantly audited so that emerging suppliers and suppliers who become less attractive are accounted for. Finally, a life cost analysis needs to be done for every part that is procured, for example, large firms offering e-procurement solutions may inform OEMs of 40

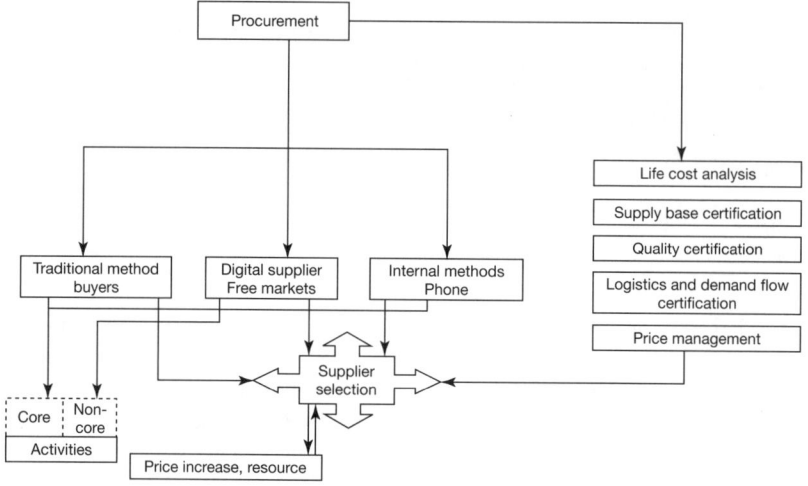

Figure 10.1 A summary of procurement

per cent savings but this figure needs to be considered in light of the changes and savings that it offers the OEM, such as in the reduction of the head count, etc.

Notes

1 Therefore, market surveys are rapidly out-dated, such as Gebauer *et al.* (1998).
2 According to IBM, in 2000, B2B will account for 78 per cent of the total revenue generated by e-commerce.
3 'We find it hard to imagine a system in which all human contact is replaced by a computer', according to R. Johnson, head of purchasing at Toyota Europe, quoted in Schlott (2000).
4 Since 1995, it has executed online auctions for over US$5.4bn, creating potential estimated savings of more than US$1bn.
5 Some portals are set up by banks and/or consulting companies to specifically support small and medium-sized enterprises (Maudet, 2000).
6 This is the strategy adopted by the French glass manufacturer Saint-Gobain that is setting up a European marketplace or vertical portal with an objective of Euro2bn turnover by 2005.
7 IndustryWeek.com
8 General Electric Appliances is currently pushing online supply auctions towards its 2,000 global suppliers which are supposed to lead to 'double-digit' percentage savings (Marsh, 2000) It has a $5.7bn turnover in 1999.
9 The correlation is indeed negative with the level of specification: the more specific the component is, the less it could be traded through Internet bidding.

Conclusion

There is an urgent need for further research on e-commerce and its impact on the automative industry structure and business models by economists as well as industry analysts and consultants before any viable business recommendation should be formulated. The new Internet-based economy is still very much in its infancy. No trends have stabilised yet. Digital procurement could well be considered a pure management guru's fashion as the lean model was ten years ago. Some observers notice that the consequences of entering such a managerial fashion without being fully prepared or without adapting it to local and cultural context can negatively impact on businesses, leading to bankruptcy and unnecessary consolidation. However, e-B2B could well be the new best practice in purchasing, transforming radically traditional business models into a more virtual and transparent system.

Bibliography

Aberdeen Group (1999) *Strategic Procurement: The Next Wave of Procurement Automation: An Executive White Paper*, July, www.aberdeen.com.

Aberdeen Group (2000) *The e-Business Supply Chain: Meeting Customer Requirements in the Internet Economy: An Executive White Paper*, January, www.aberdeen.com.

Adam, Jr. E.E. and Swamidass, P.M. (1989) 'Assessing operations management from a strategic perspective', *Journal of Management*, vol. 15, no. 2, pp. 181–203.

Adler, P.S. (2001 forthcoming) 'Market, hierarchy, and trust: the knowledge economy and the future of capitalism', *Organization Science*.

Alexander, M. (1985) 'Creative marketing and innovative consumer product design: some case studies', *Design Studies*, vol. 6, no. 1, pp. 41–50.

Aoshima, Y. (1993) *Inter Project Technology Transfer and the Design of Product Development Organisations*, IMVP working paper, Boston: MIT Press.

Araujo, L., Dubois, A. and Gadde, L.-E. (1999) 'Managing interfaces with suppliers', *Industrial Marketing Management*, vol. 28, pp. 497–506.

Arkader, R. and Fleury, P.F. (1998) 'The perspective of suppliers on advances and barriers to lean supply: a case study investigation in a developing country context', paper presented at the 5th International EUROMA conference, Dublin, 14–17 June, 26–32.

Asmus, D. and Griffin, J, (1993) 'Harnessing the power of your suppliers', *The McKinsey Quarterly*, no. 3, pp. 63–78.

Beecham, M. (1996) 'Technology partnering', *Purchasing and Supply Management*, January, pp. 32–33.

Bensaou, M. (1999) 'Portfolios of buyer–supplier relationships', *Sloan Management Review*, vol. 4, no. 4, pp. 35–44.

Berggren, C. (1992) *The Volvo Experience: Alternatives to Lean Production in the Swedish Auto Industry*, New York: ILR Press.

Black, J.A and Boal, K.B. (1994) 'Strategic resources: traits, configurations and paths to sustainable competitive advantage', *Strategic Management Journal*, vol. 15, pp. 131–148.

Blois, K.J. (1971) 'Vertical quasi integration', *Journal of Industrial Economics*, vol. 20, no. 3, pp. 253–272.

Blonder, C. and Pritzl, R. (1992) 'Developing strategic alliances: a conceptual framework for successful co-operation', *European Management Journal*, vol. 10, no. 4, pp. 412–421.

Bowen, H.K., Clark, K.B., Holloway, C.A. and Wheelwright, S.C. (1994) *The Perpetual Enterprise Machine: Several Keys to Corporate Renewal through Successful Product and Process Development*, New York: Oxford University Press.

Boyer, R. and Freyssenet, M. (1995) *The Emergence of new Industrial Models*, Actes du Gerpisa, no. 15, Evry: Université d'Evry – Val d'Essonne, pp. 75–142.

Bruce, M., Fiona, L., Dale, L. and Dominic, W. (1995) 'Success factors for collaborative product development', *R&D Management*, vol. 25, no. 1, pp. 33–44.

Burnes, B. and New, S. (1997) 'Collaboration in customer–supplier relationships: strategy, operations and the function of rhetoric', *International Journal of Purchasing and Materials Management*, Fall, pp. 10–17.

Bursa, M. (2000) 'The Internet revolution', *ISATA Magazine*, no. 9, April, p. 10.

Burt, T. (2000) 'Components: transformation underway', *Financial Times Survey*, FT Auto 2000, February, FT.com.

Capon, N., Farley, J.U. and Hulbert, J.M. (1997) *Corporate Strategic Planning*, New York: Columbia University Press.

Cash, J.I. (1996) 'Exploiting new technology', *Information Week*, 22 July.

Clark, K. (1989) 'Project scope and project performance: the effects of parts strategy and supplier involvement in product development', *Management Science*, vol. 35, no. 10, pp. 1247–1263.

Clark, K.B. and Fujimoto, T. (1991) *Product Development Performance: Strategy, Organisation and Management in the World Auto Industry*, Boston: Harvard Business School.

Cooper, D. (1975) 'Corporate planning and purchasing strategy', in D.H. Farmer and B. Taylor, (eds) *Corporate Planning and Procurement*, London: Heinemann, pp. 217–229.

Crocker, K.J. and Morgan, J. (1998) 'Is honesty the best policy? Curtailing insurance fraud through optimal incentive contracts', *Journal of Political Economy*, vol. 106, no. 2, pp. 355–375.

Cusumano, M. and Takeishi, A. (1991) 'Supplier relations and supplier management: a survey of Japanese, Japanese-transplant and US auto plants', *Strategic Management Journal*, vol. 12, pp. 563–588.

Day, G.S. (1986) *Analysis for Strategic Marketing Decisions*, St Paul: West Publishing.

Derkinderen, F. and Crum, R.L. (1994) 'Pitfalls in using portfolio techniques – assessing risk and potential', *Long Range Planning*, vol. 17, pp. 129–136.

Dowlatshahi, S. (1992) 'Purchasing's role in concurrent engineering environment', *International Journal of Purchasing and Materials Management*, vol. 28, no. 1, pp. 21–25.

Elliot, C. (1993) 'Turning dreams into specifications', *Engineering Management Journal*, vol. 3, p. 83.

Ellison, D.J. (1995) *Product Development Performance in the Auto Industry: 1990s Update*, working paper no. 95–066, Boston: Harvard Business School.

Ellram, L.M. (1991) 'A managerial guidance for the development and implementation of purchasing partnerships', *International Journal of Purchasing and Materials Management*, vol. 31, no. 2, pp. 9–16.

Fabre, R. and Manteau, P. (2000) 'E-marketplaces: le "oui" de Bruxelles', *Les Echos*, 27 September.

Fine, C.H., (1998) *Clock Speed: Winning Industry Control in the Age of Temporary Advantage*, Massachusetts: Perseus Books.

Fine, C.H. and Whitney, D.E. (1996) *Is the Make or Buy Decision Process a Core Competence?* Cambridge. MA: MIT Center for Technology, Policy and Industrial Development.

Fiocca, R. (1982) 'Account portfolio analysis for strategy development', *Industrial Marketing Management*, vol. 11, pp. 53–62.

Forrest, J.E. (1989) 'Management of technological innovation: strategic alliances in the new biotechnology industry', unpublished PhD thesis, University of Wales.

Frey, S.C. and Schlosser, M.M. (1993) 'ABB and Ford: creating value through co-operation', *Sloan Management Review*, Fall, pp. 65–72.

Galbraith, J., (1973) *Designing Complex Organisations*, Reading, MA: Addison-Wesley.

Gebauer, J., Beam, C. and Segev, A. (1998) 'Impact of the Internet on procurement', *Acquisition Review Quarterly*, vol. 14, Spring, pp. 167–181.

Gong, B.H. (1993) *Cooperative Relationships Between Assemblers and Suppliers in the Automobile Industry: A Comparative Study of Japan and Korea*, Industrial Economic Discussion Paper, no. 65, Nagoya: Nagoya School of Economics, Nagoya University.

Grant, R. (1991) 'The resource based theory of competitive advantage: implications for strategy formulation', *California Management Review*, vol. 33, no. 3, pp. 114–135.

Gugler, P. (1992) 'Building transnational alliances to create competitive advantage', *Long Range Planning*, vol. 25, no. 1, pp. 90–99.

Håkansson, H. (1982) *International Marketing and Purchasing of Industrial Goods: An Interaction Approach*, Chichester: Wiley.

Hanna, D.P. (1988) *Designing Organizations for High Performance*, Reading, MA: Addison-Wesley Publications.

Harland, C. (1996) 'Supply network strategies: the case of health suppliers', *European Journal of Purchasing and Supply Management*, vol. 2, no. 4, pp. 183–192.

Harrigan, K.R. (1986), *Managing for Joint Venture Success*, Lexington, MA: Lexington Books.

Harris, A., Giunipero, L.C. and Hult, G.T.M. (1998) 'Impact of organisational and contract flexibility on outsourcing contracts', *Industrial Marketing Management*, vol. 27, pp. 373–384.

Harrison, A. (1990) 'Co-makership as an extension of quality care', *International Journal of Quality and Reliability Management*, vol. 7, no. 2, pp. 15–22.

Haslam, J. M. (1988) *Writing Engineering Specifications*, London: E & FN Spon Ltd.

Hatzfeld, N. (2000) 'Clarifying the implications of modular production', *La lettre du GERPISA*, no. 143, pp. 3–5.

Hauser, J.R. (1988), 'The house of quality', *Harvard Business Review*, May–June, pp. 63–73.

Helper, S. (1991) 'How much has really changed between US automakers and their suppliers?', *Sloan Management Review*, vol. 32, no. 4, pp. 15–28.

Hollins, B. and Hurst, K. (1995) 'Research into user friendly specifications for effective management design management: refining and simplifying the process', *Journal of Engineering Design*, vol. 6, no. 3, pp. 239–247.

Hollins, B. and Pugh, S. (1990) *Successful Product Design*, Oxford: Butterworth & Co.

Hyun, J.H. (1994) 'Buyer supplier relations in the European automobile component industry', *Long Range Planning*, vol. 27, no. 2, pp. 66–75.

Iansiti, M. (1995) 'Shooting the rapids: managing product development in turbulent environments', *California Management Review*, vol. 38, no. 1, pp. 37–58.

Imai, H., Nonaka, I. and Takeuchi, H. (1985) 'Managing the new product development process: how Japanese companies learn and unlearn', in K. Clark, R. Hayes and C. Lorenz (eds) *The Uneasy Alliance*, Boston: Harvard Business School.

Kamath, R.R and Liker, J.J. (1994) 'A second look at Japanese product development', *Harvard Business Review*, November, pp. 154–170.

Kanter, R.M. (1994) 'Collaborative advantage', *Harvard Business Review*, July–August, pp. 96–108.

Karlson, B. (1994) 'Product design: towards a new conceptualisation of the design process', unpublished doctoral thesis, Royal Institute of Technology, Stockholm.

Kaulio, M.A. (1996) 'Specifications as mediating objects: On the tactical use of specifications in technical/product development work', paper presented at the 3rd International Product Development Conference, INSEAD, France, 15–16 April.

Keith, A.B. (1931) *Elements of the Law of Contracts*, Oxford: Clarendon Press.

Kim, D.H. (1993) 'The link between individual and organisational learning', *Sloan Management Review*, vol. 35, no. 1, pp. 37–50.

Kleinbard, D. (2000) 'Navigating the B2B maze: finding an e-commerce site or exchange that works for your small business', 23 May, *VerticalNet Web Site*.

Kolay, M.K. (1993) 'Suppliers' asset base: appreciating or depreciating?', *International Journal of Operations and Production Management*, vol. 26, no. 4, pp. 8–14.

Kotter, J.P. (1996) *Leading Change*, Boston: Harvard Business School Press.

Krafcik, J. (1988) 'Triumph for the lean production system', *Sloan Management Review*, vol. 30, no. 1, pp. 41–52.

Kraljic, P. (1983) 'Purchasing must become supply management', *Harvard Business Review*, vol. 61, no. 5, pp. 109–117.

Lacity, M.C., Willcocks, L.P. and Feeny, D.F. (1995) 'IT outsourcing: maximise flexibility and control', *Harvard Business Review*, vol. 73, no. 3, pp. 86–93.

LaLonde, B.J. and Masters, J.M. (1994) 'Emerging logistics strategies: blueprints for the next century', *International Journal of Physical Distribution and Logistics Management*, vol. 24, no. 7, pp. 35–47.

Lamm, P. (2000) 'Le New Deal de l'économie (1): l'industrie traditionnelle se dope au Net', *Les Echos*, 5 June.

Lamming, R. (1993) *Beyond Partnerships: Strategies for Innovation and Lean Supply*, Hemel Hempstead: Prentice Hall.

Larson, P.D. (1994) 'Buyer supplier co-operation: product quality and total cost', *International Journal of Physical Distribution and Logistics Management*, vol. 24, no. 6, pp. 4–9.

Lawrence, P.R. and Lorsch, J.W. (1967) 'New management job: the integrator', *Harvard Business Review*, November–December.

Lecler, Y. (1993) *La Référénce Japonaise (The Japanese Reference*, in French), Limonest: L'interdisciplinaire.

Leenders, M.R. and Fearon, H.E. (1994) *Purchasing and Materials Management*, 10th edn, Homewood, IL: Richard Irwin.

Leenders, M.R., Nollet, J. and Ellram, L.M. (1994) 'Adapting purchasing to supply chain management', *International Journal of Physical Distribution and Logistics Management*, vol. 24, no. 1, pp. 40–42.

Levy, P., Bessant, J. and Lamming, R. (1995) 'Developing integration through total quality supply chain management', *Integrated Manufacturing Systems*, vol. 6, no. 3, pp. 4–12.

Licoppe, C. (2000) 'Commerce électronique: mythes et réalités', *La Recherche*, no. 328, February, pp. 88–89.

Lieberman, M.B. (1991) 'Determinants of vertical integration: an empirical test', *Journal of Industrial Economics*, vol. 39, no. 5, pp. 451–466.

Liker, J.K., Kamath, R.R., Wasti, S.N. and Nagamachi, M. (1995) 'Integrating suppliers into fast cycle product development', in J.K. Liker, J.E. Ettlie and J.C. Campbell (eds) *Engineered in Japan: Japanese Technology Management Practices*, Oxford: Oxford University Press.

Liker, J.K., Kamath, R., Wasti, S.N. and Nagamachi, M. (1996) 'Supplier involvement in automotive product design: are there really large US/Japan differences?', *Research Policy*, vol. 25, pp. 59–89.

Lipton, M. (1996) 'Demystifying the development of an organisational vision', *Sloan Management Review*, Summer, pp. 83–92.

Llewellyn, K. (1931), 'What price contract? An essay in perspective', *Yale Law Journal*, vol. 40, May, pp. 704–751.

Major, W.T. and Taylor, C. (1996) *Law of Contract*, 9th edn, London: M. & E. Pitman Publication.

Mann, P. (1999) 'Delivering value across the Internet supply chain', *Manufacturing Systems*, July, pp. i–viii.

Markowitz, H. (1952) 'Portfolio selection', *Journal of Finance*, vol. 7, March.

Marsh, P. (2000) 'GE appliances pushes online supply auctions', *Financial Times*, 26 September.

Maudet, P. (2000) 'Internet sur le terrain: function achat: branle-bas dans le B to B'. (Internet in practice: purchasing revolution in B-2-B). *Sociétal*, no. 29, 3rd quarter, pp. 14–15.

Miller, R.J. (1999) *Impact of Internet Buying on Vehicle Manufacturers and Suppliers*, Detroit: Arthur Andersen.

Mohanty, R.P. and Deshmukh, S.G. (1993) 'Use of analytic hierarchic process for evaluating sources of supply', *International Journal of Physical Distribution and Logistics Management*, vol. 23, no. 3, pp. 22–28.

Monszka, R.M., Callahan, T.J. and Nichols, E.L. (1995) 'Predictors of relationships among buying and supplying firms', *International Journal of Physical Distribution and Logistics Management*, vol. 25, no. 10, pp. 45–59.

Mudambi, R. and Helper, S. (1998) 'The close but adversarial model of supplier relations in the US auto industry', *Strategic Management Journal*, vol. 19, pp. 775–792.

Nellore, R., Chanaron, J.J. and Söderquist, K. (2001) 'Lean supply and price based global sourcing: the interconnection', *European Journal of Purchasing and Supply Management*, vol. 7, no. 2, pp. 101–110.

Nishiguchi, T. and Beaudet, A. (1998) 'Case study: the Toyota Group and the Aisin fire', *Sloan Management Review*, vol. 40, no. 1, pp. 49–59.

Olin, J., Greis, N. and Kasarda, J. (1999) 'Knowledge management across multi-tier enterprises: the promise of intelligent software in the auto industry', *European Management Journal*, vol. 17, no. 4, August, pp. 335–346.

Olsen, R.F and Ellram, L.M. (1997) 'A portfolio approach to supplier relationships', *Industrial Marketing Management*, vol. 26, pp. 101–113.

Ponticel, P (1996) 'Supply side engineering', *Automotive Engineering*, October.

Porter, M. (1980) *Competitive Strategy*, New York: The Free Press.

Porter, M.E. (1990) 'Don't collaborate, compete', *The Economist*, 9 June, pp. 26–29.

Prahalad, C.K. and Hamel, G. (1990) 'The core competence of the corporation', *Harvard Business Review*, vol. 68, no. 3, pp. 79–91.

Quinn, J.B. and Hilmer, F.G. (1994) 'Strategic outsourcing', *Sloan Management Review*, Summer, pp. 43–55.

Reilly, C.A.O., Chatman, J. and Caldwell, D.F. (1991) 'People and organizational culture: a profile comparison approach to assessing person-organization fit', *Academy of Management Journal*, pp. 487–516.

Reinartsen, D.G. (1997) *Managing the Design Factory: A Product Developer's Toolkit*, New York: The Free Press.

Richardson, J. (1993) 'Parallel sourcing and supplier performance in the Japanese automobile industry', *Strategic Management Journal*, vol. 14, 339–350.

Robbins, S.P. (2000) 'Organizational culture', in *Essentials of Organizational Behavior*, Upper Saddle River, NJ: Prentice-Hall.

Robertson, D. and Ulrich, K. (1998) 'Planning for product platforms', *Sloan Management Review*, vol. 39, no. 4, pp. 19–31.

Roland Berger & Partners (2000) *Nine Mega-Trands Re-shape the Automotive Supplier Industry: A Trend Study to 2010*, Munich: Roland Berger & Partners, March.

Roozenburg, N.F.M and Dorst, H.K. (1991) *Some Guidelines for the Development of Performance Specifications in Product Development*, proceedings from the 8th International Conference on Engineering Design, Zurich, 27–29 August, pp. 359–365.

Rosenau, M.D. (1992) 'From experience: avoiding marketing's best of the best specification trap', *Journal of Product Innovation Management*, vol. 9, no. 4, pp. 300–302.

Sako, M. (1992) *Prices, Quality and Trust: Interfirm relationships in Britain and Japan*, Cambridge: Cambridge University Press.

Schein, E.H. (1985) *Organizational Culture and Leadership*, San Francisco: Jossey-Bass, p.168.

Schilling, M.A. and Hill, C.W. (1998) 'Managing the new product development process: strategic imperatives', *Academy of Management Executive*, vol. 12, no. 3, pp. 67–81.

Schlott, S. (2000) 'An announcement that changed the world', *International Automobile Management*, June, no. 2, p. 3.

Schrader, S. and Göpfert, J. (1994) *Structuring Manufacture-supplier Interaction in New Product Development Teams: An Empirical Analysis*, IMVP working paper, December, Cambridge, MA: MIT.

Sengès, G. (2000) 'Le New Deal de l'économie (2): un mouvement lancé aux États-Unis', *Les Echos*, 6 June.

Silverman, G. (2000) 'The urge to merge takes on a different form', *Financial Times*, IM&A Survey, 30 June, p. II.

Simon, H.A. (1976) *A Study of Decision Making Processes in Administrative Organisation*, 3rd expanded edition, New York: The Free Press.

Smith, D.G. and Rhodes, R.G. (1992) 'Specification formulation: an approach that works', *Journal of Engineering Design*, vol. 3, no. 4, pp. 275–289.

Smith, P. and Reinartsen, D. (1991) *Developing Products in Half the Time*, New York: Van Nostrand Reinhold.

Sobek II, D.K., Ward, A.C. and Liker, J.K. (1999) 'Toyota's principles of set based concurrent engineering', *Sloan Management Review*, Winter, pp. 67–83.

Söderquist, K. (1997) 'Inside the tier model: product development organisation and strategies in automotive expert supplier firms', unpublished doctoral thesis, Grenoble Business School, France.

Söderquist, K. and Nellore, R. (2000) 'Information systems in a fast cycle industry: identifying user needs in integrated automotive component development', *R&D Management Journal*, vol. 30, no. 3, pp. 199–211.

Sorabjee, H. (1997) *Automotive International*, vol. 40, Leading Edge Publications.

Stern, D. (1992) 'Core competencies: the key to corporate advantage', *Multinational Business*, no. 3, pp. 13–20.

Strauss, A. and Corbin, J. (1990) *Basics of Qualitative Research: Grounded Theory Procedures and Techniques*, Newbury Park, CA: Sage Publications.

Tait, N. (2000) 'Technical hitch stalls "Big Three" trading site', *Financial Times*, Survey Automobile, 14 June, p. II.

Teece, D.J. (1987) 'Capturing value from technological innovation: integration, strategic partnering and licensing decisions, technology and the global industry', in Tushman, M.L. and Anderson, P. (1997) *Managing Strategic Innovation and Change: A Collection of Readings*, New York: Oxford University Press, pp. 287–306.

Thorpe, C.P. and Bailey, J.C.L. (1996) *Commercial Contracts: A Practical Guide to Deals, Contracts and Promises*, Cambridge: Woodhead Publishing Limited.

Turnbull, P.W. (1990) 'A review of portfolio planning models for industrial marketing and purchasing management', *European Journal of Marketing*, 24, 7–22.

Turnbull, P.W. and Valla, J.P. (1986) *Strategies for International Industrial Marketing*, London: Croom Helm.

Venkatesan, R. (1992) 'Strategic sourcing: to make or not to make', *Harvard Business Review*, Nov–Dec, pp. 98–108.

Vincenti, W.G. (1990) *What Engineers Know and How They Know it: Analytical Studies from Aeronautical History*, Baltimore and London: The Johns Hopkins University Press.

Ward, A., Liker, J.K., Cristiano, J.J. and Sobek, D.K. (1995) 'The Second Toyota paradox: how delaying decisions can make better cars faster', *Sloan Management Review*, vol. 36, no. 3, pp. 43–61.

Wasti, S.N. and Liker, J.K. (1999) 'Collaborating with suppliers in product development: a US and Japan comparative study', *IEEE Transactions on Engineering Management*, vol. 46, no. 4, pp. 444–461.

Wernerfelt, B. (1984) 'A resource-based view of the firm', *Strategic Management Journal*, vol. 5, no. 2, pp. 4–12.

Wheelwright, S.C. and Clark, K.B. (1993) *Managing New Product and Process Development: Text and Cases*, New York: The Free Press.

Wiener, Y. (1988) 'Forms of value systems: a focus on organizational effectiveness and cultural change and maintenance', *Academy of Management Review*, p. 536.

Williamson, O.E. (1975) 'Transaction cost economics: the governance of contractual relations', *Journal of Law and Economics*, vol. 22, pp. 233–261.

Wolffe, R., Tait, N. and Bowe, C. (2000) 'Fair exchange in cyberspace', *Financial Times*, Comments and Analysis, 5 June, p. 16.

Womack, J.P. and Jones, D.T. (1994) 'From lean production to the lean enterprise', *Harvard Business Review*, vol. 72, no. 2, pp. 93–105.

Womack, J.P., Jones, D.T. and Roos, D. (1990) *The Machine that Changed the World*, New York: Rawson Associates & McMillan.

Index

Adam, E.E. Jr and Swamidass, P.M. 40
Adler, P.S. 136
aircraft industry 90–1; compared with auto industry 92–3; contracts in 139–53; outsourcing decisions in 103–7
Alexander, M. 20
Aoshima, Y. 35, 47
Araujo, L. *et al.* 22
Arkader, R. and Fleury, P.F. 134, 138
Asmus, D. and Griffin, J.J. 100, 136, 152
automotive industry, after sales/service 85–6; brand/marketing management 83–4; compared with aircraft industry 92–3; contracts in 139–53; directives 87–8; evolution of 6–8; legal demands 89–90; manufacturing 86; outsourcing decisions in 103–7; PDT leader/object group 87; product development model 93–6; project manager 86–7; R&D 84–5; risk analysis 88–9; specification process in 81–3; top management 83

Beecham, M. 134
Bensaou, M. 120, 121, 122
Berggren, C. 7
black box engineering 64, 66–7, 79, 138
Black, J.A. and Boal, K.B. 99
Blois, K.J. 135
Blonder, C. and Pritzl, R. 100
Boston matrix 115–16, 130
Bowen, H.K. *et al.* 28, 29, 30, 32, 57, 58, 76
Boyer, R. and Freyssenet, M. 7
Bruce, M. *et al.* 100
Buchholz, 156
Burnes, B. and New, S. 28
business-to-business (B2B) 169, 171, 172–3, 174–6
business-to-customers (B2C) 169

capabilities 32, 37–8
Capon, N. *et al.* 116
Cash, J.I. 138
Clark, K.B. 17, 18, 40; and Fujimoto, T. 12, 20, 30, 99, 122
collaborations, benefits of 100; risks/negative aspects 100–1
communication 19–21, 43–4, 149–50; and contracts 149–50; creative 20; early involvement 19–20; early working in the dark 19; integrated problem-solving 20; modes/dimensions 19–20; permanently open 75–6; serial/batch mode 19; understanding tacit knowledge 20
competitive advantage 101–2, 104, 105, 106–7, 111–12
component classification 121, 122–4; bottleneck 118, 119, 120, 121, 123, 126–7, 128, 129–30; leverage 119, 120, 121, 123, 126, 128; non-critical 119, 120, 123, 124–6, 128–9; strategic 119, 120, 123, 127, 129
computer-assisted design (CAD) 9
contracts 3, 113; agreement/intention/consideration 136; in auto/aircraft industries 139–53; background 133; and communication 149–50; content of 133–4; data collection 140–2; defined 133; elements of 136–8; execution of 137; and legal issues 148–9; link with specifications 139, 151–3; literature on 136–9; market mode 135–6; and negotiations 134; parameters 142–3; and payments 151; and performance criteria 147–8; purpose of 144–6; quasi-vertical integration 135; and responsibility 146–7; risks related to 137; significant aspects 155; specification flows 134; and trust 136; types of 144;

validation aspect 134–5, 137–9, 153–5; vertical integration 135
Cooper, D. 134, 135, 136, 155
core elements, define specifications 15–17, 47–8; expertise effects 17–19; specification/communications 19–21
craftsmanship 6–7, 8
critical path analysis 18
Crocker, K.J. and Morgan, J. 135, 144
customers 33–4, 46–7
Cusumano, M. and Takeishi, A. 6, 23–4, 60

Day, G.S. 116
Derkinderen, F. and Crum, R.L. 130
digital procurement 183–4; alternative strategies 174; B2B implementation strategies 172–3, 174–6; background 168; best practice 180; case study 179–83; complex rationale 174, 176–7; disadvantages of 178–9; hypotheses about major trends 177–8; infrastructure providers 173–4; potential tasks online 170–2; results 182–3; scenario 169; strategy 180–2; types of 168–77
Dowlatshahi, S. 136

e-business *see* digital procurement
Ellison, D.J. 122
Ellram, L.M. 100

Fabre, R. and Manteau, P. 179
Fine, C.H. 34; and Whitney, D.E. 33
Fordism 7
Forrest, J.E. 139
Frey, S.C. and Schlosser, M.M. 147

Galbraith, J. 11, 40
Gebauer, J. *et al.* 184
General Electric matrix 116
generation of specifications 122–4; co-development 123; detailed controlled parts 122; supplier proprietary parts 122
generic strategies 116
Gong, B.H. 30
Grant, R. 32
Gugler, P. 101

Håkansson, H. 135
Hanna, D.P. 57
Harland, C. 49
Harrigan, K.R. 100
Harris, A. *et al.* 6, 136, 142
Harrison, A. 138

Hauser, J.R. and Clausing, 79
Helper, S. 12, 151
Hollins, B., and Hurst, K. 22; and Pugh, S. 15, 35, 47, 48
Hyun, J.H. 138

Iansiti, M. 15, 27

Kamath, R.R. and Liker, J.J. 22, 23–4, 40, 56, 58, 62, 103, 124, 126, 147, 178
Kanter, R.M. 138
Karlson, B. 10, 11, 12, 20, 30, 40, 152
Kaulio, M.A. 6, 9, 16, 17, 40, 92, 136, 139
Keith, A.B. 133, 134
Kim, D.H. 30
Kleinbard, D. 169
Kolay, M.K. 138
Kotter, J.P. 29
Krafcik, J. 7
Kraljic, P. 120, 122, 128, 129

Lacity, M.C. *et al.* 32
LaLonde, B.J. and Masters, J.M. 138
Lamming, R. 6, 8, 40, 99, 100, 134, 138, 147
Larson, P.D. 138
Lawrence, P.R. and Lorsch, J.W. 10
lean production 7–8
Lecler, Y. 151
Leenders, M.R. 142; *et al.* 8, 138
Levy, P. *et al.* 138
Lieberman, M.B. 135
Liker, J.K. *et al.* 18, 25
Lipton, M. 29, 54
Llewellyn, K. 133

Major, W.T. and Taylor, C. 135, 136, 144, 145
make/buy decisions 98–9, 101; common themes/dissimilarities 107–10; competitive advantage/strategic vulnerability considerations 103–7, 113–14; exploring relationships for scenarios 112–13; Olsen-Ellram model 102–3; Quinn-Hilmer model 101–2, 110–12; Venkatesan model 102
marketing matrix 116
Markowitz, H. 115
Marsh, P. 184
mass production 7, 9
materials management 120
Maudet, P. 184
mega-systems supplier 163–7
Miller, R.J. 174

mixed specifications 108–9
models of specifications 24–6;
  goals/objectives/requirements 24;
  information-processing 24
Mohanty, R.P. and Deshmukh, S.G. 138
Monszka, R.M. *et al.* 138
Mudambi, R. and Helper, S. 25

Nishiguchi, T. and Beaudet, A. 6, 151

Olin, J. *et al.* 179
Olsen, R.F. and Ellram, L.M. 101, 102–3, 116, 119, 120, 121–2, 128, 129
Olsen-Ellram model 116–20
organisational culture 30–2
outsourcing 7, 10, 98; arm's length model 25, 103; common themes/dissimilarities 107–10; example of problem 98–9; models of 101–7; positive/negative effects of collaboration 100–1; qualititative specifications 107–8; quantitative specifications 109–10; set-based approach 25–6; strategic 99–101, *see also* visionary-driven outsourced development

Ponticel, P. 134
Porter, M.E. 101
portfolio models 3; analysis of approaches to 116–27; criticism of 116, 130; potential risks 130; strategies/action plans 119–20; supplier relationships/sourcing strategies 127–30; theoretical understanding of 115–16; as three-step approach 131
Prahalad, C.K. and Hamel, G. 99, 115
process of specification 81–2, 90–1; as central element 96; comparative analysis 92–3, 96; intervening conditions 87–90; model of product development 93–6; recommendations 96–7; role of departments 83–7
procurement matrix 111, 113–14
product design specification (PDS) 24
product development 41, 136; automotive industry model 93–6; changes in 138; models 25–6; portfolio approach 120–1; responsibility for 161–2; vision 29–30
product development team (PDT) 87
products, bottleneck 103, 116; classification of 116, 118; core/non-core 102; leverage 103, 116; non-critical 103, 116; range of 160–1; specification requirements 44–5; strategic 103, 116

project organisation, manager 86–7; PDT leader/object group 87
purchasing 120; background 1–2; Bensaou model 120–1, 122; Kraljic model 120, 122; Olsen-Ellram model 116–20, 121–2

Quinn, J.B. and Hilmer, F.G. 6, 30, 98, 99, 100
Quinn-Hilmer model 3, 103, 107, 109, 114; building on 110–12; described 101–2; relationship scenarios complementing 112–13

Reilly, C.A.O. *et al.* 30
Reinertsen, D.G. 27
requirements of specifications 44–5; customer (OEM) benefits/specifications 33–4; technology effects 34–6; traps 36
reverse auctions 180–4
Richardson, J. 6, 30, 101, 128
Robbins, S.P. 30, 31
Robertson, D. and Ulrich, K. 40
Roozenburg, N.F.M. and Dorst, K. 24, 33, 43, 44, 47
Rosenau, M.D. 36

Sako, M. 6
Schein, E.H. 17, 30
Schilling, M.A. and Hill, C.W. 100, 136
Schlott, S. 184
Schrader, S. *et al.* 17; and Göpfert, J. 17, 99
scope 18
Simon, H.A. 10, 11, 40
Smith, D.G. and Rhodes, R.G. 15, 16, 19, 24, 136
Smith, P. and Reinartsen, D. 6, 9, 22, 33, 34, 36, 38, 40, 48, 92–3
Sobek, D.K. II *et al.* 26
Söderquist, K. 15, 16, 20, 32; and Nellore, R. 147
sourcing 120, 136–7; strategies 127–30
specification case study 47–9; applying model 50; post-mortem 49–50; reflection on dimensions 50
specification framework 71–2; changes in 74–5; control 76–7; cost 75; demonstrating the model 78; governance/artefacts 76; limitations/trade-offs 77–8; participation 75–6; prototypes 78; role of supplier 72–3; technical content 73–4
specification problems 64; ambiguity 79; areas 64–5; changes in 67–8, 79;

content/causal explanations of 66–71; cost 68–9; identification of 79; integrated component development 79; interpretation/understanding of 69–70; over-specification 67; participation of suppliers in 70–1; proactiveness of suppliers 79; technical content 66–7, 79
specifications, background 6–8; commissioning/mediating perspectives 9; drawings 46; dynamic nature of 137–8; evolution 8–9; functionality 45; lack of research in 131; overview 12–13; parameters 43–7; principles 26–7; problem 41–2; process requirements 45; role of 120; survey 42–3; understanding 9–12
standards 45–6
Stern, D. 32
strategic vulnerability 101–2, 105–7; high 110–11, 113; low 111–12, 113; medium 111, 112, 113
Strauss, A. and Corbin, J. 4
suppliers, attractiveness of 119, 128; as captive 121; changing role of 6–8; and co-ordination with buyers 10–12; collaboration with 18, 100, 103; communication with 19–21; and contracts 134–5, 137–8, 139, 145–53; creation of visions 54, 56–7; effects of vision on outsourced development 53–4; involvement of 10; and link to specifications 21–4; low bargaining power of 121; and organisational culture 30–2; participation in specification process 70–1; partnership/parental/mature levels 23; proactiveness of 79; relationship with 119; role of 23–4, 30, 72–3; squeezing of 1–2; and types of specifications 21–4; vision for 30
supply management 120
systems suppliers, background 157–8; constituents 158–63; and experience 162–3; model of 164–6; and product development responsibility 161–2; and range of products 160–1; requirements 163–4; as self-sufficient 166–7; types of 164

Tait, N. 176
task uncertainty, and creation of lateral relations 11–12; and self-contained tasks 11; and slack resources 11; and vertical information systems 11
Taylorism 7
technology 34–6, 47
Teece, D.J. 135, 136
Thorpe, C.P. and Bailey, J.C.L. 133; *et al.* 133
trade-offs 38–9
Turnbull, P.W. 116; and Valla, J.P. 135, 138
types of specifications: core capabilities 32; creation of common goals 27–8; culture 30–2; establish feasibility before commitment 27; integrate by intersection 27; and links to suppliers 21–4; map the design space 26; models 24–6; visions 29–30

Venkatesan, R. 101, 102
Vincenti, W.G. 9
visionary-driven outsourced development, and core capabilities 58–61, 62; creation 54, 56–7; defined 51–2; effects of supplier 53–4; findings 53; lessons learned 62–3; matching process 56; non-identification of 54, 61; questionnaire 52; strategy component 56–7, *see also* outsourcing

Ward, A. *et al.* 12, 23, 25, 26, 68, 150
Wasti, S.N. and Liker, J.K. 35
Wernerfelt, B. 99
Wheelwright, S.C. and Clark, K.B. 19, 37, 43, 78
Williamson, O.E. 135
Wolffe, R. *et al.* 169, 179
Womack, J.P. *et al.* 6, 7, 8, 101; and Jones, D.T. 8, 12